Apples on a Windowsill

APPLES ON A
WINDOWSILL

SHAWNA LEMAY

Palimpsest Press
1171 Eastlawn Ave.
Windsor, Ontario. N8S 3J1
www.palimpsestpress.ca

Printed and bound in Canada
Cover design and book typography by Ellie Hastings
Copyedited by Sohini Ghose
Edited by Aimée Parent Dunn
Cover photo by Shawna Lemay

Palimpsest Press would like to thank the Canada Council for the Arts
and the Ontario Arts Council for their support of our publishing
program. We also acknowledge the assistance of the Government of
Ontario through the Ontario Book Publishing Tax Credit.

LIBRARY AND ARCHIVES CANADA CATALOGUING IN PUBLICATION

TITLE: Apples on a windowsill / Shawna Lemay.
NAMES: Lemay, Shawna, 1966- author.
IDENTIFIERS: Canadiana (PRINT) 20230570976
             Canadiana (EBOOK) 20230570984
ISBN 9781990293665 (SOFTCOVER)
ISBN 9781990293672 (EPUB)
SUBJECTS: LCGFT: Essays.

CLASSIFICATION: LCC PS8573.E5358 A85 2024 | DDC C814/.54—DC23

For Rob and Chloe

Contents

Objects in a Still Life

Still life is the art of the small thing, an art of holding on to the bits and pieces of our lives.

— Siri Hustvedt

Apples on a Windowsill

Our life together has been punctuated by illuminated thrills of beauty, and we have measured time in the shuffling of the dark and the light, holding a space for and giving weight to, the precarious objects balanced in a still life.

But let me backtrack a little. Rob, my artist husband, and I marked our twenty-fifth wedding anniversary in November, 2018, by going back to Italy, where we had spent our honeymoon. When we were in Rome, I posted some photos on Instagram of apples on our windowsill of the apartment we had rented on the Via di Capo le Case. A reader remembered the apples I had mentioned in my earlier work, *Calm Things*, which were placed on a windowsill in Venice, a quarter of a century earlier. She referenced the marriage proposal I received in a train station in Florence on our way to Venice. It's not everyone who receives a proposal on their honeymoon, I don't suppose?

May 1993. We realized we were on the wrong train, then dashed across the tracks to the correct train. A handsome man sang to me as I hung off the back of the now moving train and Rob schlepped our suitcases into the car. The man ran after us, his hand on his heart, saying, "I want to marry you." Or was it, "I Wanna Marry You," which is the Bruce Springsteen song. Maybe it wasn't, but I'm going to believe it was, because it was thirty years ago and I'm allowed to do that. Imagine me, then, on the moving train, hand on the railing, blonde hair blowing in the wind, my Wayfarers on, a gorgeous, tall, Italian man following (Rob remembers him as short and nerdy), hand on heart, singing.

Back in Edmonton in November, I scrolled through my iTunes and found *The River*, the album the song is on, which came out in 1980. Possibly I had the original in cassette form. I graduated from high school, which I have done my best to block entirely from my memory, in 1984. I definitely had *Born to Run,* which came out that year, but it was also on the radio and in the air and in the clubs. And oh, I was on the run. And marriage? If you'd asked me then, I know I would have laughed.

I hardly ever think of that pre-Rob time, the 80s. I had big hair, the requisite tight jeans pulled up with a coat hanger, and a leather coat. Some bad boyfriends. And I had a cool car—a beautiful work of art of a classic car, a cerulean blue 1969 Mercury Cougar, 351 Cleveland (this meant something to the guys who stopped me at traffic lights on Jasper Avenue to ask if it was a Cleveland or Windsor), with a black hardtop and a white interior, and signal lights that blink one-two-three. I felt at one with that sweet ride, long and elegant. It could *go.* And it was probably too much for me, too hot, too fast. But it was mine for a while. I owned that thing.

In Italy on our honeymoon, we visited Rome, Florence, Venice, and spent a week on Sardegna, where our friend Gio loaned us his family villa. It was my first trip to Europe and my mind was on fire. Except for the week in Sardegna, where we gazed at the Mediterranean Sea and read Italo Calvino on a stone bench and went to museums and feasted on art. Having come from the boondocks, it was all a revelation. All those Renaissance and Baroque paintings, the fountains, the sculptures! The Colosseum, the Forum, the formal gardens! The culture shock was immense for me.

Back home after our grand tour, I needed to get a job for the rest of the summer and I found work at Wedding World. This unintentionally grotesque and wondrous world of cheap and tacky wedding supplies was located in a building that was a cross between a warehouse and a strip mall. I was hired on with another young woman within hours of viewing the job posting, and the next day we went to work putting together tissue paper bells and curling ribbon around them by scraping it against the dull blades of open scissors. When the pink and teal bells were beribboned and strung together, we'd hang them from a metal beam on an upside-down coat hanger. We would also dump chalky mints whose corners had been worn off like the ancient sculptures in Rome, or frayed pastel silk flowers, into small bags. We would count murky plastic wedding favours out and then fuse them in gauzy plastic sheets with an "L-Closer," and we'd inhale the fumes from melting plastic all day. In between helping bridezillas find peach and teal and baby blue crepe paper streamers, I remember filling the plastic squares with imprecise plastic brides and grooms, crudely formed black cars, garbled flowers, and sealing them with the heat of the L-Closer. When I was interviewed for the job, I said I'd recently been married, and that was considered experience. But I didn't have any of those things at my own small wedding, just flowers—white daisies and calla lilies. I wasn't experienced in anything much at that point, least of all in the art of stocking piles of plastic-sealed brides and grooms, mints, flowers, or colour-coordinated balloons in such a way that they'd hold purchase on the narrow metal shelves.

The owner of the store kept telling us to move faster and would lean into us with her smoky, dill pickle breath and criticize us. She would say mean things to us about our appearance, our intelligence, and talk down to us, clearly unimpressed with our knowledge of feathered pens for guestbook signing or clip-on veils. We were serfs in her warehouse domain of plastic doodads, tissue paper bells, and various other colour-themed junk that would end up piled in the trash after the big event. I lasted two weeks, telling the woman hired the same day as me that I was quitting as we waited outside the wedding palace on the narrow strip of dewy emerald grass between the busy road and the parking lot one brisk early morning. Immediately she said she was quitting too. When we did, the Queen of Wedding World was livid, surprised, and refused to pay us.[1]

If I'd needed a reminder that I lived in an unsophisticated place well away from the cultural and art centres of the world, Wedding World did the trick. Soon after, I got a part-time job working in a chain bookstore at Southgate Mall, which is where I began writing my first book of poetry, *All the God-Sized Fruit*. That was my dream: to become a writer. I wanted to be Someone, someone with a capital S, the way the German expressionist artist Paula Modersohn-Becker wrote the word in her diaries, which I was reading at the time.[2] Looking back, I see those two weeks as a wedding store clerk as a gift—if I hadn't known before how little stock one ought to put into the wedding and how much more to put into the marriage, into the life that followed, that time reminded me.

I would go on to finish my English degree, write several books, have a daughter, complete an MA in English, write more books, and end up working part-time at the public library.

Rob has painted continuously. We live a life in art, with all its highs and lows. It seems a miracle that we persisted, really. Going to Rome was to be some sort of marker for just that, for that particular type of persistence. Making a life in art is its own reward, that I can tell you. But it's not exactly a picnic. It's not all calm things, though those things have been our anchor.

---

1 Eventually, though, she did after we threatened to follow up with the Employment Standards Board.
2 I also wrote a poem about it in that first book of mine.

I always imagined that we would both go back to Italy and that we wouldn't. It seemed presumptuous somehow to me to even yearn for such a thing. If I had an ache to visit Italy again, that ache would be one I could live with because life is full of such aches and it's only in the movies where the woman goes off to find herself in a Tuscan villa after the rest of her life has gone off script. And besides, I had the life I wanted. Why tempt fate with wanting more? Real life isn't like a movie, and it isn't easily contained in the narrative arc of a bestselling memoir of a trip to Italy. I love those memoirs, don't get me wrong, but our life was less concentrated on a single big gesture or moment of action. Instead, we experienced all these "shocks of beauty", to borrow the phrase from Kathleen Stewart in her book *Ordinary Affects*. But I'm the first to concede that moving from still life to still life isn't going to make a blockbuster film.

We've been to other places since. Before we had our daughter Chloe, we went to Paris and London. And after, we took her to Disneyland and Disney World, before taking her to New York twice, Chicago, Amsterdam, and Washington D.C. to look at art and museums. I'm pretty proud of us, that we, an artist and a writer, managed to make traveling as a family to look at art a priority to the extent that we were able. But with our daughter now in her twenties, and safely and productively off at animation school for her second year, we decided to book a trip to celebrate that big anniversary of ours. We knew we could neither afford nor have the energy for a trip that would recreate our original one. We somehow magically settled on two weeks in Rome in November, low season.

We rented an apartment on Via di Capo le Case, near the top of the Spanish Steps. Months later, my head is so full of all the art and architecture we saw, the colours of Rome, the food we ate, and the beauty of the streets, the tall Roman pine trees and the terra-cotta pots of cyclamen, that I don't even know where to begin. So I'll begin with our apartment, the window and its sill, the still lifes I assembled there. I'll begin with the small gestures, the daily-ness, those things that are the same no matter where one is. I'll begin with glimpsing the Roman street, swinging open the shutters, and I'll begin with the poetry of humble things. Breakfast, lunch, cookies, flowers. And coffee.

The first morning, I put my coffee and a cornetto on the windowsill and called it bliss. I took photos of it and posted it on Instagram, as one does these days. The other photos on my DSLR camera would wait until I got home. Most days, I would place something on the windowsill. Apples and pears, jam-filled cookies, sandwiches, the silk orchid in a pot that lived on the coffee table in the apartment. Back in Edmonton, I wished I'd thought to take more photos on that sill. Next time, I'll buy flowers from that touristy stall at the base of the Spanish Steps. I'll buy stargazer lilies and geraniums and cyclamen.

One morning in Rome, I had Rob take my iPhone down the three tall flights of stairs and cross the street and take a photo of me leaning on the windowsill, looking out. What you can't see is my vertigo.[3] I'm trying to look cool but inside I'm spinning a little. The walls in our apartment are a bright and modern white, but the ones outside are a washy and textured terra-cotta and seem timeless.

You'll often come across paintings of a woman looking out of a window. On our trip to Washington, D.C., and The National Museum of Art in 2012, Chloe became transfixed with one by Bartolomé Esteban Murillo from 1665, *Two Women at a Window,* and we sat and looked at it for three quarters of an hour. Which is something we often do, when looking at art as a family. Rob's habit, as is the habit for most artists I imagine, is to look long and scrutinize a particular painting up close, while we circle the room, and the next room, and sometimes even a third room, and wait for him to catch up.

I love this set of photos that I took of those things that feed us, these objects of contemplation, on our windowsill

---

3 I've always been pretty terrified of heights.

in Rome. It made me feel like I was home, in that particular way that a still life does. And when Rob took the photo of me at the same window, it made me feel like I was in a painting, that my existence was inextricably linked to the existence of others, to all those through time who had stood at a window and looked out beyond themselves.

When I returned to Edmonton, I continued to think about windows. I took my copy of Jane Hirshfield's *Ten Windows: How Great Poems Transform the World* off the shelf. In it she talks about how very often poems have a "window-moment" and things open up for the reader, as though they're standing at an open window, breathing in all the new sights and smells. The gesture, she says, "is one of lifting, unlatching, releasing: mind and attention swing open to new-peeled vistas." A work of art is always a kind of window into newly framed seeing and feeling. An opening up of the self. When we encounter a profound piece of art, one that speaks to us, Hirshfield says, it trues our vision. It changes us and it enlarges us. And maybe it creates, also, a hunger in us, for as Hirshfield says, "more range, more depth, more feeling, more associative freedom, more beauty. More perplexity and more friction of interest. More prismatic grief and unstinted delight, more longing, more darkness. More saturation and permeability in knowing our own existence as also the existence of others. More capacity to be astonished."

When I had Rob take the photo of me, I was thinking of similar compositions from the history of art, but I was also hungering for the truing of my vision. I was unshuttering, vowing to open it up, look outward, continue. In the photo, I'm leaning out, I'm daring, I'm a little off-kilter, I'm breathing in. I'm listening to what's out there. The entire trip, when I think back, was a window moment. I have only just begun, I felt, and I was thinking to myself, more beauty, more beauty, more beauty. So, of course, it makes sense that the window moment and the still life moment overlap, because in writing an essay about how our marriage has been punctuated by the beauty of still lifes, it's apparent that it has also been a life of being open to seeing and to understanding how we can look outward but still feel content with the apples on our windowsill.

When we arrived home from Rome, I thought to my monstrously jet-lagged self, well, there, that's another one of your dreams crossed off the list. We'd thrown our coin into the Trevi Fountain all those years ago and we had indeed made it back. And, of course, we threw another one in, because Rome is now under our skin. I can't see not going back. Yet, after the jet lag passes, you settle back into your old life quite quickly after a return from a trip. You hardly remember being away. But Rome still feels like a determining moment. One of my favourite poets, Charles Wright, asks, "What are the determining moments of our lives? / How do we know them? / Are they ends of things or beginnings? / Are we more or less of ourselves once they've come and gone?" And I do feel like I'm more of myself, right now. How long will that feeling last? Was our mere two weeks in Rome the end of something or the beginning?

I've been trying to get in shape. Our good dog of twelve years left this world and so my outdoor morning walk has been gradually exchanged for a walk on the treadmill. I'm fifty-two and this isn't the easiest thing in the world. I've let myself go. Or maybe it's that life is intense and though it is punctuated by beauty, astonishing moments filled with light and clarity, it has also been permeated with the more or less constant worry you would pretty much expect for a couple who chose the path of artist and writer.

And so it ends up that I'm on the treadmill, and for whatever reason I'm listening to Bruce Springsteen, watching YouTube videos of him in interviews and in concert over the years. I'm seeing his long relationship with Patti Scialfa. I'm thinking about how strange it is that you can sort of catch up with a career in art like this. But you don't really know what their real life is like. You feel like you know the artist.

You don't. You do. You find out some things. You know their art, rather than them. Their art is real but they are fakes, in a certain way, and Springsteen even says something to this affect in his Broadway show. This is true for all artists. It's true for me and Rob. We're not all flowers and pretty pictures and trips to Italy. Leonard Cohen in a poem says, that out of all the poets, "maybe one or two / are genuine / and the rest are fakes, / hanging around the sacred precincts / trying to look like the real thing." Naturally, he aligns himself as do we, in the following way: "Needless to say / I am one of the fakes." But you know, we're fakes with dreams.

In an interview Springsteen says, "What do you do when your dreams come true? What do you do if they don't?"

I've been sitting with those excellent questions ever since hearing the interview. Because you reach that moment in your life when you know that if your dreams were going to come true, they probably would have by now. And how do dreams work, anyhow? You have a dream when you're young and you work toward it. But then this or that gets in your way, or things simply arise. They're not necessarily bad things. I'm not a Springsteen expert by any means, but a lot of his music is about those for whom dreams were waylaid or stifled. I'm interested in the ways our dreams evolve and change over time. Circumstances cause us to modify our dreams, and it's not always for the worst.

There's a line in the iconic song "Born to Run" that reminds me of what the German poet Rainer Maria Rilke says in his *Letters on Life*. You can listen to the song yourself, but Rilke says: "…in a good marriage each person appoints the other to be the guardian of his solitude and thus shows him the greatest faith he can bestow." In a good relationship, we guard each other's dreams, and souls, and solitudes. In a comparison of the two lives, Springsteen's and Rilke's, Bruce seems to have achieved this more sufficiently than Rainer.

I've not reached any kind of Rockstar fame, and in fact, very little even in the Canadian literary community. And Rob isn't a household name either. This was never a dream for either of us. What we dreamed of was being able to do our work. We're not recognized personages but we have felt, at times, known. We have aligned ourselves with the still life, which is traditionally the overlooked genre. It's the genre of ordinary things just barely seen or noticed, of pretty flowers—some a little past their prime—and of chipped vessels. Sometimes a curious cat will swing in, or a butterfly, but it's the genre of loneliness and solitude and quiet. It's the genre of calm and silence and equilibrium. It's the genre of flying under the radar, of the next to invisible, but at the same time of things being seen deeply and reverently.

Noticing still lifes is a worthy activity because they make us feel the weight of everything we can't see. Or know. When done well, they are shards of recognition, quick and startling openings into a life lived. They wake us up to what we wouldn't have seen or understood otherwise. Still life is the genre of quiet astonishment. They contain and gently, tenderly hold the details, the fragments, of a life. We might not all experience rock stardom, the fast life in a fast car, but we all experience still lifes. The toothbrush and toothpaste on our bathroom vanity each morning. The box of cornflakes and a bowl and a spoon reflecting our faces each morning. The way light falls on the folded newspaper on the coffee table on a Saturday afternoon. On the bedside table, a book, a vase of dandelions the kids picked, a bottle of pills, eyeglasses.

A few years ago, Rob started experimenting with painting the figure from found objects, from the covers of books and magazines. This led to thinking about movie stars and the ephemeral nature of those fashion magazines you see in grocery store checkout aisles. And this led to paintings of movie stills and iconic stars caught in a fleeting big-screen moment. The common theme was the stilled moment. So, I was pleased to find a book that made the connection between film still and still life. In *Ordinary Affects*, Kathleen Stewart talks about the "charge" or the "quivering" of a still life, or a stopped moment in a film. She mentions Hitchcock and the way he focused on "a door or a telephone" and how this produced a "powerful suspense." Stewart talks about remembering her childhood as a series of "beauty shocks." She says that "when a still life pops up out of the ordinary, it can come as a shock or as some kind of wake-up call."

Rob titled his series of movie still paintings *Big Screen TV,* which played with the idea that TV screens have replaced paintings in the contemporary home. People hardly blink when handing over their hard-earned cash for a huge flat-screen TV. But for many, buying a painting, original art, seems an absurd luxury[4].

While Stewart accurately calls them shocks of beauty, I also like to think of those moments when we encounter something ordinary that inhabits and transmits the magic of the extraordinary as thrills of beauty. Does a thrill last slightly longer than a shock, reverberate a bit longer? I want to get at the tremolos, the vibrations and frequencies of the universe, the pleasurable shiver of that particular moment when we experience such beauty. A thrill is a sensation or a wave of excitement. We seek thrills as we seek beauty, and in this day and age, it almost feels dangerous to be on the side of beauty. It feels a little bit out there, a little bit irresponsible or reckless, I suppose. If the world is coming to an end, do we want to spend it looking at the way light falls on a bowl of oranges, the unwinding rind of a lemon, on the reflections of a spoon sitting beside a coffee cup and a sugar bowl?

My answer is yes. I've spent a lifetime looking for still lifes, being alert to them, keeping a sharp eye out for them. We must

---

4 Suggesting someone should buy art sounds elitist and snobby. Which is just fine really, because I don't think it's the artist's job to go around telling anyone to buy their art. The artist's work is to make more paintings. Warhol's dictum fits: "Don't think about making art, just get it done. Let everyone else decide if it's good or bad, whether they love it or hate it. While they are deciding, make even more art." And this is what has happened. There has been a steady stream of paintings being made in our house, regardless of anything else.

have every book written about still life paintings in our library. When we started out, there weren't too many, and now we have stacks of them. I remember poring over Norman Bryson's scholarly *Looking at the Overlooked* when it first came out and Mark Doty's more intimate *Still Life with Oysters and Lemon* in which he wrote about the painting by Jan Davidsz. de Heem housed at the Metropolitan Museum of Art in New York. Both of these books seemed so fresh when they first came out and they're still vibrant. They each get at the poetry of still life in their own way, as well as the silent conversation that a painting of flowers and objects can draw the viewer into.

Then there are the paintings made in our basement. A succession of peonies, snapdragons, sweet peas, roses, and daisies. A succession of grapes and plums and peaches and pears and cantaloupes. A succession of silver dishes, and skulls, and platters bought at Winners. The paintings are made painstakingly, a square inch at a time, and hours and hours are spent in this labour. Rob works from photographs that he's taken, usually in our kitchen. Some of the photos are spur of the moment, but most are the product of meticulous staging, arranging, and waiting for that elusive light that touches or permeates the objects to just the correct degree. The process is really intense. Our daughter has often teased Rob about putting the pain in painting, but we know that any pain is balanced with joy.

When we go to a museum, we gravitate toward the still lifes, or to the part in a larger painting that has a still life. Maybe you do, as well. Often, it's the details that comes to mind later. It's similar to the way we remember an image or a line from a poem. We'll remember details in a painting, such as the particular colour of the ruby wine in a goblet. The gesture of a lemon peel unwinding over a table's edge. The way the milk pours in a thin white line from the jug, and the way the bread lies on the blue tablecloth in Vermeer's *The Milkmaid*.

One day in October of 2018, there was no avoiding the news. I was on a writing day, trying to work on my novel, while tuning in to the proceedings of the United States Senate Judiciary Committee hearing regarding Brett Kavanaugh's Supreme Court Nomination and Christine Blasey Ford's allegations of sexual assault. She testified that Kavanaugh had sexually assaulted her in 1982 when they were both teenagers. It was difficult to look away. It was difficult to watch. The words by Christine Blasey Ford that resounded for me as I watched the live feed of the proceedings were: "My responsibility is to the truth." Also unforgettable was her comment on the details that had been "seared" into her: "The details that bring me here today are the ones I will never forget. They have been seared into my memory and haunted me…"

In *A Chorus of Stones* by Susan Griffin, a book on personal and public trauma related to World War II, she talks about how every life bears in some way on every other life. She talks about the minute consequences of an action and the way it will ripple forever outward. "Were you to trace any life, and study even the minute consequences, the effect, for instance, of a three-minute walk over a patch of grass, of words said casually to a stranger who happens to sit nearby in a public place, the range of that life would extend beyond the territory we imagine it to inhabit."

And in another book by Griffin, *The Eros of Everyday Life*, she says: "To speak falsely, even with a false cadence, is to betray oneself. One aims for the language that resonates at exactly the same pitch that one feels. Perhaps whatever is said in this pitch is right." Truth is in the cadences in which we speak and write, and truth is in the details. I keep coming back to this quotation from W. S. Di Piero in his book on art and poetry, *Shooting the Works*:

> The mystery of details. The satisfaction of painted particulars. We enter a familiar museum or gallery and go at once (or pretend to drift) to a favourite picture, because in the picture is a detail we love, as we love lines or phrases in poems, we can hardly remember the entire drift of.

Di Piero also says: "An artist's concentration is such that certain details will suddenly bear, unexpectedly, a full sense of existence. A hat, an ear, a phrase."

Let's go back to Susan Griffin, and another passage from *Eros of Everyday Life*. In it she talks about a friend who lost her apartment, her partner, and has been weeping. As one does in times of loss. They also joke: about getting back "to the serious things" like "who does the shopping."

> And then we laugh again because everyone knows that who does the shopping is just a detail, and all that loss is the serious thing. But is this really so? For loss is experienced through detail, when, for instance, one shops alone if before one shopped for the night's food with a lover.

For loss is experienced through detail. The fullness of life can be captured in a detail, well-rendered. Details can haunt. Once shared, our truth moves out beyond us and resonates into future lives in ways we can only imagine. Sharing these details is worth our persistence and it is worth our bravery.

I mention all this here, because still life is understood to be outside narrative. And yet we instinctively know that this is where life happens, where our sense of self and home are centred. When Chloe was an infant, I would sneak away for an hour or two to write upstairs and leave Rob playing with her. I always came down to find her toys arrayed in front of her in unusual combinations, precariously stacked into imaginatively mismatched towers, into what was essentially an elaborate toy still life. I have photographs of when she was a toddler and Rob is setting up his own still lifes on our old scratched up coffee table, dragged into the bright light streaming through the kitchen window. Rob is taking photos of what was on the table, and Chloe is helping. She's wearing an outfit with giraffes and bears and monkeys and her hair is wild and curly and in spots there are tiny matted strands, which at the time made me feel like a terrible mother. She's composing purple and red plums on a silver platter, and Rob is kneeling on the ground in front of the scene. There are flowers, green grapes, pears, silver dishes, and a glass with an orangey-red juice in it.

Reading Bruce Springsteen's biography, I'm delighted by the passage where he talks about Patti Scialfa, his wife, telling him he's going to "miss it," and when he asks what, she replies, "The morning, it's the best time, it's when they need you the most." Springsteen wakes up to this fact and finds himself taking up the role of short-order cook dad. I'm imagining the toast, the children, the light shining on the scene, on the knives and spoons, and glinting off the jar of peanut butter and raspberry jam. For me, this is a scene of extreme beauty, it's a scene of splendour. That's some kind of rock 'n' roll, baby.

For a brief time, in high school and even shortly after, I entertained the dream that I could be a news reporter. A journalist.[5] But what that dream transformed into instead is that I now report on the extreme beauty of the world as it manifests in shards of the ordinary life, in still lifes. I find it in the early morning light at breakfast, on our kitchen table at noon, and in the backyard at the golden hour. When I don't find it, I attempt to make it happen. I set things up and wait. I photograph books, flowers, a glass of milk and a plate of cookies, a mooncake, teacups galore. You can make a sliver of beauty appear, I have found, by lavishing attention on a simple and ordinary thing, turning it and moving it so that the light finds it. It's a magic trick that anyone can do, and I've followed my dreams one ordinary magic trick at a time.[6]

After painting other subject matter for a couple of years, Rob returned to painting flowers. The mood of the world called for flowers and flowers called to him once again. He

---

5 I even took an evening course at the community college toward that.
6 Did I mention that I also take photographs? I've always been taking photographs. Even in my writing, I'm taking pictures. So.

realized he had more to say about flowers, after nearly a life-time of painting them. A scene from last summer: in the kitchen, he takes photos of some weather-worn but colour-ful flowers from our garden, and then stuffs them into an old Marzano tomato tin when he's done. I look at them for a couple of days and then I take them outdoors and sit with them one morning on the patio, the tin can of tea roses precariously perched on the bistro table. It occurs to me that I'm not done thinking of still life, either. One could spend a lifetime thinking about flowers. They say so much.

I'm always alert to mentions of the subject. This from Adam Zagajewski's, *A Defense of Ardor*:

> The connections between high and low are complex. Let's take a look at one of Chardin's still lifes, per-haps his beautiful Still Life with Plums, which hangs in the Frick Collection in New York: what we'll see is apparently only a tumbler made of thick glass, some gleaming enamelware, a plate, and a bulging bottle. Through them, though, we'll come to love singular, specific things. Why? Because they exist, they're indif-ferent, that is to say, incorruptible. We'll learn to value objectivity, faithful depictions, accurate accounts – in an age so adept at exploiting falsehoods, particularly in Central Europe.

This was published in 2004, and we can see that the words live on, can be newly interpreted and extrapolated upon. In this new/old age of falsehoods, the age of Trump[7], perhaps the still life is of interest once again. We love its incorrupt-ibility, and we love the specificity of the still life.

What does the still life signify in the early dregs of the twenty-first century? How do we evaluate and measure our

---

7 I'm reluctant to use his name because I wanted to write about beauty here.

desire for the incorruptibility of flowers at this time? To what degree has the public realm crept into the private and how are we surviving this? And what does it mean to inhabit that dreaming scene, if only briefly? What is our allegiance to "objectivity, faithful depictions, accurate accounts?" I have so many questions to which, perhaps, still life has some answers.

While I'm writing this, the news of the day is that while congress is shut down in the United States and the kitchens of the White House are unstaffed as a result, Trump has entertained a champion university football team with a dinner of cold fast-food hamburgers and french fries. The news and social media are full of photos of the table piled high with boxed Big Macs and other wrapped fast-food burgers, packaged dipping sauces in silver gravy boats, and elaborate gold candelabras. The abundance is grotesque, incongruous, but perfectly symbolizes the current administration. The burger still life is front and centre, not at all being overlooked. Is it incorruptible? A faithful depiction? As Zagajewski points out, the "connections between high and low are complex."

Here, I can't help but think of Michelle Obama's words: "When they go low, we go high." Which of course refers to a different kind of high and low but are, at the same time, connected. In contemporary still life, low can be high. The humble objects of the modern world are often elevated in hyper-realist works of art. The Dutch painter Tjalf Sparnaay paints images of burgers and fries and ketchup bottles that are sold for impressive prices in a New York art gallery. In his high gloss, hyper-realist images there is, at the same time, truth and authenticity. This is how the world is, the paintings seem to say. We love our burgers and fries, but we have an uneasy relationship with them. The paintings don't so much glorify fast-food as remind us of how it is glorified, how it is accepted as part of our culture. The viewer knows you can put a glossy sheen on the surface of it, but it does bad stuff to our bodies. That super-sized Big Mac meal is a quick hit of empty calories that trigger the pleasure centre of our brains and stimulates further cravings for fat, sugar, salt. We eat it because we're stressed, short on time, and because it's cheap and addictive. It's terrible for us but we consume it anyway. The poor eat fast-food, but so do the rich, if to a lesser extent.

The White House burger display is neat and tidy. The burgers are boxed and wrapped and stacked into piles like office towers, or a city of burgers, and Trump can't help but mention that he paid for them out of pocket. The usual grease one finds soaking through fast-food wrapping is missing. The burger chains, no doubt, took some care in this matter, foreseeing that the images would go viral. The viewer doesn't get to see the food, only the wrapping, though the french fries have been repackaged and displayed in White House branded paper cups. A feast without the food, without nourishment. It's all packaging, and what could be, but isn't, empty boxes. Or, boxes full of empty calories. The symbolism isn't hard to unpack.

I want to leave the contemporary out of this. I would rather write an essay about how the beauty of still life has punctuated our life, the lives of an artist and a writer and their daughter. But still life has always had something to say about the time and place in which they are created. One still life will speak to another still life, and even if they're outside of narrative, they tell a story and convey a broader picture if looked at together. The seventeenth-century Dutch paintings, for example, told a story of abundance and trade with distant lands in their depictions of tulips and Persian carpets, wild game, and other delicacies on silver platters and drinks served in jeweled goblets. And yet, the beauty is there in the details of the elaborately designed carpets, the gorgeous colours of the jewels, and the tantalizing reflections in all the shiny silver. The fast-food still life at The White House is a shock, but not one of beauty. Rather it is altogether perverse.

Still life can capture startling moments of beauty as well as abundance, at times opulent, at times grotesque. And it is in the details of these pictures that a faithfulness to truth resides.

My own life has been a succession of flowers, bouquets. Which is, of course, a privileged thing. I often bought them because Rob needed them for his still lifes. Even when we couldn't afford them, I brought home flowers and arranged them in vases. I planted them in our garden. They seemed like a necessity. I have always found flowers necessary. I have found them to be persistent. Insistent. I have found them to be good and sturdy and elegant and dignified company.

I treasure Virginia Woolf and her famous lines from the end of *The Waves*: "How much better is silence; the coffee-cup, the table. How much better to sit by myself like the solitary sea-bird that opens its wings on the stake. Let me sit here for ever with bare things, this coffee-cup, this knife, this fork, things in themselves, myself being myself." And always I hear this line in my head when I go to buy flowers, the line from Mrs. Dalloway, "…she would buy the flowers herself…" Once, a rare occasion years ago, we had a party for which I went out to buy flowers, and my friend Lee called me Mrs. Dallemay, which I found to be delightful.

What I've been looking for is this balance between metaphorically and literally going out to buy the flowers, and being able to stay home at my table, with my coffee cup, with bare things, getting down to the essence of me, myself being myself. Woolf has her bird sitting alone on a stake but opening its wings. And Rumi says: "Something opens our wings. Something /makes boredom and hurt disappear. / Someone fills the cup in front of us. /We taste only sacredness." I've tasted a lot of sacredness and I've been accompanied by flowers, which very often, I bought myself.

In Rome, we arrived at our apartment in the dark. We unpacked and put the books and journals, maps and pens we each brought on the coffee table by the two decorative silk ferns. Over the two weeks we were there, other objects accumulated. Postcards of the Caravaggios that we bought at Santa Maria del Popolo and San Luigi dei Francesi. Apples and pears. The small replica bee plaques from the Barberini Palace gift shop. A package of cookies, a bag of potato chips.

A glass of water, a glass of wine. My camera. My cell phone and tangled earbuds.

I prefaced readings for my novel, *Rumi and the Red Handbag*, with how some now forgotten academic had written that in literature "men go out on quests, while women run errands." And how reading that had in part inspired my book.[8] But maybe it has also informed my life. Maybe it informs many of our lives. I would argue for the nobleness of the errand, for the grandness of the overlooked, for the flowers we buy ourselves, for the bare things that are just themselves, nothing more. When I read from my book, I talked about the quest for the holy grail and "what if" the purse was the grail or the vessel we were looking for, and it was there all along? We carry it along with us on our errands.

Here we were in Rome, out in the world. A quest, or a very big errand? The word errand derives from the Old English and holds within its meaning, "message, mission." And the message is? What if the message, or mission, is flowers? What if the message is that you don't need to go on an elaborate quest, that what we're searching for is often right on the table in front of us, right on our own windowsill?

Kristjana Gunnars was a professor whose class in creative writing I attended during my BA in English. In her book, *The Rose Garden: Reading Marcel Proust*, she talked about having an appointment with herself. The setting for the appointment is a rose garden in Germany. In a certain way, going to Rome felt like keeping an appointment with our younger selves.

We've been in a conversation with still lifes for our entire marriage and the still lifes seem to be in conversation with each other. They usually start as objects on our kitchen table. A vase of flowers picked from the garden or brought home from the florist or grocery store. Some apples or pomegranates. Rob will wait for a particular light to come in through our back window. At different times of year, the light is

---

8 *Rumi and the Red Handbag* was an attempt to write against that trope.

completely different, arrives at different times. In winter, the low light has to peek through the tall houses behind us. In summer the light is patient and high. And in the spring and fall it's difficult to keep track of, changing all the time. Waiting for the correct light is just one of the stages.

Rob takes photos of the flowers and then uses that photo to grid up a canvas of the same proportions, down in his basement studio. He paints for a week or two depending on how large the canvas is, looking at the photograph, looking at the paint palette, and then the canvas. Part way through, he'll bring the canvas upstairs to our living room and set it on the sideboard. He climbs the stairs to our bedroom and looks at it from above, or he'll sit by the front window and look at it from that vantage point. It goes up and back down the stairs to the studio a few times until, finally, it's finished and finds a home for a while on the sideboard, propped against the wall. Then the process begins again.

We've kept our appointments with still life. We've sat with tulips and peonies and roses and hydrangeas. We've waited for the light to illuminate their colourful petals. And afterwards, we sat with the flowers, watched them fade and drop petals, droop and dwindle. We stayed with them long after their prime. They go from exuberant and bold to poetic, to tragic. We have a pact with them to wait it out, to be there, to make it to the ends, to see them through.

The light of January is surprising at latitude 53, perhaps the most surprising light of the year. It comes in low and reaches further into the house than at other times of the year. I was thinking about who knows what when I walked into the dimly lit kitchen late yesterday morning to find the tops of the purple grocery store tulips alight and aglow. It was as startling as it would be fleeting, which is also a quality of winter light. "Huh," I said out loud to no one. I wondered how long the tulips had been radiantly waiting for me to come out of my study, out of my reveries. It reminded me of how a child might wait, holding a precious rock or shiny object in their palm, waiting for you to turn around and notice. That kind of bright, innocent patience.

Still lifes take us out of time and wake us up. The Egyptians painted still lifes on the interior of tombs because they believed that in the afterlife the fruit would become real and the deceased would have something to sustain them. Still lifes were in the homes of the wealthy in second-century Pompeii and symbolized hospitality. The images from Pompeii are not that different from the bowl of fruit I currently have on my kitchen table. Which are not that unlike the bowls of strawberries or peaches or plums that Chardin painted in the early 1700s in Paris, or the arrays of apples and pears and lemons that Paul Cezanne painted in the nineteenth century. Isn't it amazing to think of the conversations these images have through time? And isn't it wonderful the way a bowl will be just a bowl until something, some spark, ignites and it seems as though the still life is on fire, or that we are on fire, awake to it.

Still lifes have traditionally been emblematic of themes such as "memento mori" and "tempus fugit." Maybe anyone looking back over their life can see it as a series of still lifes, but I know that I certainly do. We're not racing in the streets trying to outrun time. But neither are we incognizant of what's going on in the world outside of our own small corner of it. Instead, we're looking at objects on a table as a way of measuring time, racing against time, slowing time down.

In an essay on Chardin, Siri Hustvedt notes that in his painting of a coffeepot, garlic, and a glass of water, "these objects are imaginatively reinvented as essences of human dignity." She sees in his work, "the presence of a man who worked with both intelligence and love." She evokes Marcel Proust's comment, too, "that in Chardin one feels the affection a tablecloth has for a table." There is nothing heroic, I suppose, in spending a lifetime conveying the essence of a vase of weathered roses or a drooping peony, or in attempting to communicate the affection one has for the objects of everyday. But it is dignified.

We've travelled, but we've stayed. There is the narrative of the artist who leaves, becomes famous, and the one of the artist who stays. But no one is interested in that one. They should be.

I would argue for something more than the narrative of the tortured, starving artist, the loner, the misunderstood misfit who leaves town to make good, to find herself, and whose glorious quest feels, perhaps, ordinary. I mean, leave town if you so desire, but know that staying can also be a satisfying option. Find a way to be happy in your own way. As Rilke said, "I basically do not believe that it matters to be happy in the sense in which people expect to be happy."

An ordinary life can be a work of art unto itself. I have found happiness in this life of running errands to buy flowers, and in appointments with a bowl of peaches or roses cut from our garden, and in asking for more beauty. I've looked for the truth in still lifes, in the details of a life, and I have listened in on the long conversation of still lifes through history, including contemporary history. I have some faith in the incorruptibility of objects on a table. They open up the conversation beyond us in time and tell a beautiful, sometimes thrilling, and occasionally grotesque story of the way things are.

By the Still Life Painter's Wife

Sun tremolos on the white table, I set the strawberries down.

These are early days in our relationship, morning in my old and rundown bachelor pad with hardwood floors, deep windowsills, a view of the gravelled parking lot, downtown Edmonton. Birdsong and the neighbours' fighting and making up, the soundtrack. A round, white Ikea table is next to the window and right beside that, the bed. The light flutters in and I get up, make coffee, take out strawberries sliced the night before. There are three pots of African violets and a vase of gaping orange and red tulips. I make toast, set out strawberry jam amid the shadows cast by the flowers. The necklace I'd worn the night before is on the table where I happened to leave it. My Pentax MX loaded with film, 36 exposures, is on the nearby chest of drawers.

Rob gets out of bed and sees something in this scene and asks to use my camera. Sure, I say. The colors are good. The blue design on the Chinese mugs works well with the orange and purple of the flowers, which makes a nice counterpoint to the red of the strawberries. He adjusts a few things, places the knives on the edges of the plates with toast. I watch as he leans over and in, the strap of the camera hanging down, and even now I remember the satisfying sound of the shutter.

He talked about wanting to paint still lifes again, which he'd done in his student days. He'd had success painting outdoor patio scenes, and views from the Muttart Conservatory—glass pyramids housing temperate, tropical, and desert plants year-round. He began exhibiting his work right out of art school. We'd met through mutual friends at a few parties and he'd mentioned he was having a solo show. I went to it by myself one afternoon and I liked his work.

We were young then, but the feeling was that we weren't getting any younger. And yet trying something new felt risky, heavy, and momentous. We were 23 and 27 at the time and something big had to happen. Something good. We really didn't know anything then. The way that life can move so slowly, and the way that one object on a table shifted slightly to meet the sun can be enough.

I took the photos to be developed, a painting was made. And then it was exhibited in his next solo exhibition where it sold to the Canadian Embassy in Beijing. As far as I know, it's still hanging there. We were dating then, but eventually, I became the wife of the artist.

There have been many novels about the "wives of." *The Pilot's Wife, The Time Traveler's Wife, The Photographer's Wife.* I'm certainly not the first to remark on this trend. In a 2007 article in *The Guardian*, Judith Evans points out, "So all these novels seem to take the reader with them in a little conspiracy: others may think that the time traveller, kitchen god or Greek tycoon is the main attraction—and indeed, they're pretty intriguing—but come with me and I'll show you the wife or daughter in the background who really deserves the attention." The woman-as-sidekick is something that Evans is skeptical about. Isn't it time, she asks, for women to be the centre of attention? Why can't the wife also be the ringmaster, the alchemist, or the tycoon? she asks.

I recently read Meg Wolitzer's novel *The Wife*, which is popular again because of the movie starring Glenn Close, who won numerous awards for her acting in the film. I hadn't read a single review of the book, but I knew how it would end when I read the first sentence in which the narrator, who happens to be "the wife" of the novel's title, announces that she has had "enough" and is leaving her husband, the famous novelist. Reading the first sentence, we are alerted to the tone in the title; she is not X's Wife, she is The Wife. In a certain way, she's the ringmaster, but it's complicated.

In 2014, Jessica Dawson asked why the art world "ignores wives" in a piece for *The Daily Beast*. She discussed video artist Bill Viola, who at the time had a retrospective in Paris, and who produces work in collaboration with his partner Kira Perov, the executive director of his studio. When Dawson asked Perov about an article in the *New York Times* that Dawson thinks gives her "inordinate credit," Perov replied that "the characterization didn't go far enough." Her roles are listed as bookkeeper, archivist, and collaborator and I imagine the list could be expanded. Still, when the author later asked if she "felt any wish for co-authorship," Perov left the email unanswered. Regarding the retrospective, the articles ends, "Did Perov ask for co-billing, or does she even want it? We don't know. What we do know is that Bill Viola has a major show on view at The Grand Palais and Kira Perov doesn't."

In Wolitzer's novel, the narrator says, "Everyone needs a wife; even wives need wives. Wives tend, they hover." She goes on, "Wives bring broth, we bring paper clips, we bring ourselves and our pliant, warm bodies." Wives are the ones who say, "everything will be okay." "And then, as if our lives depend on it, we make sure it is." I wasn't terribly surprised by the revelation at the end of the book as to the extent of the wife's contribution to the preening, prize-winning husband's writing. The lack of surprise is perhaps the biggest surprise.

James Tissot's painting *The Artists' Wives, 1885* depicts a gathering on a cafe terrace in Paris on varnishing day, when artists apply a final coat to their paintings that will hang in the annual *Salon* exhibition. Rob also varnishes his paintings and looking at this image, I can smell the recently applied varnish. But I also think about the word varnish, which is quite close to vanish, and is used to indicate a superficial appearance. For all that the painting is about the artists' wives, and sure there they are in the foreground, there is a higher percentage of fellows. And, in fact, it's Auguste Rodin, lurking with his beard and top hat like a photobomber, who is named in descriptions of the paintings; in the Chrysler Museum's catalogue entry on the painting, the wives are referred to as "female companions."

Rob has had over thirty solo shows and he's been in numerous group exhibitions. I've attended most of the openings, as his wife. I'm useful at these things. I'm actually great at them. I talk to the relatives and to those who would like to tell him stories about how their rosebush is infested with aphids. Occasionally, there are art buyers who want to meet me. I'm often asked, are you a painter too? Oh god no, I want to say, that would be a disaster... but I don't. It's hard enough to follow up with, "I'm a writer," and see the expressions that that produces.

We've had a good long marriage, the still life painter and me. I consider myself an expert on what it's like to be married to an artist, given that we've lasted over twenty-five years at the writing of this essay. I have a pretty grand sense of humour about the whole thing, always have.

Case in point, the poem in my first collection, *All the God-Sized Fruit*, published in 1999, titled, "By the Still Life Painter's Wife." I'd been reading up on the still life painters of the seventeenth century and onward. I remember waking up at 4 a.m. and grabbing the legal pad that I kept on my night table and writing the poem almost as is. A poem arriving in this way is a miraculous thing for a writer and I love it for this reason, and also because I think it's amusing the way these objects appear somewhat magically for the artists.

By the Still Life Painter's Wife

Did Willem Kalf's wife say
look, i have brought home this nautilus cup
filled with light
from my merchant brother's house.
On it Neptune stands on a fearsome whale head
and below Jonah dives from the monster's jaws.
Or, here is a lemon carefully peeled
the rind a curling ribbon.
And here is a lobster, darling,
i have cleaned all the meat from it
so you may have it in your studio
the brilliant smooth orange-red.

Did Chardin's wife say
i baked this splendid brioche today
and trimmed it with mint leaves
from the plant in the backyard.
I'll leave it for you on the sideboard
by the candy dish, decanter, apples and cherries.
In case you're hungry, dear man.

Did Rembrandt's wife say
the slaughtered ox has been trussed up in the shed
will you go and inspect it, my darling.

And the wives of de Heem and Aertsen, Bosschaert and Brueghel.
Did they
gather flowers in ditches
arrange them on the console
bake fussy confectioneries
and bread just so
barter assiduously at market for exotic fruit
place it carelessly
in unusual china bowls
buy pears with attention

to length and curve of stem
coax juice from wasting fruit
blend the concoction until pink-orange-red
some unnameable colour.

Reader, I have spent my life bringing flowers home from the grocery store. I have looked for pears with unusual stems. I have arranged apples and grapes in a bowl. I have practiced the peeling of lemons, and I have cleared the table so as to make of it a blank canvas. More importantly, I have made the making of paintings the priority in our household. I have held space for it with superhuman powers. I have also documented his career, maintained his website, and facilitated his social media. We like to say that he works in his basement studio in the sixteenth century, which is when oil paints were invented. I have contributed to making sure his work is seen in the twenty-first century. Have I shaped his work in some small way? I think so, and he doesn't disagree.

Here's the thing: he also shapes my work. I have a name, and it's on the front of all my books, many of which are about art, living with art, still life, and living a creative life. In short, he shapes my work as much as I shape his. There is no one more interested in the photographs I take or the words I write. We each work to make the space for each other.

When my essay collection *Calm Things* came out in 2008, a reader wrote on Amazon, "This small work is a journal written by the poet Shana Lemay on the subject of 'Still Life'. As her husband is an artist who focuses on painting Still Lifes it is also an effort at description, revelation and perhaps promotion of his work." You will notice the misspelling of my name. You will notice that my writing makes "an effort." And you will notice that I've been relegated to someone promoting my husband's work.

Does it bother me so much because it's partly true? When I wrote *Calm Things*, I was trying to create something in the realm of what Annie Dillard does in *Pilgrim at Tinker Creek*, or May Sarton in her *Journal of a Solitude*, or Anne Morrow

Lindbergh in *Gift from the Sea*. I was making a considerable and freaking graceful effort to utilize the material at hand. I was trying to make something of my life. In the second chapter Lindbergh writes that one of the goals in writing her book is "to be at peace with myself. I want a singleness of eye, a purity of intention, a central core to my life that will enable me to carry out these obligations and activities as well as I can." She was seeking a life lived "in grace." I wanted to say that my life lived through still life is also steeped in grace, deeply contemplative, and even elegant. I wasn't writing to hawk my husband's art.

Meanwhile, though we're all the way into the twenty-first century, we're still asking the question Linda Nochlin famously asked in 1988: "Why Have There Been No Great Women Artists?" in various permutations. In a *Forbes article*, Erin Spencer writes about the question Wilhelmina Holladay, the founder of The National Museum of Women in the Arts, began asking in the 1970s: "Where are all the women artists?" The NMWA is the only major museum in the world, she says, solely dedicated to women's art. She also quotes a 2017 study "that found that just 13.7% of living artists represent in galleries in Europe and North America are women." Granted, we can't rewrite history and insert more women artists into the seventeenth century.

I thought more would have changed by now. I published *All the God-Sized Fruit* in 1999 and our daughter was born in 1998. I thought by now—she's in her 20s—she'd be living in a world that esteemed women artists. In my book, I inhabited the voices of women artists, reimagining their lives and the lives of their paintings. It was through the voices of artists like Artemisia Gentileschi, Rachel Ruysch, Rosa Bonheur, and Paula Modersohn-Becker, that I began to imagine my own life.

There's an article on *Salon*, written in 2015 by the writer Anne Bauer, titled "'Sponsored' by my husband: Why it's a problem that writers never talk about where their money comes from." She lays out her money situation in the first paragraph: her husband has a well-paying job with fancy perks like a gym membership. This allows Bauer to work intermittently, and to spend the rest of her time writing. She details examples of writers who have inheritances, rich and connected parents, or, like her, a well-off husband.

Rob and I have often joked about why we only had one child, saying it must be illegal for an artist and a writer to have more than one. We've not received any inheritances from long lost uncles and neither of us have made money on the stock market or from the patent on a secret invention. Mainly we fly by the seat of our pants, and worry a lot, and save our money, and buy everything with cash, and try to live simply. There is the Oscar Wilde line I'm fond of quoting, "When bankers get together, they talk about art. When artists get together, they talk about money." But when artists do talk about money, it sounds needy. For painters, if you're not successful, or seem to be, then your art isn't deemed worthy by collectors. If you seem too successful, the other artists are resentful. Being an artist means you're almost always living on the edge.

I'm photographing two ranunculus—one dark pink, one a light ballerina pink—but the stems are too short and I don't want the vase in the photo. I could MacGyver them, Scotch tape them onto the vase so they sit higher up. But, instead, I have Rob hold the flowers. He understands immediately what I want. Something poetic, a gesture between the two flowers. He twirls them and manipulates them until they're in the light I want, and also assuming that poetic gesture. When I post the photo on Instagram, I don't mention his involvement. It doesn't even occur to me that I might have.

I frequently bring home flowers but Rob also gathers his stems, goes flower shopping. These days, I often use his castoff flowers for my photographs, and sometimes he uses mine. I think of them that way, "castoff flowers." When they have been manipulated, and prodded, and coaxed to pose for photos, they have a secondhand feeling to them.

When I wrote *Rumi and the Red Handbag,* which is set in a secondhand store, I had in mind an essay by Hélène Cixous from her book *Stigmata.* In the essay Cixous talks about James Joyce's "wombtext"—Ovid's *Metamorphoses.* In Ovid's account of the story of Icarus, his father forges wings composed of melted wax and feathers he collects when birds drop them. She quotes from Ovid: "…he came too close to the blazing sun, and it softened the sweet-smelling wax that bound his wings together. The wax melted. Icarus moved his bare arms up and down, but without their feathers they had no purchase on the air." Later, she quotes Joyce, "Mother is putting my new secondhand clothes in order." The essay is full of tracings and resonances, but I have lived with this line for some time, "There is no artist without castoff feathers." We inherit the feathers, the clothes, of previous artists. We all begin our creative lives packing our suitcases with secondhand clothes—trying on, in my case, the frocks of Virginia Woolf, the black turtlenecks of Clarice Lispector, the kimonos of Georgia O'Keeffe.

Earlier, I said that as artists, we're flying by the seat of our pants. But Rob and I, we're really flying by castoff flowers.

I've never really thought of myself as the wife of the still life artist. But I wonder if society's understanding of the way art is produced has evolved?

On Instagram you will see young women posing in various locales looking sensational but spontaneous. Rarely does the viewer wonder who is behind the camera. The photograph has likely been taken by what is known as an "Instagram husband," who may be "any gender and sexual orientation, and he doesn't have to be your actual husband" according to an article in *The Atlantic* titled, "The Instagram-Husband Revolution." The men who are behind the camera now want to get their due. They've begun organizing in the form of Facebook groups, Instagram reveals, and hashtags (#instagramhusband). Being an Instagram Husband for an influencer (who might make in the millions) is a full-time job requiring a wide variety of skills, including photography, but also scouting locations, making videos, shopping, online marketing. In reference to one such husband, the article notes that "it can be hard for some men when their wife finds fame." He emphasizes that his role isn't "demeaning yourself; it's about building something with your wife."

I find it interesting that Instagram Husbands are concerned that their role might be considered a demeaning one, a role without dignity. Their invisibility causes embarrassment. Obviously, the dynamics of every single relationship are unique and artistic relationships are no different. I can't help but look back at that review of my book and my offense at it being called promotion for my husband's work. Because when you make a life in art, you really are building something, and it's rarely done alone, in spite of the persistent myth of the solitary and temperamental artist.

I have lived, so far, a life in art, a life steeped in the making of art. Ten years into our marriage, I wrote a poem titled "Daring Instruction," which used still life as a metaphor for our marriage. The constant shifting, the impermanence, the precariousness, the way you add and take away, recompose, that speaks to what it is to cohabitate over time. The focus in the poem is the dailyness, the light that comes and goes, and the sturdy table at the centre of it all.

Still life is a useful lens through which to look at how art is made, too. There is the absence of humans, but human touch is everywhere in it. While outside of narrative, a still life is often placed at the emotional core of a story, saying something unsayable. We might view art-making as a solitary, romantic endeavour but what makes the practice possible is friends, like-minded people, family, and partners, a neighbour handing you a flower or a bowl of tomatoes over the fence. And like the art-making practice, a still life comes together very often thanks to a community. It's a mash-up of the public and the private. The strategies of still life are a "particularly productive focus for exploring the way the distant affairs of the world might reach into the life of the individual," says Bonnie Costello in *Planets on the Table*. She says the still life is a "threshold genre" and connects the private and public spheres. Rob's still life paintings are made in our home, comprised of things from flower stores and grocery stores, imported from all over the world.

Still lifes holds a trace of all who have touched the objects, whether it's the farmer who picked the lemon from the tree, or the potter who turned the bowl. While a still life isn't labelled with arrows saying where the flowers were grown, or marked up with the provenance of the objects, these are all intrinsically part of such a painting. So many forces come into play to make a single picture that it's astounding. And it's the magic trick of still life: when you're looking at a painting of a bowl of plums beside a single pink rose in a narrow vase, all you're thinking about is the way the light hits each of the objects and the way the shadow sprawls out on the tablecloth. Sure, someone pricked their skin when plucking the rose, someone washed the plums under cold water, arranging them just so, but the lived moment of the painting dominates. Arresting are the paint strokes, made by another human hand practiced for years, in conjunction with an eye noticing, refining the ability to mix and apply colour to capture the tones, shapes, forms, depth, shadow, and light of an object. You're hovering in front of the painting, held by the force of the paint, and by all those castoff feathers and petals. You have gained purchase on the air.

Should you wish to email me after reading this and ask if I'd like some portion of credit for Rob's work, would I leave it unanswered? Yes, yes, I would. I'd like credit for my own work. More importantly, I'd like the space to do my work. I'd like women from all backgrounds to have the space to do their work. I'd also like Rob to continue to do his work. I love the back and forth that we've developed, the flowers that we share, the objects on a table. The way, at lunch, one of us will gently push the bowl of plums on the kitchen table, into the light.

Affection for the Table

Proust was captivated by Chardin's paintings when he was twenty-four, well before he came to write about madeleines and lost time. In a short essay, Proust talks with such pleasure about the tenderness with which light caresses the old and worn tablecloth in Chardin's domestic scenes, the "amity" between one thing and another, and between people and things. In a room, the table is where people gravitate and congregate, and light, too. We can imagine through Proust's writing, Chardin's tablecloth being sorted, the shaking out of it, the lift and loft and soft caress when it becomes flat on the surface of the table. The hands of the woman, both in real life and in the painting, that smooth the cloth as though it were the skin of a loved one. The comfort and the affection captured in the mundane task of spreading out a tablecloth holds meaning—I know this in my bones, in my soul. At least, I want to find meaning in this moment that is so ordinary because then maybe this world, and us in it, maybe we're going to be okay.

I have this idea that the beauty in an ordinary moment can act as a disruption in the political landscape of divisiveness and hate that we're all more or less helplessly tuned into. I have this idea that these small jolts of beauty can remind us of our human connection. I put my hope in the gestures of the human hand: the hand reaching out for another hand, the hand holding a paintbrush, and in the hands that flap out the tablecloth for a Sunday dinner. I put my hope, too, in the human daydream, the reverie, and the moment of the madeleine. A still life can provoke a fissure in time and compel us to drop into the state of the dreaming self. In *Ordinary Affects*, Kathleen Stewart says that a still life can act as "an alibi for all the violence, inequality and social insanity folded into the open disguise of ordinary things." Time slows down when we look at the beauty of something still and allows us to think about the fast-moving world in a different rhythm.

In *Mysteries of the Rectangle*, Siri Hustvedt notes in another essay on Chardin, for we will never weary of looking at and considering Chardin, that "I am certain that these strokes made by a paintbrush lie at the bottom of Proust's comment that in Chardin one feels the affection a tablecloth has for a table." I cling to the words, *I am certain*. It's good to be certain about what one has observed, especially in contrast to the unmoored feeling I seem to constantly have.

Do we not still have affection for one another? Despite evidence to the contrary, I want to place my belief in this. In my own family, and maybe it's a coincidence that the strife began at the beginning of the Trump years, there has been discord to the point where many of us no longer see each other. In short, I haven't spoken to my sister in years, except in some texts around the time my dad had heart issues and a pacemaker operation. At this moment, I don't see us ever reconciling. I've reached the point in my self-therapy[9] where I'm wishing her well and meaning it. But we can't go back in time, so I'm moving forward and sending good thoughts out, as per the advice of Pema Chödron, who reminds us via

---

9 We're not in the income bracket where an actual therapist could be a thing.

Shantideva to "Be calm and call to mind, / That everything arises from conditions." I don't know what my sister's conditions are, and she doesn't know mine.

Amity is the word Proust uses in his short work on Chardin, or *amitié*, in French. The translator, Jennie Feldman, mentions that the word is used in talking about the rapport between people and things. There is a feeling of goodwill, understanding, and interconnectedness that Proust conveys in his discussion of the amity in a scene from Chardin, and which I have lost with my sister. We won't be sitting down to a family dinner together any time soon.

In a still life, the table is the element most likely to be overlooked, but I have a fondness for tables. There's a particular old scratched up table I feel affection for. It has the requisite paint stains from having lived part of its life in the painter's studio downstairs. When I first got my present camera, I practiced by taking photos of the table itself, bare. It's an old table, the kind that pops into two pieces for storage, though we always have it out. It's on a bit of a perpetual slant because of its design, because of the hard use and neglect too. We bought most of our furniture secondhand and that was twenty-five years ago, so almost everything in our house sags or slants or dips or is chipped or has tears or is frayed. I think this must be preferable to ordering a home out of a design magazine.

What's interesting to me is that we can retain an affection for things, my old table, for example, but lose faith with and in our fellow human beings. Less complicated are tables, obviously, however many meals you've shared around one, however you've adapted to and learned to accommodate each other's sags and creaks.

I'm not alone in noticing tables. In Clarice Lispector's most recently translated work, *The Besieged City*, she says: "… behold the table in the dark. Raised above itself by its lack of function." In another book she talks about the aura of things, their spirit. This aura, she says, is "…a halo. It is a breath. It is a breathing. It is a manifestation. It is the freed movement of the thing." I think of my round table, the halo of it, of all the things it's held, will hold. Right now it's in my kitchen by the window, holding all the flowers left at the end of summer. It's late September and we've already had snow, and so we brought in terra-cotta pots of geraniums, and filled small vases with dahlias, and roses, and veronica. All summer, it's held books and flowers, glasses of wine and glasses of water, notebooks, and sunglasses. The table is a round O, a breathing. I get up in the middle of the night when I can't sleep, and there it is, glowing in the dark, holding whatever I have asked it to hold. In the first light of morning, the sun slices through the window over the kitchen sink and illumines the plants and flowers resting there. Later in the day the sun comes in from the opposite window, filtered now, but still surprising. The table comes alive when the light touches it. It could be levitating. The flowers are radiant now, they sparkle, they smile and gleam, like jewels in a treasure box. Whenever I enter the room, my eye goes first to the table by the window, so that I might note the drama unfolding.

In traditional Dutch still lifes, piled up with treasures and valuables, the table itself, Norman Bryson says, becomes like a "bank-vault" or a "graveyard." But really, in a still life, who ever really notices the table? The whole magic trick of still life is that we forget who put the stuff on the table, and how it was arranged and composed, and we don't think about the table either, the sturdy surface holding up the objects. We might take note of the light and shadows falling upon the table, but we usually take the surface for granted.

Usually. But there are those who have considered the table. Neruda, for example, in his ode says:

Tables are trustworthy:
titanic quadrupeds
they sustain
our hopes and our daily life.

He goes on:

> The world is a table
> engulfed in honey and smoke
> smothered by apples and blood.
> The table is already set,
> and we know the truth
> as soon as we are called:
> whether we're called to war or to dinner
> we will have to choose sides,
> have to know
> how we'll dress
> to sit
> at the long table,
> whether we'll wear the pants of hate
> or the shirt of love, freshly laundered.

The table for Neruda, is not just a site for collecting treasures, it's the world. Whatever the world is, so the table is. What happens at the table, happens in the world. And the question is, how do you want to come to the table? Joy Harjo, addresses this as well in her poem, "Perhaps the World Ends Here." In it she says:

> The world begins at a kitchen table. No matter what,
> we must eat to live.
> The gifts of earth are brought and prepared, set on the
> table. So it has been since creation, and it will go on.

The poem ends:

> Perhaps the world will end at the kitchen table, while
> we are laughing and crying, eating of the last sweet bite.

Who is invited to the table? What will you put upon it? Who will feel welcome? Who will bring love? Who will talk loudly and who will speak quietly and with assurance? How will we become more human and teach those we love to be more human at this table? With whom will we share and how much? How fulsomely will we give thanks? Who is missing from the table and why? Even if we can't always answer the question "why?" it must do some good to ask it. To sit at the table with plates and gravy boats filled with questions.

If we really looked at the tables that we sat at, and not just the fruit bowls, the dishes of cookies, and the cups of tea, what would happen? What would happen if we cultivated amity between people and things? I can't help but bring to mind the surrealist painting by Remedios Varo, *Still Life Reviving*. It was her last painting before she died of a heart attack at the age of 54.[10] The painting depicts fruits, plates, a candlestick levitating in an orbit over the table. Some of the fruits have collided and seeds have erupted, sprouting into small plants. The tablecloth is alive and dancing to some rock and roll music, spiraling and whirling. Let's get the party started, let's get living, let's blow this whole fucking thing apart, is what I can't help hearing in my head. If we were to be asked to dine at this table, and were asked to choose sides, I could only shout out—we've got to be alive to things!

The painting is about rebirth and resurrection, with the "dead nature" of still life exploding into life. Almost all of Varo's paintings include a human form, but not this one, which is why art historians find it eerily prophetic. The surreal world of the table that she created went on without her, ending and beginning all at the same time.

Tables are trustworthy, says Neruda. The world begins at the kitchen table, says Harjo. Lispector says things have an aura, a spirit. At the table we will choose sides. And it is at the table that we will know the affection the tablecloth feels for the table, and perhaps we'll be able to extend it to each other, or perhaps we will find it insurmountably difficult. At the table it is possible that the world will end, but it can also begin again, rising up from the tablecloth, rearranging itself, while those assembled don the "freshly laundered shirt of love."

---

10 It's probably not important to note that I'm currently 53.

The Magic Trick of Still Life

You stand in front of a painting of a table, a bowl of plums, and an open window. The light on the plums is so sweet and golden. After you look at it for a while, you close your eyes and imagine how when a breeze comes in, the light would modulate, flickering, softening, brightening. Years later, you can still close your eyes and see this scene in your imagination, though you can't remember what museum you were in when you saw it.

Knowing what goes on in setting up the trick doesn't change the fact that still life is magic. Maybe all good art is an iridescent magic trick of the soul. The magic of the still life is potentially this: the viewer feels that time has stopped, that the ordinary is astonishing and even transcendent, holy. A painting is a kind of window itself, and the window of a painting is simultaneously tangibly real and makes us feel we are standing in front of one of those openings in the universe, a pane through which beauty shines, into our astonishing decrepit world from another more serene realm. In short, the magic trick is that we forget for a second or two that we're looking at a painting. We're in the painting.

I don't know much about stage magic. I'm unschooled in the pulling of rabbits from hats, the sawing of a lady in half, or the pulling of coins from ears. I know little about parlour tricks or escapology. Sleight of hand, misdirection, and the application of various other tricks of the eye are quite mysterious to me. While other people might feel delight at seeing—abracadabra!—a rabbit pop out of a hat, or—poof!—a dove emerging from a colourful handkerchief, I admit that these tricks make me feel uneasy and unsettled. In general, I'm the kind of person who dislikes surprises or having the wool pulled over my eyes, and I really feel queasy around fakery. I don't enjoy being fooled or duped and I don't have the patience to figure out where the secret compartment is, or how my eye has been misdirected.

But the illusion of a painting, the way a viewer can be drawn into the world depicted in the confines of a rectangle or window-shape, which is made out of a canvas pulled over a wooden stretcher, and then covered with colourful pigments suspended in oil, having a muddy or gooey texture—shazam!—this is for me.

I am ready to fall for the illusion of the rectangle every time. I was not brought up around art or paintings. In the 1970s and 1980s in Edmonton,[11] I knew no one who had a piece of original art on their walls. We had some kind of a knock-off Frederic Remington repro painting of a horse in a Western setting that would have come from Sears or some now-defunct furniture showroom. It was big, though, and it probably went with the orange and brown tones that were prevalent. I don't remember looking at it very much. I couldn't describe it for you now without making the whole thing up. I didn't imagine myself in the scene and I didn't fantasize about falling into the picture, such as in the passage from *The Narnia Chronicles: The Voyage of the Dawn Treader*, where Edmund and Lucy and Eustace are looking at a painting of a ship. As they're looking at it, the waves come alive, the ship moves, and the three of them land in its waters, in Narnia. As a child it made perfect sense to me that you could make it to Narnia through a wardrobe or

---

11 And then on an acreage outside Edmonton.

through a painting, and maybe ever since then, I've always been hoping to get through to another realm.

I was twenty-three when I met my husband Rob, the artist Robert Lemay. And since, I've lived with original art in my life for longer than I have lived without it. I've seen the other side of that magic trick, all the things that go into making up the illusion. I've seen the pigment squeezed out of the tubes, the colours mixed, the canvas being pulled taut over the stretcher. I've seen the grid being drawn in pencil on the canvas, and the threads used to grid the working photo. I've seen the photos being taken and the flowers being arranged. I've even watched the flowers grow in our backyard or selected from the cooler at the florist. I've waited for the light to change so the photo could be taken, and I've waited for the long hours for a painting to be completed, looking every day at the progress, a few inches of paint applied one day, a few more the next. When the painting is done, it's brought out of the studio and upstairs where we can look at it in a different light, at a different distance. I've looked at the paintings for weeks while they dry, and seen them packed up in a box, shipped to one of the galleries that represent Rob. And sometimes I've seen them hanging up in the gallery where they've been sent and watched other people looking at them.

Rob has very often been asked by viewers how he does what he does. How does he make the flowers he paints look so real? He usually talks about getting the tonal values correct up close and when this happens, you can back up from the painting, and it will read realistically. If you get the tones right, he says, the colour will take care of itself. When you look at the brushstrokes up close, they're quite poetic, they flow. Especially with a larger canvas, it really is surprising to move back and see the realism or the illusion come together.

Siri Hustvedt quotes David Freedberg who says that he was "concerned, above all, by the failure of art history to deal with the extraordinarily abundant evidence for the ways in which people of all classes and cultures have responded to images." She goes on to talk about how art transfixes people who have little background in art theory or art history. Museums are full of people from all sorts of backgrounds, just enjoying and looking, intently viewing, and once in a while becoming captivated by a single canvas.

I'm interested in all the ways that ordinary people look at and experience art and whether or not they think about the magic trick of it, or if there are other things that they find enjoyable about looking at art. Maybe my viewpoint and experience are interesting to others. I think I'm in a fairly unique position to talk about the magic trick. I've spent a lot of time "behind the scenes" of art, seeing it made and living with it in my home, but I'm also a writer, with that sensibility, and I have spent a lot of time practicing photography, developing my eye that way. I'm not an art historian, but I've been looking at art and reading about it and living with it for thirty years. I like thinking about the differences between paintings and photos. The way paintings take so long to make, and how that time is built into brushstrokes, the pigment. The drying time can be long, too, and some colours take longer than others. When we view a painting, we usually walk back and forth in front of it, if it's larger, and then we step back. The time it takes to physically look at every inch of a painting is part of the experience of looking at it. A photograph is experienced differently. Sometimes a photo is enlarged and presented in a more monumental scale. But usually, a photo is more intimate. Most of us will be more likely to experience a photo in a book—held in our hands or balanced on our lap— reproduced on glossy or matte paper. And we know that the capture, the photo, is an instant. We also know that it's possible that many photos were taken on each side of this instant and were deleted or discarded, in favour of the one we are now looking at.

I think it's possible to fall into a photograph, or a reproduction of a painting. But it also seems to me that there is something about viewing a painting up close and personal that makes this experience more likely. Who knows why the illusion of space on a flat canvas created with daubs of coloured mud works upon us in this way, but I do know that I've stood in front of Monet's water lilies and felt that I was there. I've stood in front of Vermeer's milkmaid and felt as though I was in the room with her. I've also felt this quite regularly, looking at still lifes.

Still life has this added illusion in that they depict objects we're familiar with or that could be in our own homes, and so we feel as though we know them—plums, lemons, wine glasses, bowls. Maybe we haven't experienced a pond of waterlilies in France, but most of us have placed fruit in a bowl, arranged flowers in a vase or pitcher, put out bread on a cutting board. Not only that, but as Siri Hustvedt notes in *Mysteries of the Rectangle*, "in solitude objects are the company we keep." When we feel alone, we can turn to the objects in our own humble lives for contemplation. John Berger says, "We live in a world of suffering in which evil is rampant, a world whose events do not confirm our Being, a world that has to be resisted. It is in this situation that the aesthetic moment offers hope, that we find a crystal or a poppy beautiful means that we are less alone…"

The magic trick of art, and perhaps particularly still life, is to remind us above all that there is beauty at the same time as evil. Evil is a given but beauty persists. The magic trick of still life is that it reminds us that we're not alone. The magic trick of still life is that it's not really a trick at all. There are no hidden compartments and even the artist marvels at the illusion they have created. There is no one saying "abracadabra" and no "poof" of smoke. What there is: the feeling of going deep, being in the presence of something calm and lovely. Our breathing alters. Looking at a painting of a bowl of plums we might, transported, sigh.

The Loophole

"Daily life contains within itself the abuse of daily life: daily life has the tragedy of the tedium of repetition. But there's a loophole: that the great reality is exceptional, like a dream in the entrails of the day."

– from *A Breath of Life* by Clarice Lispector

The now-instant of a still life can be a loophole. A bowl of peaches or a stack of books beside a vase of lilacs can be a fissure where the light gets into the daily, a dream in the entrails of the day, a shortcut to the marvellous, an opening through which to shoot beauty's arrow.

The word loophole is used to suggest an ambiguity in the system or law, a site of circumvention. The word comes from the design in a medieval fortress known as an arrowslit or loophole, a usually narrow cross-shaped interval through which an archer may launch his arrows, while still being protected from incoming arrows. In the absence of conflict or action, the loophole is a crack where the light gets into the castle. It's a slim threshold between the private stronghold and the threats of the world outside.

Ordinary life interests me. But I'm also a junkie for the marvellous and the transcendent and the poetic. When I am not at home writing or taking photographs, I have a day job where I'm an anonymous ordinary person. This state is not dissimilar to my role as a minor writer, of course. I work at a public library, talking to people who have a myriad of everyday concerns. The work can be absurdly mundane. Countless recitals of how to use the photocopier, how to print a document, or how to save a file. The tasks are repetitive, but the people are never so. Each one is unique and working on something of importance to them. I find this interesting, and I like feeling useful. And I like it when a small task you've helped someone with lifts a weight and you are both charged, energized, renewed by this brief encounter. I've been asked what it's like to be a writer in a public library—with the intimation that I might be better known than I really am—and my answer is that Margaret Atwood could be working the front desk and people would still just be wanting her to hurry up and put fifty cents on their print account. They'd be tapping their fingers on the desk.

I find so-called ordinary life to be fascinating but you might enjoy contrasting it with the experience of Anaïs Nin, who said:

> "Ordinary life does not interest me. I seek only the high moments. I am in accord with the surrealists, searching for the marvellous. I want to be a writer who reminds others that these moments exist; I want to prove that there is infinite space, infinite meaning, infinite dimension. But I am not always in what I call a state of grace. I have days of illuminations and fevers. I have days when the music in my head stops. Then I mend socks, prune trees, can fruits, polish furniture. But while I am doing this, I feel I am not living."

Because I need my day job to sustain my writing life, I have had to find ways to make it not just palatable, but meaningful. I work hard to do this even if I don't always succeed. But my goal is to find the beauty in work, the poetry in work, and I have come to believe that one feeds the other. If I can't find the beauty in my library work, how can I find beauty in my creative life? I need to be the person who can find beauty without separating one part of my life from another. When I'm not writing or being creative, I don't want to think that I'm "not living." I can't compartmentalize. I need to let one part of my life flow into the other part. This is when interesting things start to happen anyway.

Half of my working life is spent at the library and the rest of my time is spent writing and taking photographs and thinking about the beauty of the world, as juxtaposed with the not always so beautiful parts of the world. My husband's studio is in the basement and he paints flowers, huge bouquets of peonies and roses. The still life is at the centre of our life, and I'm interested in the way these arrangements, and being attentive to them, affect us. I like thinking about still life paintings, which distill and refine a grouping of objects into a silent presence that can be described variously as poetic, calming, enlightening, transcendent, meditative, contemplative, or profound.

I'm also interested in the history and secrets and stories of things themselves. The way objects speak, silent and still, persistent and bittersweet, powerful and cold, holds my attention. I like rocks and odd china ornaments and chipped cups and smooth bowls. I like pearl earrings and old weathered chairs and water pitchers. I like fading flowers and green bottles and books. I like things. I like listening to the music and silence in things. What do they say about us, and what are they whispering to us about our lives and this world, this planet? The still life can be a small world that speaks about the larger one. It can be witness, consolation, a secret message, the arrow you launch through a narrow opening, a dream we once had or will have. A still life is in time but it also stops time, is out of time. A still life can exist in what seems to be another realm and it can be an instant that circumvents tedium.

The still life is sometimes a question. And sometimes it provokes other questions: What are the dreams in the entrails of your tedious day? What is your exceptional reality? Where is the loophole in your daily life? Where is the holy ordinary, that sweet spot? Which way to the transcendent?

I think the marvellous is there at all times and we just have to be in the correct state to witness it. But I also believe that this is something we have to constantly relearn and constantly seek. We need to remain open to this possibility. It's also useful to know that there will be dead times, flat ones, stretches where we are dulled to the great magic of the universe, to the magnificence, and to the real beauty of being merely alive—alive on a blue planet circling a sun in a universe we know next to nothing about, to be expansively imprecise.

Even if we don't remember to be on the lookout for those moments where, as Emily Dickinson once said, she felt "physically as if the top of my head were taken off," it will happen anyway. You'll come around the corner in your own house and a pile of laundry is illuminated, or your cat sits in the window and blinks, or the bowl of oranges casts a beautiful shadow on your kitchen table, and everything drops away. So what? you might think. The world has these little pockets of surprising beauty. Big deal.

Many people will feel indifferent to beauty and sometimes even hostile toward it. At the very least, it's possible to hold yourself aloof from beauty, feel superior to beauty, or to feel that beauty will let you down, or that the world's ugliness and sorrows and pressing and seemingly impending ruin must take precedence. Our relationship to beauty is complicated. Which is why I waffle between feeling that I should be making a coherent and extensive case for beauty and that I should be apologizing for my insistence on it. Or maybe I should be talking my reader into the necessity, yelling out and howling on beauty's behalf, shooting arrows of beauty through my stronghold's loophole. And I feel as though I should make excuses for myself, for wanting and needing it so. But if we don't have beauty, what do we have?

You deserve beauty in your life. Every single living soul does.

If we can recognize the slivers and shimmers of beauty out there in our everyday lives, maybe we have a slightly better chance of seeing and feeling our own beauty. Which I have the feeling most people don't do. I know I find it difficult to think of myself that way. And if I can't think of myself as having beauty, being worthy of beauty, then how do I look outward and see others as beautiful?

One thing I've learned in both my library and writing life is that: People are beautiful; they are poetry.

I'm very fond of the lines by Gustave Flaubert: "There is not a particle of life which does not bear poetry within it." When I'm asked about poetry at work, which is more often than you'd imagine, I sometimes want to tell the person—well, you're poetry, this entire place is poetry, filled with poetry.

The American poet Philip Levine writes,

> . . . our lives, any life, is worthy of poetry
> the experience of any human being
> is worthy of poetry.

And what I ask myself is, how to make of our lives poetry? How to see the poetry in others? How to let people know that their experience, their very existence is poetry, is worthy of poetry. The loophole is there, the marvellous and astonishing world is always there, and we need to map the shortcuts to it.

I'm attentive to the still lifes at the library, the actual objects on surfaces. The thumbed through and abandoned stacks of books and magazines on a worn table in the morning light. The newspaper perched on the edge of an armchair. The takeout coffee cups on the shelf of a carrel. The backpacks propped up against the computer desks. The purses, gaping open and revealing. The Slurpees and Doritos and Dairy Queen burgers and french fries and chocolate bar wrappers beside the computer screens. The piles of documents and identification. A well-loved stuffed animal forgotten by a child on a table in the children's section. The makeup bag open and lipstick and compact beside where a young woman applies mascara, looking at her muted reflection on the computer screen.

When I come home, I make my own still lifes. The not-so-deliberate ones, such as my work bag, the book club books I bring home to read, car keys, purse. My endless stacks of books on the night table, the coffee tables, the table in my study, and also on the floor. I usually wear a scarf to work and that's tossed into the mix too. On my days off, I'm more deliberate. I take photos of things for my blog. These arrays are very much staged. It's helpful to be married to a still life painter, as our basement is full of props and we often have flowers. Lately, I've been photographing my strange arrays of candy and books and junk food and Rob's castoff flowers against a black background. I'm trying to say something about the state of the world, though I can't say exactly what. I'm waiting for the correct light and—putting everything into them that I can think of—the sweet, the salty, the kitsch, and the classical and the contemporary.

In this practice, it occurred to me that the words of Joseph Campbell, which I've quoted in a previous book, have stayed with me throughout my life. He says, "Any object, intensely regarded, may be a gate of access…" In an interview with Bill D. Moyers, Campbell says,

> Usually you think of a thing in practical terms, but you could think of anything in terms of its mystery. For example, this is a watch, but it is also a thing in being. You could put it down, draw a ring around it, and regard it in that dimension. That is the point of

consecration . . . Do you really know what a thing is? What supports it? It is something in time and space. Think how mysterious it is that anything should be.

I can't help but feel the connection between the objects I observe at the library, and in the still lifes in my home. The objects might say something about our economy, about how people live, and what forces come into play in the variousness of our private lives. But they also speak to the mystery, too. The other realm is not beside this one, *it is* this one, and we only need a little light, a sense of composition, a love of the inadvertent, an appreciation for the humble, and there it is. Look, there's a worn and grubby backpack, a sheaf of lined paper and a newly sharpened pencil, a perspiring Slurpee leaving a red ring on top of the paper. There's the mystery, the loophole. Here are some flowers I clipped from my garden, some books, the seashells my neighbour handed me twenty years ago.

Why is it that this moment of transcendence induced by a still life, this seeing through to the other side, this opening or loophole where we drop into the sheer mystery of being, is so interesting to me? I think it's because it also contains the promise of the moment after. A still life stops time, is out of time, occasionally offering the viewer that rupture/ rapture. It is also suspenseful. The question hovers: what happens next? And it gives us an interval to dream new possibilities. It affects us, and it affects how we walk through this world, into the loophole, beyond the threshold, our eyes open, awake.

Look at Me

On Claiming Your Expertise

I am exactly rubbish at claiming my expertise. If you'd asked me when I was seventeen what I thought I'd be good at in my fifties, I might have shrugged my shoulders. More likely, I might have said, I don't think I'll live so long. In high school, I didn't think I'd ever go to college. Looking back, I'm a little surprised that I did make it to college and university. Several years of depressed and rather hopeless partying, dancing in basement clubs to Depeche Mode and The Smiths until I didn't remember my name, drinking with a lot of the wrong people, walking home alone, sauced, in the dark, eating brownies with friends who just gleefully waited for my awful trip, hopping into cars without looking at the driver and finding it wasn't who I thought it was, going for rides on dark highways with guys I barely knew in their Camaros and Jeeps, and other death-defying feats punctuated my late teens and early twenties. The idea of expertise in relation to myself would have seemed laughable, then.

These days, I'm happy to go along in a pretty low-key, anonymous way. I prefer it. I don't need to use fancy words to prove I'm clever or to brag about the places I've been.[12] I wasn't always this way. There were times in my long career of

---

12 Not that many but you know what I mean.

customer service jobs[13] and waiting on tables that I wanted to say to someone who was talking down to me, "Hey, I'm Somebody, you know!" Does this mean I'm more evolved than I once was? Maybe. I like the words by Hafiz, translated here by Daniel Ladinsky: "Greatness /is always built upon this foundation: /the ability / to appear, speak, and act / as the most / common /[wo]man."

One of the things I'm quite good at is talking to ordinary humans, the people that come into the library where I work, many of whom are part of an at-risk population. While it feels good to just be anonymous and down-to-earth, it's also important to claim one's expertise. When I'm not working at the library, I write and I take photos. I had begun thinking about taking a series of still life photographs long before I set the first one up and clicked the shutter. I even tried talking myself out of doing it, for who would be the viewer? Various random people scrolling by on my Instagram feed? In the end I decided to let the photos say, persistently, and quietly, I know some stuff.

How has the question of "who is the viewer of a still life?" changed through time? Norman Bryson, referring to a Willem Kalf painting *Still Life with Nautilus Cup*, asks about "the kind of sociality the painting assumes." Is the viewer the owner of the painting, whose gaze might be one of satisfaction? Or do we imagine the picture being shown to others who may covet the objects, or dream of them—a dream which Bryson says is likelier to "isolate than to bind individuals together" because of the competition this sets up. As for my photographs, they're available on the internet. What I'm hoping is that some viewers might see their lives, past or present, reflected in these pictures, or just think about lives that aren't quite the same as theirs. I might also hope that the viewer believes in me. This is what any artist or writer hopes for—that the viewer believes in you and your expertise enough to go along for the ride, see what happens next, and to look with you through your particular lens.

---

13 Selling piles of self-help books or five-hundred-dollar fountain pens.

I often think of my knowledge base in terms of what I don't know, the degrees I don't have. I'm not an art historian and I'm not a trained photographer. When I work at the library, I feel awkward when I'm referred to as a librarian, which is technically someone who has a Master's degree in library science. I feel a bit of a fake. Why does it feel equally fake to say what I do know, though? I started off, in my early twenties, by getting a diploma in Library and Information Management and then went on to get a BA in English Literature. After I'd written a couple of books and had a child, I also obtained an MA in English Literature. As for my photography cred, well, I've been taking photographs off and on since high school, when I bought my first camera, a Pentax MX. Maybe it's enough to say I've taken four or five good photographs in my life.

I remember reading the manual for the Pentax multiple times before threading that first roll of film through it. My subjects were trees, leaves, horses, hay bales, our black lab. When the guidance counsellor had us write a report on a career we'd pursue after high school, I chose photography, because I didn't think writing could be a career. What I learned was that my marks in chemistry would preclude me from getting into photography at the technical college. The two things I was interested in, writing and photography, seemed utterly unattainable.

I can measure out my life by the cameras I've owned. Many of us can do this. I took the Pentax with me when I moved out at eighteen. I would take black-and-white photos of friends in front of old buildings, of cigarette butts, and of my lipsticks in a row reflected in the bathroom mirror. I'd not heard of Irving Penn at that time. The camera came with me through several moves to crumby apartments. Near the beginning of my relationship with Rob, he used it to take a reference photo for his first still life painting as a professional artist, one that ended up in the Canadian Embassy in Beijing. We took that camera on our honeymoon to Italy. When we had our daughter, I bought a Canon Rebel SLR. After that there was a Lumix point-and-shoot, which I never really did get the hang of; we weren't simpatico. When DSLRs appeared, we bought a Nikon D50. Both Rob and I used that Nikon for ages, each of us having our own lens for it. My latest camera, a Nikon D610 is mine alone, as Rob has moved on to using an iPad for his reference photos.

Before I bought the D610, I had the idea that I would try to learn how to paint and then write about that. But painting well is difficult and I don't have the heart to do it horribly. I've watched my husband go to his basement studio to paint for thirty years, almost every day. And then when our daughter made getting into animation college a goal, I watched her draw endlessly, until she did get in. She was rarely without a pencil or stylus in her hand, going to figure drawing classes, drawing the flowers in the front yard, the dog, her own hands. I thought of the thousands of hours I would need to learn to just draw, before I could really make a solid go of painting. It occurred to me that photography was attainable because I've been doing this all along. I've been composing and seeing through a lens since high school and learning about digital photography for years. Still life also seemed to be the subject right before my very eyes. It's a subject I've read about alongside Rob all these years. What was holding me back? I didn't want to step on his toes or infringe upon his subject matter. But since I started to take these photos, he has been as delighted by them and as interested in them as I am. A photograph, after all, has only so much in common with a painting. I felt free to begin practicing my practice.

The photograph I'd had in mind when I began this project was this one:

As soon as I saw that mind-boggling image of Trump and his fast-food spread, I knew I wanted to take some photos of burgers. I wanted to mix it up with traditional motifs, the cat, the tropical fruit and flowers, the unwinding lemon.

Fast-food is cheap, it's terrible for us, but it's designed to give us a quick, feel-good hit. It's easy to be moralistic about it, but it persists. We can know how truly awful something is and still be okay with it, collectively, because it's an industry, it's larger than we are, and there's a feeling of helplessness before all that. And meanwhile, some of us have fewer choices than others. When I see kids who spend most of their summer in the library playing video games on the computers, I never judge them for consuming their giant bags of chips, Slurpees and, on rare good days, the burgers and fries. It's what they can afford.

Maybe if we could figure out the nuances of our addiction to fast-food, we could figure out how we got to where we have politically. You'll notice in my photo how the orange of the cheese is picked up in the flowers and how the red french fries box is a counterpoint to the magenta of the ranunculus. The porcelain cat is never going to get a morsel. And the lemon is the same colour as the M on the cup. If I were to have left all this as pictured, the lemon would have rotted, the flowers would have wilted, but the fries and burger would remain. That stuff never decomposes, never goes away. Nevertheless, memento mori.

Is there still beauty to be found in all this? Does the presence of the fast-food spoil the other elements and make them less beautiful or interesting? Are we left feeling satisfied in our looking? or do the empty calories translate there as well? How hungry for beauty are we? How hungry for something of substance? Questions.

One of the first still lifes I constructed was a bit of a free-for-all. I went to the 7-Eleven and purchased all the junk food I could think of. When I paid for my bags of Hawkins Cheezies, Doritos, Hostess Ding Dongs, processed cherry pie, sprinkle-covered pretzel, and powdered mini-doughnuts, the clerk didn't bat an eye. I picked whatever flowers were growing in my yard that day, some dahlias and a bouquet of mock orange blossoms, and I arrayed them along with copies of *Jane Eyre* and *Pride and Prejudice*, a classical bust, and a peeled and unwinding lemon.

Thus began my practice. In other attempts I put in things that would appear in traditional still lifes, but in different forms. Goldfish crackers or Swedish fish to stand in for the bream prevalent in Dutch still lifes. Cats were regularly depicted in still lifes by artists such as Chardin, Clara Peeters, and Frans Snyders. I added a cut melon, another standard still life object, in a painting with a hotdog and a Slurpee from the 7-Eleven.

What interests me in still life is that while it's all just stuff on a table and has been for hundreds of years, those things can say a lot about our time, how we live, about our level of wealth, and how we understand and interact with beauty. It also says something about the consumer market, what we desire, what we hold dear, what is actually available to us. The Sev in our suburban neighbourhood is a hotspot. You run into people you know there as you're grabbing your milk and a lottery ticket. Sometimes you just need some junk food. They don't call them convenience stores for nothing. It's not a Roman piazza, but it's what we have.

While traditional still lifes might show off an opulent lifestyle—think oysters and expensive cheeses, think golden goblets and abundant fruit—I wanted to see how a can of wieners and beans and cup noodles might signify, and how they would hold up to the beauty of a vase of flowers.

The repeating ingredient in most of my experiments is a stack of books. The first book I read about still life was one of Rob's titled *Looking at the Overlooked* by Norman Bryson, published in 1990. The books in my photographs signal to the viewer, perhaps, an accumulation of knowledge, the importance of reading, the prestige of the books. Maybe the viewer finds this pretentious. I'm saying that I've read these books and lived with them over a decent period of time. I'm claiming my expertise.

I throw in modern, less conventional items, along with the traditional. In doing so, I'm trying to say something about the way we live. I'm trying to say something about wealth, abundance, the way things seem versus the way they are. How appearances regarding wealth can be deceiving. I want the objects to speak for themselves and I want to dwell on the possibilities and disparities. These strategies aren't all that different from those employed by painters of historical still lifes. They, too, were commenting on wastefulness, abundance, the perils of decadence, the precariousness of wealth, even as they were painting scenes to bring prestige to the owners of the pictures.

I'm wondering how a digital photograph of a still life reflects things back to society versus how a painting does. The number of frames that an SD card holds, and the quickness, the immediacy of a digital photo is in contrast to a painting that takes weeks to construct. To even own the kind of camera I do is a sign of a certain level of wealth and privilege. We live in a Marie Kondo–inspired world, where if a thing doesn't spark joy, we're advised to ditch it. But this, too, is a very privileged stance. You have to have stuff in the first place to ditch it.

I'm conscious of this after having worked a shift in my library branch which is full of people who are precariously low-income as well as those who are houseless. I come home to my lower middle-class abode, which feels pretty decadent, in comparison. I have some pretty complicated feelings around all of this, let me tell you. It's not always easy navigating these disparities, nor should it be. A lot of this swirls around in my mind on my nights with insomnia, to which I am prone.

Along with the 7-Eleven and McDonald's still lifes, I also wanted to do a Kraft Dinner still life. Shooting it, I couldn't get the song from The Barenaked Ladies out of my head, "If I Had a Million Dollars." If you were rich, would you still eat Kraft Dinner? Of course…not. The song tells the same kind of joke that still lifes tell. It's no big deal being rich, because we're still just like you. But I can pretty much guarantee you that rich people don't have late night KD parties or live on cup noodles at lunch.

I spend a lot of my time blogging about beauty and attempting to justify it as a counterbalance to my despair at the ugly things going on in the world. There is a poem by Lia Purpura in which she talks about "beauty's terrible plumage" and how it has the ability to disturb or disrupt our despair. And maybe this is something else for which I'll claim expertise—as a curator for the beautiful, as someone who persistently reminds people of the beauty in the ordinary and the everyday.

So here is beauty's terrible plumage, as plucked from my garden one afternoon this summer. It's not an extraordinary image, but I did have an extraordinary time photographing it. I felt these flowers. And I think they felt me. Maybe it's because I had a week of lesser and greater nights of insomnia, but it was an emotional experience. When I was done, I just set the camera down and felt like crying. That feeling. Beyond being able to weep, even. I sat with the beauty of the flowers and the news of the world and it was all too much and, at the same time, this other thing occurred: the aesthetic experience. And that's how it is these days, everything all at once all the time.

In photographing this particular still life series, I'm carving out my unique skill set, I'm claiming my expertise. It's all coming into play. Almost all of my writing has been about art, in one form or another, including work on ekphrasis. I've blogged for over a decade, incorporating my own photographs with the text. I've not only thought and written about how text and image work together in the internet age, I've enacted it. And so this latest project, which unfolds on social media and on my blog, models a kind of learning that is public, of the moment, and contributes to a live conversation. I'm muddling through the questions of how we find beauty, how we make beauty, and how to do so meaningfully while interrogating how it fits into an ordinary day, into the world right now. And I'm insisting that we look at the terrible plumage of things against the darkest background possible. I insist that your ordinary world is beautiful.

An Ugly Woman

"There is a time when you must take a picture of yourself."

– Clarice Lispector

When I was younger, I might have wasted one of my three wishes on being beautiful.

We know at a young age that beauty is currency, and I certainly knew that my life trajectory would have been different if my teeth had been straight, if my nose wasn't so large, if my skin was clearer, if my features were more uniform. In high school I had the usual crushes, but as one of the ugly girls, tall and inelegant, I knew it would be unrequited love. In my early twenties, a friend wanted to take a modelling course and, knowing it would lead to nothing, I went along. It was a fantasy. I knew what I looked like, and I knew what the young women looked like who got picked up by the international modelling agencies. We read *Vogue* and *Elle* quite religiously, then. I knew what I was.

But did I?

As part of this modelling course, we got a free headshot session with a local photographer. Once our course was over, he asked me and my friend Dawn to sit for him because he was building up his portfolio and needed models for practice. I still have a folder full of the contact sheets and prints he gave me, which seems incredibly generous now. I was twenty-one years old then. I remember, or misremember, a conversation I had with this photographer about beauty. I was self-conscious about my teeth, and he said, it doesn't matter, you don't have to smile anyway, it's not important. That was revelatory.

I look back now at those photographs that are in a folder in my closet and wonder at the fact that I felt ugly then; I felt fat; I felt unattractive. Because, honestly, they're not half bad. Actually, they're amazing. Would that I looked so good now. There are studio photos, photos taken at the airfield in front of prop planes, lying on the beach and floating in the river scenes, and sitting in the forest looking pensive. I looked good. I looked interesting. I looked svelte. But at the time I felt anything but.

I remember the photographer, Peter McClure, said something about beauty being just about knowing how to turn your face. How to turn your face toward beauty. He said that sometimes the ugliest woman is also the most beautiful. I aligned myself with that ugliest beautiful woman as an act of self-preservation. Because as Simone Weil said, "A very beautiful woman who looks at her reflection in the mirror can very well believe that she is that. An ugly woman knows that she is not that." While I felt ugly and weird and awkward because of my height, I also knew that I was not that. I was not *that*.

In one of the first photos I posted of myself on Instagram I'm wearing a black turtleneck on a black background. I was about to head out to meet a friend for lunch, and I felt like myself—that rare feeling. I set up the camera and had Rob snap a few photos and off I went. I posted them later saying that I thought it was important to share photos of what an ordinary woman looks like at 53. I received many comments about how I was not at all ordinary.

But I am. I'm not a movie star or a model or a rockstar or an Instagram influencer. I'm not a celebrity of any sort.

I'm not even a famous writer. I'm a super minor Canadian writer, which is the truth rather than self-deprecation. As someone who is past middle-age, I'm okay with who I am. I have deep wrinkles around my eyes, my eyes never have matched,[14] and I am not my ideal weight. I haven't been inside a salon in years. I am utterly ordinary. Which is a lovely thing. It's what most of us actually are. Maybe when I'm 70 I'll look back at the photos of myself in my 50s and think, wow, you were beautiful, just as I now look at photos of myself in my 20s and think about how I didn't know what my powers were. I hadn't a clue.

I've worn glasses since grade three, and then contacts for years beginning in my teens. After childbirth though, I scratched my cornea badly and wore an eyepatch for several weeks. My eyes were so dry I could no longer wear contacts comfortably and gave up on them. It's only in the last few years that I began wearing them again. When I wear glasses, I feel less like who I am and more like I'm wearing some kind of disguise. I don't recognize myself when I'm wearing glasses. There's the famous line by Dorothy Parker that I've always been fond of: "Men seldom make passes at girls who wear glasses." There are so many reasons why this is funny, partly because it's true, and partly because it's not. Sometimes glasses can be a bit of a shield from unwanted attention. When you wear glasses, you can be ordinary, like Clark Kent.

A lot of writers wear glasses. It seems to go with the territory. But they don't always wear them in their author photos. A lot has been written about the importance of author photos by marketers of books. Adam Zagajewski's poem about photographs of poets is a delight to me. He says, poets are photographed, "but never when / they truly see" and "never in darkness, / never in silence, / at night, in uncertainty / when they hesitate" or when they experience joy. I

---

14 I have heterochromia, that hardly anyone notices but which, in all honesty, I enjoy.

guess they're most often captured when a book is about to be published.

I remember being so nervous about my author photo before my first book of poetry came out. The poems were about beauty, about the way women have been historically portrayed in art. It seemed crucial to me that my photo said something about my critique and unpacking of the themes in the poetry. Lo and behold, the publisher decided that this new series of books would not include author photos. Which, in the end, for me, said exactly the correct thing. Still, I was a tiny bit disappointed; I felt vain. I expended a lot of energy getting images of the art to which the poems referred included in the book. This was the late 90s and having pictures in a book of poetry was almost unheard of. So, you'll find, in black-and-white, paintings by Paula Modersohn-Becker, Artemisia Gentileschi, Rachel Ruysch, and Rosa Bonheur, but no photograph of me.

Looking back at my author photos in subsequent books, I cringe. There's not one that I like, that seems real, that seems like me. But there's always the next book, that hope. Though maybe the problem is that it's impossible to see oneself. The Zagajewski poem gets at this. So much of who we are is internal—it's the silence that's missing, the joy, the constant worrying.

There are a lot of articles on the internet about the need for a good author photo. It should signal something about you as an author, apparently. If you're writing about vampires, you're going to want dark moodiness and red lipstick, and if you're a nature writer, make sure you're standing in a forest with leaves in your hair. You should look serious, obviously. Though I haven't studied this in any scientific way, it seems that if you're a woman, you might be more likely to smile than if you're a man.

The photographer Annie Leibovitz notes that "There are not many smiling people in my pictures. I've never asked anyone to smile. Almost never." She talks about the way the subject of a photo is often asked to smile for the birdie, to say cheese, and of course that sort of smiling on demand is fake, forced. There's nothing more lovely than a natural smile, but a put-on one is heartbreaking.

I'm fond of the song "Cynthia" by Springsteen because she doesn't smile and that's alright. Likewise, Mary ain't no beauty in the song "Thunder Road." But women who don't smile and aren't conventionally beautiful in real life occupy space differently than those who do. There aren't that many songs about them.[15]

I don't love seeing photos of myself, though at the same time, I think it's good to keep a record of who we are as ordinary women, ordinary humans. Most of us don't hire a professional photographer when the occasion arises that we need a headshot. We don't get our hair and makeup done by someone else beforehand. Usually, we have a partner or friend take the photo. I'm interested in photos of women who aren't movie stars or models, though I often like those, too. I'm interested in the ways a photographer will see someone and how we ourselves want ourselves to be seen.

I like the self-portraits of Vivian Maier. I like the paintings of Paula Modersohn-Becker. I like the self-portraits of Alice Neel, who said, "The self, we have it like an albatross around the neck." I like the photographs by and of Annie Leibovitz. I like Stieglitz's photographs of Georgia O'Keeffe. Let's not forget the portrait of Michelle Obama by Amy Sherald and the little girl who upon viewing it thought Obama was a queen.

I'm interested in all the reasons we take selfies. I'm interested in how women are portrayed in the news. I'm interested in those of us who like photographs of ourselves, and those who don't. I'm interested in the truths that can be found in photographs of women, vulnerable, strong, honest, and kickass.

---

15 It's the twenty-first century and women on popular TV and in movies and in magazines are still predominantly young and white and of a type.

When I was in Banff with my family recently, we went to Lake Minnewanka and spent time just hanging out. My daughter skipped rocks and I took photos of her and of other people taking selfies. I found it to be poignant that so many people come to this spot from all over the world and want a record of themselves in front of the mountains and the lake. They clamber on top of rocks for glamourous unselfconscious poses. They hold their phones out and use selfie sticks and frame the shot so the mountains would also have a moment.

I want to say that I think selfies are potentially beautiful and ridiculous and fun and ultimately sublime attempts to capture your own soul when others have perhaps failed. We're not movie stars but we exist right now at this exact moment and one day we won't. We exist now in this world where every thirty seconds we're told in one way or another that we're going to hell in a hand basket. And once in a while we find ourselves in front of ancient rocks and know ourselves to be as small and insignificant as ants, and we can celebrate that, too, and be creatures full of joy and awe.

The ability to take a selfie isn't new. In 1839, Robert Cornelius took a photo of himself in Philadelphia, according to an article in *The Guardian*. In the 1970s there was Andy Warhol and his experiments with the Polaroid. On our honeymoon in Rome in 1993, Rob and I held my film manual focus camera out in front of us and took several shots, which we developed when we got back home to Edmonton—a miracle any turned out. Fast forward to Flickr and Facebook and Instagram. Posting selfies or photos of yourself taken by a mysterious and often unnamed someone is prevalent. To dismiss the phenomena as narcissism without considering the art of this form of self-representation, without considering the ways in which it empowers and makes visible and disrupts the phenomena of the male gaze, would be bloody foolish.

When we scroll through Instagram, our selfies occupy the same space as someone famous, as a celebrity. Sure, we don't have the reach, but there is your photo (potentially) in the same feed as your favourite rock star, actor, or celebrity chef. Of course, we're looking at them but they're not looking at us. They can't see you, or at least, they're unlikely to. Even though you absolutely know that your phone or computer is a one-way mirror, sometimes it's still possible to forget, to still feel connected to celebrities in ways that weren't possible before social media.

When we're taking selfies or appearing in a photograph and then curating our images on social media, I wonder if we're modelling those photographs after celebrity images. What models or references are we working from? In what ways are we subverting these models in our own modes of self-representation?

In Cesare Ripa's *Iconologia*, the handbook for emblems used by artists in the seventeenth century, the allegory of painting is described as: "a beautiful woman, with full black hair, dishevelled, and twisted in various ways, with arched eyebrows that show imaginative thought, the mouth covered with a cloth tied behind her ears, with a chain of gold at her throat from which hangs a mask, and has written in front 'imitation.'"

Artemisia Gentileschi painted herself in *Self-Portrait as the Allegory of Painting* when she was invited to London from Italy in 1638, leaving off the cloth tied behind the ears. To achieve the complicated and dynamic pose, scholars say that she would have had to position two mirrors to view herself while working. The radical act of depicting herself as the allegory of painting, something her male contemporaries could not do, seems mind-blowing now, and I can only imagine the response to the painting at the time. In a letter to a collector of her work, she wrote: "I have painted my portrait with the utmost care." And no way was she going to represent herself as a silenced woman.

In many of the typical selfies on Instagram, you might see someone wonderfully adorned, with the utmost care taken on hair, nails, smoky eyes. But there are also those selfies where that glamour is demystified. Women posting pictures without makeup, for example, or after a workout. As well, there are plenty of photos of ordinary people, which is what I'm interested in. When you post a picture of yourself, regardless of who took it, this says something about how you wish to be represented.

There are the portraits that emulate those of celebrity selfies, but then there are other entire modes of representation out there that I don't think have been catalogued. In a certain way, everything we post online is something of a self-portrait. When we post a photo of our coffee cup beside a small vase of handpicked flowers, or when we post a picture of a sunset, or the book we're reading, we're telling the story of who we are. There's a poem by Charles Wright in which he says: "The poem is a self-portrait / always, no matter what mask / You take off and put back on."

Oscar Wilde said, "Every portrait that is painted with feeling is a portrait of the artist, not of the sitter." With all the photos we take and post online, I think we're trying to get at something about our life. We're trying to say something about our time. In an article about Annie Leibovitz in *The Globe and Mail*, the writer says, "What is a portrait of a famous person? Is it an attempt to unearth the personality behind the official role, or is it a glorification of the person's office, of the mask itself?" Leibovitz talks about photographing celebrities: "I have a problem with the word 'celebrity'," she says. "I don't think of Stephen Hawking as a celebrity. It sounds cheap. … I like to think of myself as a portrait photographer of our time."

My question is, what is a portrait of an ordinary person? Is it an attempt to unearth the extraordinariness that each ordinary person possesses? I'm interested in photos of people who are not airbrushed, who have wrinkles, and other tics and quirks. I'm interested in going deep and getting real. I'm interested in that moment that shuffles between ugly and beautiful, darkness and morning light.

Georgia O'Keeffe was famously photographed by Alfred Stieglitz, beginning when they met in 1916. She was in her late 20s and he was 25 years older than her. I've probably internalized the one of her in a black turtleneck with her hands holding the shirt above her chin where she's looking down and off to the side. After she split up with Stieglitz, she would still be regularly photographed by well-known photographers such as Todd Webb, Ansel Adams, Cecil Beaton, and Richard Avedon. My favourite photos of her are in her old age, wrinkled, and still incredibly stunning, holding all her silences, all her seeing.

In *ARTNews*, the fashion designer Tom Ford talks about a photograph of O'Keeffe that he owns. He met her as a boy, and recalls, "I thought she was the strangest person I ever met in my life." He goes on to say, "My grandmother was from Texas, and she wore makeup and always had her hair done. I didn't understand this creature at all. If we were in Santa Fe, I'd lead you to my bathroom, and right there, next to my mirror where I get dressed, is a Warhol Polaroid of Georgia O'Keeffe. And she is fucking cool-looking, just covered in wrinkles."

What would happen if we were all able to imagine our wrinkled selves as fucking cool-looking? What would happen if those of us who don't look like models or movie stars could think of ourselves as fucking cool-looking?

In novels, I'm fond of the less beautiful characters. Perhaps the reason so many English literature lovers get caught up in the story of *Jane Eyre* is because of the unlikeliness of her as a heroine. The famous declaration to Mr. Rochester arrested me when I first read it: "Do you think, because I am poor, obscure, plain, and little, I am soulless and heartless? You think wrong!—I have as much soul as you,—and full as much heart! And if God had gifted me with some beauty, and much wealth, I should have made it as hard for you to leave me, as it is now for me to leave you." Of course, for the match to be made, the madwoman in the attic must die and Rochester must be disfigured. Plain women don't get to pair up with handsome, rich powerful men.

When we encounter plain women in novels, it's memorable. In *Look at Me* by Anita Brookner, Frances Hinton, a medical librarian, says, "Sometimes I wish it were different. I wish I were beautiful and lazy and spoiled and not to be trusted. I wish, in short, that I had it easier." She also says, "For I want more, and I even think I deserve it. I am no beauty but I am quite pleasant-looking. In fact, people tell me that I am 'attractive,' which always depresses me. It is like being told that you are 'brilliant,' which means precisely nothing." The novel hinges on the character's looks. Near the end of the story, she gazes into the mirror and notes that she looks "odd." She says, "I looked, in fact, rather chic but rather plain..." She discovers that "My appearance, which I had accepted ever since I decided that I could only get by on style, no longer pleased me." What the character discovered is that her solitude is due to her lack of beauty. She has been "rendered invisible" but it's writing that is her "way of piping up."

In one of my favourite books by my favourite author, Clarice Lispector, resides the most amazing character: Macabéa. Early in the book the narrator says, "I am the only person who finds her charming," and she is said to have "the expression of someone with a broken wing." When her workmate, Gloria, asks her, "Is it painful being ugly?" she replies, "I've never really thought about it, I suppose it's a little painful. How do you feel about it being ugly yourself?" She's not disputing anything but she's not bloody having it either. She can take it and she can dish it out.

At 55, I wouldn't change the way I look or my imperfect smile. If you were to give me three wishes today, one of them would not be, "Make me beautiful." There is an essay by Hélène Cixous on Clarice Lispector which ends with some thoughts about being a woman and being patient. It's about waiting. Cixous says, "...that the day will come in which the women who have always been— there, will at last appear." So, there's my wish, one of them. That women will at last appear, be visible. That ordinary women will pipe up, continue to pipe up, in whatever manifestation suits. In photos, I wish for women to wear glasses or not to wear glasses, to smile or not to smile, to show their wrinkles, or cover them up with concealer. I wish for women to be bold and silly and joyful. To be plain, or chic, to use utmost care, or none at all. I wish for women to be as strange and weird as they choose. I wish for them to dish it out.

I wish for you to appear. So that someday the self will not be an albatross around our necks. So that someday we can all think of ourselves as fucking cool-looking.

A Year with Springsteen

I was eighteen in June of 1984 when "Born in the U.S.A." arrived in the world. I had dreams of being a writer, but they were so unrealistic I knew deep in the madness of my downbound soul they would never be cashed in.

When I left home that summer, I hit the highway from my small town to the not-so-big city of Edmonton in a cerulean blue 1969 Cougar with a 351 Cleveland. I'd drive down Jasper Avenue and some guy would pull up beside and say, "Cleveland or Windsor?" I had no real idea what the difference was, but they were always impressed it was the Cleveland. That car was poetry. Elegant, classy lines. The signal lights blinked one-two-three. The horn was a thin silver half-moon around the bottom of the steering wheel. The interior white and spotless. That beauty, that suicide machine, is part of my chemical makeup and some days I yearn for it. The previous owner had installed a cassette deck, a pretty decadent addition, and in it was "Born in the U.S.A." I also have the distinct memory of driving down Highway 16 listening to "Born to Run" from 1975, feeling it so hard. But even a distinct memory can be wrong.

That time between eighteen and twenty-three was vulnerable and embarrassing and I've kept it private for no reason other than it was weird and messy and full of a soughing longing and despair. I hadn't really lived in my own skin at that point, it hurts to look at it even now. Even so I had an instinct for saving myself. I began learning that if you can fall in love with one thing, you can fall in love with another, and if you keep falling in love with things, eventually you can learn to love yourself.

I remember driving down that crepuscular highway in my '69 Cougar, the road empty for miles coming and going, and putting my foot down hard. I remember the car rumbling and imagining it coming apart at the seams and feeling afraid but not easing off. This could be it, I thought, this is how you give up. And then I did ease off. I turned the car around. I drove home. The car held together; I held together. Maybe I was born to hold it together. Maybe that was fine.

In the 1980s I saw Bruce Springsteen out of the corner of my eye but for all sorts of reasons, I rejected his music. What I didn't know is that it would be there all along, and that thirty years later it would revitalize me. As I delighted in Bruce at all ages and stages, I would come to love this earlier version of me, this young woman in the blue car. I had no idea how powerful that simple act of loving my young self would be and how much more at peace in my soul I would be because of it.

In the cringe-worthy 80s, moms packed lunches for their kids in liquor store bags. We did our jeans up with coat hangers, and if the jeans weren't tight enough, we ripped seams and hand sewed them up tighter. We went to bush parties near the bog where a rare wild orchid was rumoured to grow and we drank to the point of blacking out. Someone would occasionally fall into the bonfire and be fished out. "Back in Black" played constantly. We drank at the tennis court near the high school, and sometimes at lunch we'd hop into one of the cool guys' muscle cars and go to McDonald's, which was new to our small town. I sometimes got invited because I helped a guy on the hockey team with his English homework. We drank swamp juice—the skimmed off alcohol from multiple bottles. Rye, rum, vodka, all together. I had a terrible complexion and a string of bad haircuts but I made an attempt to feather my hair like the women in *Charlie's Angels*, though my cowlick resisted. I was skinny and I thought I was fat. We'd buy a sheet of brownies or a discounted birthday cake someone forgot to pick up from Safeway—*Happy Birthday Roxy!*—and eat the entire thing. Some purged, but I never did. One weekend I stayed at a friend's acreage and we camped out in a tent in the yard. She borrowed her sister's hash pipe and in the middle of the night we saw Jesus in the ditch beside the gravel road. I swear to God we met Jesus. I was in love with this one guy with a souped-up shiny black muscle car. I was smart but my grades were abysmal and I didn't know anyone going off to university or college. I surely was not. I tried to smoke cigarettes so I could hang out with the leather jackets in the designated smoking area but my suppressed coughing monologues curtailed this. I was full of such a thick despair and dread that I would now find terrifying.

When I moved out, I worked jobs I had no feeling for, lived in a green shag carpeted bachelor apartment downtown where my rock-hard futon bed resided behind a glamourous band-aid coloured screen, and silverfish on the ceiling worked on their MTV choreography. I started going to nightclubs almost every night. My complexion improved slightly. My hair started cooperating. Once in a while someone would say how cool they thought my mismatched eyes were. And here's Bruce. I met my first boyfriend in a bar while "Dancing in the Dark" played. The dance floor was raised and there were twinkle lights above, and off in the distance, if you rashly looked out into the night, you'd see planes or shooting stars. I would later learn how much the boyfriend loved Springsteen, and when any Springsteen song came on, he insisted we dance. I can still clearly picture the studied way this guy danced, just like Courteney Cox. The night we met I was wearing blue capris and a top that showed about half an inch of my midriff. My blonde hair was back-combed and my eyeliner and mascara were on point, which is to say thick and smudgy. The table was full of greyhounds and I had had too many and only paid for the first one. I was a curious mix of shyness and low self-esteem tempered with a steely regard for myself and knew I was smarter than mostly everyone I spoke to. I was also feeling supremely intellectually wanting, smothered, stymied. I lived in a dump and there was no script I could see writing for myself that would create the sparks I would need to get out of it. I had no faith in the magic of the night.

So that guy? Bad. When he started dealing drugs, I realized I needed to incrementally break up with him, which probably says all you need to know. We all know what incremental breakups mean. I was no bird, and I exerted my will to leave. Things got better, also incrementally, as things do. But I also had to leave Bruce in the dust for the reckless and unexamined self-preservation of my mad and swaying soul.

There was a gym in a sketchy part of town. Mr. C's was old school, free weights, basic machines, endless mirrors, loud music, a lot of sweat, and it was in a basement, cave-like. In rotation was Springsteen's "I'm on Fire" and "Dancing in the Dark." There was no longer a Mr. C. but the name stuck perhaps because of all the logo T-shirts he left for sale. I fell into unrequited love at Mr. C's Gym, hanging out gawping at the juice-bar guys' delts and traps with my fellow blonde gym ladies after a workout. That was a good thing. I needed unrequited.

Eventually, the juice-bar boys left and the gym moved to a swankier non-subterranean location. I became the juice-bar girl for a while, blending Joe Weider protein powder with frozen fruit and bananas and off-brand juice, and wiping sweat off the mirrors. I made new friends and we went to parties rather than nightclubs.[16] I ending up with a friend

---

16 Here, let me say that I've skipped over telling you about three seedy apartments. I've skipped over a couple of boyfriends, genuinely sweet roommates, various terrible choices. I skipped over how I pawned my

group of truly decent guys from Mr. C's who hung out with me and my then-roommate at skating ponds and movie nights and restaurants. That group of people probably saved my life. Thanks to them and the friend-of-a-friend scenario, I met my husband at a party at a sculptor's house in the backyard under a full moon. The scene was so romantic I distrusted it completely. Romance wasn't meant for someone like me, someone who woke up at 3 a.m. and turned on the lights to mentally record the silverfish scurry around like inebriated line-dancers at last call. Magic wasn't for weird unschooled girls with heterochromia, blending protein powder drinks and writing poetry about the controlled pain of lifting weights and the way ripped bodies looked broken in mirrors. Who tore the poetry into strips, placing it in the garbage with banana peels so that no one could ever dredge it up and find it legible. In the years that followed, when Springsteen came on the car radio, I changed the channel.

To condense a lot of what happened after the gym years: There were years of listening to Billy Bragg, feeling that everyone was better than me, wearing clothes from Le Château, taking a modelling course with a friend, and enjoying a subsequent impromptu and short-lived gig as a photographer's model, feeling always ugly and gawky and self-conscious about my bad teeth. I went to college, then university, married, had a daughter, published multiple books, and lived happily ever after, in the usual messy and complicated sense of that phrase. In my extended family and friend group I have experienced or witnessed most of the statistically probable elements: recovering alcoholics, suicide, mental illness, divorce, estrangement, friend breakups, ghosting, early deaths, late ones, some divisions that occur because of politics or boredom, other riffs occur because of childish but irrevocable behaviour. Does anyone escape

---

flute, which I played poorly in high school band class to pay rent the month I'd spent too much money on booze, trading in my wings, and trying to get them back again. I skipped ditching my unsavoury pals.

from these types of things? It felt as though life, whatever that was, was coming at me from all directions. Back then I imagined I would always feel as though I were on top of the scrapheap.

So here we are now, wondrously not on the scrapheap—which leads us back to Bruce Springsteen and perhaps a bit more about my obsessions with books and music. I tend to get a bit obsessed with things. I've read *The Stream of Life* and *A Breath of Life* by Clarice Lispector, over and over. And I'm the same with music. I trace this behaviour back to when I drove a Volkswagen Fox[17] where a cassette had become lodged in the player: *Beggar's Banquet* by the Stones. I couldn't afford the cost to extricate it and I would later sell the Fox with the cassette still stuck in it. When I gave anyone a ride, they always wanted to hear *Beggar's Banquet*. I still listen to "Factory Girl" and I'm right back there in that car.

In 2016, I popped Leonard Cohen's *You Want it Darker* into the CD player of my current car, a silver Fiat 500, and it stayed there for about a year. I drove to work singing the title song. Leonard Cohen died and then Trump got into office. I've never cried in my life over the death of a celebrity; I wept when Leonard Cohen died. I was also weeping for the state of the world. I loved that album, but after a year, felt it might have been contributing to my melancholy.

We have a picture of Leonard Cohen on our fridge. "Is that your uncle?" I've been asked. "Spiritually, yes." There's also a picture of Clarice Lispector, and the Barry Schneier photo of Bruce at the piano in 1974. Family is where you find it, goes the saying. It's a bit lonely when your family is either in the afterlife or New Jersey, but I have to be fine with that. I wonder if Clarice Lispector would like Bruce's music, his broken spirits, his hot-rod angels. And I reread her with his lyrics in mind. She says, "For anything can happen and damage the most intimate life of a person. What will have

---

17 A couple of cars after the Mercury Cougar.

been done to my soul next year? Will that soul have grown? and grown peacefully or through the pain of doubt?" I imagine Bruce would like Clarice, but I'll never know.

The writer Anne Boyer once tweeted the line "Born to Recluse" and ever since I've wanted to steal it. The phrase encapsulates my life after that brief stint of feeling born to run. Maybe it's like that for most of us, especially those who want to become writers. I spent years trying to cultivate silence, reading about silence, listening to medieval chants, trying to drown out the sound of the freeway that we happen to live ridiculously close to. In the summer when the sun doesn't set until 11 p.m., you can hear the motorcycles racing. All day long semis rumble, the commute of SUVs and Ford F150s. After twenty years of living in this same house, I can filter out the noise from the highway and find my inner silence.

And this is where I arrive back at Bruce in the present, because I'm no longer going for hour long walks with the dog. I started walking on the treadmill in our basement and working out with dumbbells. After a while, I made a trip to Canadian Tire and bought some heavier dumbbells. Lifting weights, I listen to Springsteen's *Greatest Hits*. It's perfect. When I'm on the treadmill I start watching videos of Springsteen in concert, interviews, you name it, if Bruce is in it, I watch. I fall in love with young Bruce, and all the Bruces through the years. I fall in love with the E Street Band. I fall in love with Patti, and Clarence, Stevie, Nils, Max, Garry, Roy, Soozie. I'm fond of Charles Giordano. I'm sad when I belatedly find out about Danny Federici's death and while I knew about Clarence, I hadn't really known that his nephew Jake Clemons joined the band. I allow myself to become a fan, mooning and swooning over them all.

I don't really think about what I'm doing; I'm just going with what I love. I'm allowing it. And the more I listen and watch, the happier I become, and because I like the feeling, I am loath to analyze it. I just keep going. Normally, when I get this interested in a subject, it means I probably need to write a book about it. But I could never write a book about Springsteen because I'm a Springsteen fraud, especially in comparison to the legion of hard-core fans who follow his work and know about it in incredible detail. I've never experienced one of his legendary heart-stopping, earth-quaking shows and I know I'm too much of a recluse to handle one. His fan base is—understatement—dedicated. Since I am not writing a book, I experience his music through a different lens. My story of loving Bruce is a story about coming to love something with joy and openness and finding that it's okay to just happily and adoringly swoon over someone in a world gone mad. My story of loving Bruce is about embracing all the darkness at the edge of town but remembering also to crank the tunes and dance to "Cadillac Ranch" in that strip of light that comes low into my house in January at latitude 53 at 11 in the morning, like an annunciation.

I have a hard time connecting my new fitness regime with my Bruce fondness. Back in my 20s, I ditched the crumby boyfriend and I ditched Bruce, after which I worked my way through things by pumping iron. Lifting weights again, reclaiming the music, felt empowering as hell. But I hadn't really left anything behind. As Springsteen says in his memoir, *Born to Run*: "No one you have been and no place you have gone ever leaves you. The new parts of you simply jump in the car and go along for the rest of the ride." I thought I'd left certain memories behind, but sure enough, they were all there, in my car. But if the car I was driving was that 1969 Mercury Cougar, then maybe I could find a way to be compassionate to that young woman with the back-combed hair and jeans she ripped herself.

I downloaded the albums from iTunes, one at a time. *You Want It Darker* came out of the CD player, and I played Springsteen's *Greatest Hits*. If I had it to do over again, I would have been methodical. I would have started at *Asbury Park*. Later, I would read one of Steven Van Zandt's tweets about Springsteen's *Western Stars*, where he says that the proper way to listen to it would be one song per day. To just absorb an album like that. And I wish I would have done this with Springsteen's oeuvre.[18]

I could have started anywhere, but I started with *Tunnel of Love*. In Brian Hiatt's book *Bruce Springsteen: The Stories Behind the Songs*, he says that Springsteen "scoffed at the idea of 'married music' just a couple years earlier, but now he was intent on making some." I fell for Springsteen via his married music. Maybe my favourite songs aren't his most known, but I love them wholeheartedly. I love "Tougher Than the Rest" from *Tunnel of Love*. I love "Better Days" and "If I should Fall Behind" and "Leap of Faith" from *Lucky Town*. I love "Happy" from *Tracks*. I mean, where has that song been all my life? I was a bit mad at myself for ignoring Springsteen all those years in my thirty years of marriage. These are songs to live with and to listen to when things are amazing and the sky is blue and when things are dull and seem precarious, and maybe especially when circumstances require us to be tougher than the rest, not just for each other but against the rest of the world, together. It's not that my marriage hadn't been just lovely before, it's just that Bruce and Patti would have been good company.

Now, because I have read many books about Bruce, interviews with him, his memoir, a collection of philosophical essays, as well as watched (on Netflix) the Broadway show and *Western Stars*, and *Blinded by the Light* in the movie theatre, I know I have nothing new to add to Springsteenalia. At a cocktail party, I could hold my own in a debate about whether Mary's dress waves or sways (it sways), or whether or not Wendy in "Thunder Road" is Wendy from Peter Pan. I can talk about the way his songs can be simultaneously happy and sad, full of angst and full of joy, passionate and desperate,

---

18 I should say here that I know more about silence than I do about music. I know little about the music scene, I can't sing, and I play no instruments. You'll remember what happened to my flute. I would say, though, that I have enthusiasm and that prolonged listening to Springsteen inspires even more enthusiasm.

depressing and uplifting, melancholy and fiery. His songs live in the multiple registers, just like we all do every day. Others may feel his work is more like prose than poetry, but I think I could make a good case for the poetry in his songs.

There are feminist readings of Springsteen's work, and it's fine to say that it's of its time. Isn't that the goal in writing anything? To capture what it is to live in a precise moment in time. Would it be possible, even, to write many of the songs featuring a woman's name (others have made the count to be so far 29 give or take) today? As Rebecca Traister has pointed out in an article on *Vulture* about his memoir, "... a lot of us have also long heard (or perhaps wanted to hear) in Bruce something more nuanced and appreciative in his portraits of the Candys, Marys, Janeys, and Rosies. We have loved that he doesn't just sing about perfect beach babes, but about women who've been around a time or two, who put our makeup on and our hair up pretty, who push our baby carriages down the street and drink warm beer, and may not be beauties but are alright nonetheless." In his music, she hears his respect for women. My personal favourite is Cynthia, who is "an inspiring sight" who doesn't have to "smile or say hi" because it's enough that she exists.

What I learned from steadily listening to Bruce Springsteen's music for a year and more now, is that the soul goes on in disrepair, that we go on repairing it, and this is what it is to be human. Throughout my adulthood, I have constantly posed the question to myself—what constitutes a good life? Springsteen says, "Nobody wins unless everybody wins." I have spent the last several years working on a novel about angels that investigates the idea put forth by Clarice Lispector, in an essay on annunciation, that, "each of us is responsible for the entire world." Maybe my novel will end up being as informed by Bruce as it is by Clarice.

I didn't turn to Springsteen's music to learn anything but rather to feel things I hadn't allowed myself to feel. I didn't specifically or intellectually know that music was for this—to filter your life through. Yet I learned that you could come back to these places where your spirit was hurt or broken or leaking out, and you can replace those missing or damaged parts with something more joyful. That there are more ways to heal than one, and that in looking back at moments in a life, and holding them for a bit, you can laugh a little at how you were and who you are now. We get to reread our own selves, the stories of our lives, with tenderness and forgiveness.

In a video of a 2013 show in London, before he properly begins "I'm Going Down," Springsteen says to the audience, "help me out" and then gives that great laugh of his. Sometimes just saying, "help me out" can be a kindness. People want to feel useful, and when you ask them for help, it's saying, I trust you to help me, I trust that you have my back. I believe that you can do this thing. Sure, I'm fine on my own maybe but it would be better with a little help. Thanks to Bruce I learned to be kinder to myself; I learned to say *help me out*. I wrote the following out and taped it onto my computer monitor: "Speak to yourself with tenderness. Call yourself honey, baby, darling, as though you are the subject of a Springsteen song." I learned that you've got to be okay with yourself. You've got to just reach a deep sort of acceptance of yourself because you are not going to be here forever. Your life is a rock and roll show, and baby it won't last all night. In an interview on *Esquire* about figuring things out in his forties, Springsteen says, "You're trying to take all this misunderstanding and loathing, and you're trying to turn it into love—which is the wonderful thing that happens when you're trying to make music out of the rough, hard, bad things. You're trying to turn it into love." Maybe I'd had the same realizations myself at some point, but here they were from Bruce.

There is a fan-recorded video of Springsteen doing "Reason to Believe" in Paris, 2016, and midway through, he just sort of breathes into the microphone. It could be interpreted as a lot of things. The deep sighs from the underbelly of the universe. When you first listen to the song you might think that it's designed to be uplifting, but as Brian Hiatt says in his book on the songs, it's "the bleakest song Springsteen has ever written, almost dangerously so." The song, says Hiatt, is "the artist mocking his own past certainties, wondering aloud if everyone is fooling themselves. The song is an existential cry for help…" It was on the 1982 album *Nebraska*, but in 2016 this performance of it adds another layer. There he is breathing for the audience, breathing with. *Breathing with.* Or maybe it's tonglen—a Buddhist practice used to awaken compassion—on the in-breath you take in the pain of another, and on the out-breath you send them love and relief. The song is bleak, sure, but it's also about resilience, about believing, even when life shows you you're a fool to do so. In a lot of Springsteen's lyrics, he's able to be in two or maybe more places at once, which is the gift of his storytelling, his poetry. The fictional Author in Clarice Lispector's book, *A Breath of Life*, has created the character Angela, with whom he speaks in tandem, but separately. Sometimes Angela hears the Author's monologuing, and sometimes it's more secret. They go back and forth, one breathing, then the other. The premise is that the fictional Author has created Angela, and he says, "I've discovered why I breathed life into Angela's flesh, it was to have someone to hate. I hate her. She represents my terrible faith that is reborn every single morning. And it's frustrating to have faith. I hate this creature who simply seems to believe." And later, "I am looking for somebody whose life I can save. The only one who allows me to do that is Angela. And as I save her life, I save my own." Of course, the Author and Angela are parts of Clarice Lispector, the writer, and none of them are each other. They are all one and all separate. They go back and forth, each one in turn saving the others' life, Lispector's life, the readers' lives. Mine.

I have the worst memory but I know all the words to "Racing in the Street," and when I drive to work, sometimes I play it on repeat, three times at 6:56 minutes, because it calms my nerves. I want to exuberantly reveal that both Nils Lofgren and Amy Aiello Lofgren followed me back on Twitter. I want to brag about the blurb I was asked to do for an anthology of writing about Springsteen, titled *Shut Down Strangers and Hot Rod Angels*, and how ridiculously excited I was to do it. Not that I thought Bruce would ever read my blurb, but it means I am aligned with people who love his work as much as I do. I wish to tell you about all the sweet people in the Springsteen Facebook group I'm in where they coach each other to be inclusive and respectful. I want to talk about the way I love how Bruce lets people in, how he lives the contradiction of being the rich man in the poor man's clothes in a way that reminds me of the lines from Hafiz: "Greatness / is always / built upon this foundation: / the ability to appear, speak, and act / as the most / common / man." I want to say that when I began posting flower photographs on Instagram accompanied by Springsteen lyrics, so many Springsteen fans among my acquaintance came out of the woodwork and shared their Springsteen-love with me. I bonded with people in emails and DMs about favourite songs and the ones they love to sing. I want to talk about how watching the video of "Dream Baby Dream" in black-and-white by dvddubbingguy is a religious and healing experience that cracks me open inside and my response to it is both thank you and I love you, which can be translated into: Bruuuuuuuce!

At another point in my life, in someone else, I might have dismissed all these moments as lame fan behaviour. Or maybe I would have found it all charming but slight, and I would have smiled when someone recounted these connections and thought, cute, or who cares?

I didn't start listening to Bruce Springsteen and reading everything I could get my hands on about him because I wanted to learn any great truths; I wanted to sing in my car and dance to "Hungry Heart" between sets of bicep curls. I ended up in Springsteen school and didn't even catch on until about halfway through that "three-minute record," which is funny, because many of the things I learned I'd already worked through in my study of poetry. But coming at these truths via Springsteen added a layer to my understanding for which I'm grateful. The Irish poet, Paula Meehan says, "I think the whole river of poetry is a history of the dream life and the dreaming of the human species. I think we can solve things through dreaming, I think we can embed important memories, survival strategies, through dreaming. It's the place where everybody is a poet, in the dream." She goes on to say, "Just as a poem can contain a complete mystery of the universe," it can also be a kind of salvation. "There are poems that tell stories but there are also poems that just give you a moment of vision or transcendence or colour even, or just an image that you can carry around with you. Two lines. Two lines can save a life, I believe it."

Poems can save a life, I've come to believe, but they won't change the world. Patrizia Cavalli says: "Someone told me /of course my poems / won't change the world. / I say yes/ of course / my poems / won't change the world." Which is to say, of course they can change the world, or at least the world of the reader. We can work things out in a poem, we can work things out in dreams. When you write a poem, or a song, or a novel, or anything, I think it helps if you know what the stakes are: you're able to save a life. In an interview in *The Guardian,* Springsteen says, "And you can change someone's life in three minutes with the right song. I still believe that to this day. You can bend the course of their development, what they think is important, of how vital and alive they feel."

You've got to live this life with joy, I've learned. You've got to transform the ugly stuff into love. The more I fell in love with Springsteen, the more I re-fell in love with other writers. I was reinvigorated by the lines from Rumi: "Because I love this, I am never bored. / Beauty constantly wells up, a noise of springwater, / in my ear and in my inner being." When you love Springsteen, you are never bored!

What I have found in Springsteen's songs is that he bears witness in a unique and absorbing way. His songs have been described as cinematic and he is known for his love of certain movies—*Badlands, Thunder Road.* There is no shortage of darkness in his lyrics, but without being stated, there is also light, a cinematic focus. His songs act like a camera, or a lens, a spotlight. The photographer Robert Adams said, "The job of the photographer in my view, is not to catalogue indisputable fact but to try to be coherent about intuition and hope." Adams talks about the poet William Carlos Williams, who "said that poets write for a single reason—to give *splendour* (a word also used by Thomas Aquinas in defining the beautiful). It is a useful word for a photographer because it implies light—light of overwhelming intensity." I find in Springsteen's music not only intuition and hope, but splendour. I have found room to dream baby dream, and room to run.

In listening to Springsteen this past year, I am reminded that when you are creating something, the stakes are high; they are beautiful, a dream. I am reminded to write with joy, toward splendour, toward beauty, the light. I am reminded to write recklessly, under such a spell of wild and zestful joy, that it could infuse another soul with this juice welling up in me. I find it wonderful that the things you love are often magically in conversation with each other and that when you hear the convergences even in unlikely places, say a mash-up of Lispector and Springsteen and Rumi, it means the universe is handing you a message. The message might be: you've got to take everything you've got, every last dream and every last bit of spirit and breath and madness in your soul and pour it into a useful vessel, and then share that potion. You've got to stay alive; you've got to be splendid, babies.

The year I spent listening to Bruce Springsteen was a year of allowing myself to be absorbed by something without questioning why. It didn't so much change me as remind me about a lot of things that I knew in one way but needed to learn in another. My torn soul became easier, the ride smoother, the car I was metaphorically driving became cooler. I asked myself the age-old question—what were you born for? Was I born to run? Born to hold it together? Born to recluse? It didn't even have to be just one thing. But in the end the answer was right there. Born to love.

Women's Lives,
Women's Still Lifes

No one clamours. No one has asked me to write an essay about the lives of women writers and women who paint still lifes.

I've decided to write this at my kitchen table of my own accord, for my own sake. On the table, I've spread the lace tablecloth my mother-in-law gave me when she moved houses. When I began writing, there was a bouquet of coral peonies and another of pink and yellow ranunculus on the table, and I took a photograph of the flowers with the books I've gathered on Mary Pratt, Audrey Flack, Mary Hiester Reid, Anne Vallayer-Coster, Clara Peeters, and Rachel Ruysch. I have the catalogue from an exhibition in 1995 titled, *Nothing Overlooked: Women Painting Still Life.* I have a book of essays on art by Siri Hustvedt. I'll start with art and move on to writing—this is how I imagine it will go, but of course it doesn't, because as Virginia Woolf once said, "…for interruptions there will always be."

Making art, writing, as a woman means that you're always looking at how to construct your own life with an eye to how others before you have done so. You're stealing from them, you're taking caution from their lives, you're expending energy to find ways to get to the page or easel, but also in keeping the confidence up, keeping your nerve up, to justify doing so. I've been writing for close to thirty years, and I still find it difficult to even imagine writing an essay on women and making art. I have so many lines that rattle in my head from women about making art, the process, about living as a creative person, but maybe the one I come back to most often is the line by Georgia O'Keeffe, "I've been absolutely terrified every moment of my life and I've never let it keep me from doing a single thing that I wanted to do." She also said, "It's not enough to be nice in life. You've got to have nerve."

Months have passed since that time when I sat at my kitchen table and took notes from these books. I'm sitting here now staring at the pages of notes, trying to remember what it was I wanted to say. I remember I was getting angry. I remember thinking I was in a terrible place geographically to be writing any such essay. Still life is the overlooked genre and women artists still go on being overlooked, and then, still life is generally a history of white male artists, and many of the women still life artists, few though they are, are also white. I'm white too, of course. And I live in the boondocks, away from major art centres. I'm not an art historian either, so my expertise does not lie there. I keep thinking maybe someone else should write this. I think, my audience is so small, anyway, that what's the point even in trying to gather my thoughts on the subject. The only justification I can find to write this is thinking that maybe it could be a jumping off spot in the future for another person, someone sitting in a room wondering if she should bother. I want her to know that she should.

I set the books aside. I set my notes aside, other things call, and then a pandemic arrives, leaving us all in our domestic spaces, in quarantine. I planned to start by talking about the seventeenth-century artists, Clara Peeters and Rachel Ruysch. I would talk about the subjects they painted, flowers, fish, butterflies, a cat that slips into the picture. Then perhaps, I would move on to Anne Vallayer-Coster and her splendid still lifes of shells and corals, florals in the round, and the fruit pictures that remind the viewer a little of Chardin. I would bring it back home to Canada and talk about the Canadian Mary Hiester Reid, who in the catalogue of an exhibition of her work in 2000 was said to be "the most prominent woman artist in Toronto through the late nineteenth and early twentieth centuries…" Also remark upon: "On the one hand, Reid enjoyed a commercially successful working life as an artist; on the other hand, she has nearly disappeared from the historical record." Few Canadians even recognize her name or her work. Contemporary critics noted of her work the "power of interlocking accuracy of detail and poetic insight."

I hadn't heard of Mary Hiester Reid or seen any of her work in reproduction until one summer when we visited our daughter, who was going to college in Oakville, and we took the train into Toronto to go to the Art Gallery of Ontario. The three of us, Rob, Chloe and I, looked at art for a couple of hours, and then decided we needed lunch. It was busy, so we put our name in at the restaurant. We were seated in a pretty posh setting, on two couches with a coffee table in between. On the table was the catalogue I've been quoting from which was from a past exhibition. I was immediately struck by the detail of the cover and found the reproduction of the painting *Roses in a Vase* 1891 inside. The painting should have been no big deal. I've seen hundreds of paintings in my day of roses in a vase. But the level of realism was lovely, the poetic arrangement startling, the palette pleasing.

Hiester Reid's husband was a painter as well, and he was better known and more respected at the time, but George Agnew Reid isn't exactly a household name these days either. It seems like a story we're all extremely familiar with, that of the woman artist being subsumed by her partner's reputation, compared to it, only to be found lesser. Of another painting, *Roses in an Antique Jar*, not reproduced in this catalogue, a reviewer of the exhibition called it, "suitably but timidly executed," and gave the advice, "Dare to be bold, young lady."

That day in the restaurant of the AGO, we ate our food, drank our wine, and looked at the catalogues and fashion magazines on the coffee table, my artist husband and daughter studying animation. At the end, the waiter brought us our bill and asked us to sign for it, which is when we realized we had somehow blundered into the members lounge, where we had, apparently, no business being. The waiter had to rush off and find the manager, who came and looked at us leaning back in the couches reading our magazines and catalogue raisonné as though we hadn't a care in the world. The table of women wearing exuberantly patterned blazers, whimsical eyeglasses, and bright lipstick near us were looking at us and then at the manager and waiter, finding the whole thing amusing, one of them leaning out to wink at me, perhaps in commiseration, perhaps in a "way to pull that one off" gesture. There had been a much longer line-up at the other restaurant.

At other times, earlier in my life, I might have been embarrassed, but instead we laughed. It felt as though we'd inadvertently crashed some sort of party, and no way was I going to feel bad after the fact. We shrugged our shoulders and felt quite good about having sipped prosecco on the posh couches. If nothing else, I wanted our daughter to dare to be bold, or to at least not worry about social faux pas. I wanted her to not care about not belonging in a place. I wanted her to remember what it's like to find yourself in a place where you're not supposed to be and to find it amusing rather than awkward. I wanted her to somehow feel that belonging isn't something that can be bestowed upon you, and that being in the right place was relative.

I went home and ordered a copy of the catalogue. While it's unlikely that Mary Hiester Reid will ever become a household name, or even particularly well-known among art lovers, discovering her startled me. I saw myself in her portrait. Her work felt deeply poetic and I felt a shock of recognition simultaneously with despair for her exceedingly low profile[19]

Mary Pratt is a beloved Canadian artist who died in 2018. I can't say her name without having her miraculous paintings of jam jars, lit as though from within, pop into my head. She painted portraits and landscapes as well, but the still lifes linger. She's there in our kitchens as we're prepping meals and the light comes in and lands on our bowl of fruit. When we make dinner for our children and make them wait before they can eat it so we can take a photo of the hotdogs and ketchup bottle. And for those women who are alone after a divorce, Pratt's poignant and yet empowering *Dinner for One* from 1994 will resonate. There is such care and precision in the image, such strength and resolve. Even in the face of a personal challenge, we must eat, we must continue to see the beauty of the life before us, the painting seems to say. Don't let anything stop you, is what I hear when I look at the reproduction.

Did Mary Pratt know the work of Mary Hiester Reid? The year after Hiester Reid's death in 1922 there was a memorial exhibition of over three hundred of her works at the AGO, "the first one-person showing by a woman artist ever held at the Gallery." When a survey of Canadian art was published in 1943, even though her work was included in a previous volume, Hiester Reid was left out.

Mary Pratt was married to Christopher Pratt, whom she met in art school at Mount Allison University in New Brunswick. When he went to art school in Glasgow, she was disallowed because she was pregnant. They had four children together and her career would be secondary to his. Lawren Harris once said to Mary, "Now you have to understand, in a family of painters, there can only be one painter, and in your family, it's Christopher." Both of them painted

---

19 After I set this essay aside for the two years of the pandemic, Molly Peacock released a book entitled *Flower Diary* about MHR in 2021.

a model, Donna, who is well-known to have had a relationship with Christopher, though it was another woman who would ultimately cause them to break up. They would divorce and Mary would remarry and divorce again.

Mary once said, "I intend to have children and to have food on the table, and I intend to do the ironing, but I will have time to paint." Later, in an acceptance speech for an honorary degree, she would say, "Do not be deceived by the woman standing patiently before you. She only appears to be the epitome of modesty, composure, and reticence." At a certain point, Pratt stated that she no longer wanted to be "regarded as a kitchen housewife painter" but as a painter. In biographies of women artists, as in all biographies, there are things said and things unsaid and then there is what can be read between the lines. Any woman who has tried to make a life in art knows how much work goes on behind the scenes to carve out the space to make art. And then there's the matter of finding and keeping one's nerve, one's confidence. To believe in oneself is a monumental effort and women have done it without the level of ego-stroking and encouragement that men often receive. I'd like to think that things have changed radically, but we all know they haven't, not radically anyway.

In the book *Art and Soul: Notes on Creating*, published in 1986, the American artist Audrey Flack tells the story of how one of her large canvases, *Jolie Madame,* painted in 1972 and exhibited in the show *Women Choose Women*, was said by critics of the day to be "the ugliest painting of the decade." She was also said to be a "greedy person" due to the subject matter: an abundance of jewelry, perfume, a compact, a vase, a rose. In another note, she tells the story of visiting the home of a famous collector, Morton Newman, and noticing that he had only one work by a female, and it was a small painting, hanging on a door in the kitchen. She told her art dealer that if Newman wanted one of hers it would have to be a large work or nothing.

She refused to have it "hang on the other side of the kitchen door."

There isn't anyone reading this essay who will be surprised by these stories. We're all used to reading the biographies of women from the history of art and how they are positioned as the daughter of or the wife of. If women in previous centuries managed to paint it was usually because their father was an artist. In the seventeenth and eighteenth centuries, women often painted still life because they were prohibited from painting the nude, which was considered to be the training ground for painting the figure. When I look at a female artist, one of the first things I wonder is, what was she thwarted by? Did she have ten children like the Dutch seventeenth-century painter Rachel Ruysch? Did she die young, as Paula Modersohn-Becker did, dying at 31 of an embolism following childbirth in 1907? Modersohn-Becker is known for her expressionistic style, and for being the first woman to have painted a nude self-portrait. I imagine most of us who have aspirations to make a life in art are curious about the conditions that made this possible for those who went before us.

I remember reading the biographies of women writers when I was starting out, looking to see how many of them had children, and if so, how many, and then, how did they negotiate things to continue to find time to write.

Because I married a still life painter, I've always had my eye on still life. I'm interested in how people talk about it, through history and in the present. You would think that the whole "still life as the lesser of the genres" thing would have dissipated by now. You would think that we would have freshened up our thinking on still life as a gendered space a bit. But all these years, there have been kindly made remarks, intimations, about men painting still life. Which is interesting because the still life resides fairly firmly in the domestic space, the private realm, often in the kitchen, in the home. And of course, it's the twenty-first century now, so we might like to think of that space as being shared equally by all.

In the catalogue essay to the 1994 exhibition of women still life artists, Janet Marquardt-Cherry says, "…whatever other qualities they may share, these works are all romantic in their own way, offering us a chance to refresh our appreciation of the day-to-day world." I will only say that when there are exhibitions of male artists, their work is rarely called romantic. Siri Hustvedt, in her book *Mysteries of the Rectangle*, says of Chardin in an essay, that "his art is separate from the story of his life." I don't know that a male reviewer would have said that. In the introduction to the book, Hustvedt also notes that there is a "failure of art history to deal with the extraordinarily abundant evidence for the ways in which people of all classes and cultures have responded to images." And one of the responses to a lot of work by women is to ignore it. Historically, creative women have been trivialised, especially those who had more than one talent.

I'm thinking here of Charlotte Brontë. Jonathan Jones in *The Guardian* mentions seeing a self-portrait. He says, "Of the most unsettling works of art I have seen for a long time is a small sketch in a school atlas that was identified last year as a self-portrait by the young Charlotte Brontë. Why is it so unsettling? Because of the talent it shows. Could she have been an artist as well as a great writer—and how many other talented women have found their ability to draw trivialised or suppressed through the centuries? Brontë found her voice in literature, of course, as did her sisters, while her brother Branwell tried to become a professional artist. Why was it the boy, in this brilliant family, who got to call himself an artist? And why is it that while women have often been able to pick up a pen and become great writers, visual art was an almost entirely male preserve before modern times?" It's nice to see these questions being posed as pertaining to a nineteenth-century writer and artist. In what permutations do these questions yet persist? Why does it feel unfashionable to even pose them at this current juncture?

It makes sense that so many women painted still lifes. We do still occupy the domestic sphere more fully, in general, than men do. What are the conditions necessary to make art? Although I also had artistic leanings early on, I had no artistic background. I grew up not knowing a single thing about art or having any exposure to art at all. It's amazing that I made it to literature, but that somehow seemed more possible—you could do this alone, with a pen and paper. It could be hidden. Which is why reading about Jane Austen hiding her work under her blotter, the supposed creak that alerted her to another's presence, always spoke to my heart. I wasn't bold. Not in the least.

Deeply imbedded in me is the poem by Eavan Boland, "The Rooms of Other Women Poets." The way she begins—*I wonder about you: whether the blue abrasions / of daylight, falling as dusk across your page, / make you reach for the lamp*—is so beautiful. Because we all wonder about each other, how we are able to do what we do, how we are able to continue, what the minimum circumstances are in which to thrive and make a poem, simultaneously. In her wondering, I felt encouragement, curiosity, companionship. How I wish to give that to anyone, someone, you! That would be enough, really, to know that you could reach out through words and metaphorically hold someone's hand or know that your being at your desk, sometimes lonely, sometimes sad and desperate, sometimes so full of joy that it brims over…that this could reach another one such as you have been, hope to be.

I have thought a lot about how to be a writer, a woman writer, over the years. I have spent my entire adult life contriving to find time and energy (the energy!) to write. I have looked closely at the lives of women writers trying to find the secrets to apply to my own life. I have asked, how can I do the work I want to do, the work I'm able to do, and what is the work I am "allowed" to do? What is the work I will be hindered from, the work I will be given credit for and the work I will be erased from having done, what is the work that I will be thwarted from, and who will thwart me? And given all those variables, how will I refuse to be thwarted, and how will I manage to work in spite of, because of, *because of.* How will I continue, how will I contrive my own particular set of circumstances so I can say what I want to say, however small?

We just want to work. I in my room, you in yours. I don't want to be in competition with you, but to send my good wishes to you so that you can send yours to me. This is what I learned from reading Eavan Boland. How to wonder about you, the importance of that wondering, and to remember that you are wondering about me.

Heterochromia, or Seeing through Mismatched Eyes

My left eye is blue and my right eye is blue with a sizeable smattering of green. Someone once said my right eye resembles the earth as seen from space. On other occasions, I've heard that my right eye looks like a marble, and I've been asked if I was a cat in a previous life. I'm always trying to get a good photo of my mismatched eyes, but as romantic novelists have pointed out through the ages, one's eyes appear to change colour depending on mood, location, light. Having heterochromia is, of course, something of which I was always aware. As a child, I have a distinct memory of another child telling me my eye colour meant I was a witch. I didn't take it as an insult but filed it away as interesting information.

I can't remember not knowing about Mengele's experiments in Auschwitz and his horrific fascination with heterochromia. He wanted to "unlock the secret of artificially changing eye colour" according to the *Holocaust Encyclopedia*. He "collected the eyes of his murdered victims," which isn't a fact I knew at a young age, but I did know the experiments weren't humane. I'm not sure how or exactly when I learned about the experiments, but I do remember reading *Anne Frank's Diary* at some point in grade two and having a nightmare (which became recurring) and sleep walking afterwards. I have no clear memory of learning about the holocaust, but the dream involved being put on a cattle car to go to a death camp. I know I was in grade two because we moved houses when I was in grade three.

Last night we went for a walk around the neighbourhood and a dog had gotten loose from its owner and Rob caught it and returned it. The dog had one blue eye, one brown. Friend! The guy who owned the dog, when I said, hey I too have mismatched eyes, was like "yah whatever who cares" and kept walking. No problem. I was bonding with the dog anyway, not him.

On the internet, pets become celebrities in part due to their heterochromia. There are lists of human celebrities who have heterochromia with descriptions of colouration and if it's sectoral heterochromia that's also described. Inevitably David Bowie also comes up and the fact that his eye colouration is not heterochromia but a result of a punch to the eye as a youth which caused his pupil to remain dilated. Mismatched eyes occur in less than 1 percent of the population, so not super common, but not that rare either.

Actors who have played Superman and Lois Lane, Henry Cavill in *Man of Steel* (2016) and Kate Bosworth in *Superman Returns* (2006), both have heterochromia. Apparently, previous to her role in *Superman Returns*, Bosworth often wore coloured contacts to hide her heterochromia. The dolls of Lois Lane depict her natural eye colour. How could anyone see Clark Kent and not know that he's also Superman? I never got this as a kid—I ended up just believing that adults couldn't see things clearly. I did like that part of his disguise was glasses, just ordinary old, black-rimmed glasses. I mean what a terrific disguise! And you know, for a long period in my adult life I wore glasses, and rarely did anyone notice my eyes. When I started wearing contact lenses again, it became a regular thing, and I realized how much I missed having that as part of my identity. I didn't want it to be the secret that it had quietly become.

When a fictional character has heterochromia, according to the website *TV Tropes*, this might mark "the character as special in some way, whether as magical, nonhuman, or something else entirely." A number of Anime characters have heterochromia, but it doesn't crop up that often in literary fiction. I do remember reading *Solomon Gursky Was Here* by Mordecai Richler in a CanLit class in my undergrad and noting an instance of the mismatched eye trope.

The two questions I have been asked most frequently: Did you know your eyes are different colours? (Umm, yes …) And, do you see differently through each eye? This second question is obviously the more interesting of the two. The answer is no but I think it speaks to our desire to be able to see things differently. Once, someone asked, "Does that give you anything?" and I responded, "magical powers."

Having heterochromia doesn't so much give me anything special but, at the same time, it's given me a lot. As a kid I would look through my blue eye, then my mainly green one. I'd close one eye and look at the world sort of like artists do when they're holding their thumb up to see if a painting would work better without a particular element. Having mismatched eyes meant that I've always been attuned to the fact that there is always more than one way to see things.

In David Foster Wallace's commencement speech, "This is Water" he talks to college grads about the upcoming tedium of their days. The boring stuff. Standing in line at the grocery store, enduring long waits, grumpiness, people screaming at their kids. He says, "But if you really learn how to pay attention, then you will know there are other options. It will actually be within your power to experience a crowded, hot, slow, consumer-hell type situation as not only meaningful, but sacred, on fire with the same force that made the stars: love, fellowship, the mystical oneness of all things deep down." Sure, he goes on, maybe it isn't that way, but consider it's possible.

At my day job at the library, I've brought this story with me to routine, dull interactions. The endless showing people how to use the computer mouse, the walk-through of how to use the photocopier. I've also brought the fact that I can only see what I can see right now in my interactions with people. I try to remember all the myriad of possibilities in this person's life, but also remember to just think about them in the right now. For example, someone who has been recently incarcerated brings in their papers to get a library card or to clear the fines on their account. We talk about hitting the reset button. We don't need or want to know what happened, but we can give them a fresh start with a new clear library card. I'm looking the person in the eyes and saying, we're good. Let's move forward from here.

I can imagine things about the person I'm speaking to or I can just see them. And I admit, as someone who writes novels, I'm prone to imagining possible scenarios. Yes, I have concocted entire time-travel narratives at certain points, but I've also learned that being present is usually more useful.

How do you say to a person, I see you? How often do we take a split second to register someone's eye colour? We're looking, but are we seeing? Does it even matter if we notice if someone's eyes are blue or brown? Are we too jaded and unpoetic these days to consider eyes as the window to the soul? One of my favourite lines in English literature is the moment in *Pride and Prejudice* where Miss Bingley is goading Mr. Darcy into declaring his admiration of Elizabeth Bennet. Miss Bingley is mocking Elizabeth's family, and suggests Darcy is thinking similarly. But he says, "My mind was more agreeable engaged. I have been meditating on the very great pleasure which a pair of fine eyes in the face of a pretty woman can bestow." This is the earliest moment in the book where the reader is given an inkling of the taciturn Darcy's feelings.

Clark Kent's glasses were such a great disguise that he was unknowable as Superman when he wore them, but he was still Superman. "Don't ask questions about longing," says Rumi, "Look in my face." But I always misremember the line as, "look in my eyes." It's romantic, maybe, to think that we can know someone by looking them in the eyes, but there's something to it, too. And maybe it's less what you see, and more that the person you are looking at feels seen. One day at the library I had been helping a mother and elementary school–aged daughter with getting a library card. As they were leaving through the front doors, I heard the girl say to her mom, "Did you notice that lady had two different-coloured eyes!" I found this to be delightful and memorable and also a reminder that people are seeing you when you're not even particularly aware of it. That small, good feeling of someone seeing me has stayed with me.

I think I could write a long poem about the gestures and small details of things I notice at the library that don't otherwise have a place. They don't belong in an incident report, and they don't belong in an essay. I'm not an expert in body language, but I notice things. Tense shoulders, nervous ticks, fingernails bitten to the quick, ripped earlobes, stains, dirt, excessive blinking, dilated pupils, greasy hair, secondhand clothes. Because at the library, your privacy is everything. We workers don't get to know what happens next. We get to see what happens in a given moment and help out but after that the story is not ours. It never really was. What replays in the mind later are the details. We don't get to know. And that has to be okay.

The way we see has always been of interest to me and you could say that it's been the through-line of all my writing. These days, I'm wearing contact lenses for much of my day and this both expands and limits my vision. When I wear my glasses, I can take them off and look at things without them. My vision is crisper up close with my glasses, too, because I have progressive lenses. But wearing glasses means one's peripheral view is obscured.[20] And then when I'm looking through the various lenses of my cameras, that changes my perspective on the world I see, too. There are so many ways that we see the world, through so many lenses. Andy

---

20 The degree depends upon how strong one's prescription is and mine is quite so.

Warhol wrote about the time before people wore eyeglasses and I think about his words all the time. He said, "It must have been weird because everyone was seeing in different ways according to how bad their eyes were. Now, eyeglasses standardize everyone's vision to 20-20."

We see in all these different ways, but we also fail to see so much. And how do we know how the person standing next to us is seeing the world? It's more evident on our ubiquitous digital screens, but not dissimilar. We're viewing movies, websites, photographs in a digital environment, but the quality is all over the place, and that's without allowing for the different settings on a screen for light and colour. Is the monitor old or new? Latest model or old dinosaur? Is our phone cracked or pristine? Are we looking at the screen in a darkened room or a bright one? We all think we're looking at the same thing, watching the latest superhero movie, but are we?

When I was a child, walking home from elementary school, I would often close my eyes for a block at a time. What would it be like to not be able to see at all? Or just a little bit? I would open my eyes a slit to navigate the end of the street. Secretly, I have always considered my ability to see and notice small details as my superpower. When you are looking to see if people need help, as I have done at the library, and trying to discern what type of help, there are often small details that are cues. I don't make assumptions about those things I see, but I file them away, in case they indicate something. I might probe a bit deeper or wait a bit longer. Or try to strike up a sidelong conversation.

I've always had this belief that if we could see well, if we could really look, and look at things in more than just one way, through different lenses, squinting with one eye then the other, if we could look into the shadows and notice the bands of light, if we could notice the holes in a person's shoes, or the way someone's eyes meet ours, if you could put all these things together, it would somehow be useful.

Christopher Reeve (the original Superman) didn't have heterochromia, but he did have a deep insight into the character of Superman. In an interview, he once said that what drew people to Superman was that he was a friend, which sounds simple, but I think most people would think about how he saves people. But that's just a one-off, being saved. And as Clark Kent, he really cared, without needing credit or fanfare. He wanted to anonymously care for people and he did that by noticing what was happening, then doing what he could. He didn't just have super-powered seeing; he noticed, which is a completely different kind of skill.

There's something to be said for just seeing people where they're standing. You might see them one way and then another, upon closer deliberation. In a certain way, this kind of seeing is the seeing of a poet: you look for patterns, rhymes, gestures, beauty, oddness, something quirky, off-kilter, something that would typically not be noticed, or if noticed, go generally unremarked upon.

I admit that having heterochromia has always made me feel a bit special. I ask myself, does that give you anything? I don't have magical powers or superpowers. What I do have, and most people have this, is knowing that if I can see things in one way, I can also see them in another. That I can't see everything, but I can see what is right in front of me and there is a lot of information that can be collected from right where I stand. I've learned to trust in those things that jump out at me as poetic observances because they might mean something at some point in the near future; they might be useful. Of course, they might not be of any use other than to contribute to the practice of seeing, noticing. Seeing isn't knowing, but a long practice of this offers up slivers of understanding of what's happening in the immediate world.

Ordinary Life

Ordinary Life, Still Life, Library Life

The question, *what will happen next?* is something that can be asked of both a still life painting and ordinary life. But ordinary life is people moving through space, interacting with other people, hoping, hurting, loving, noticing, and trying to make do, survive, do their best. An ordinary person is working hard, trying to get better, hustling, trying to find and mine their everyday life for moments of transcendence, joy, or a gorgeously shocking poetry with layers of meaning. Something is always happening next, even if that something happens to be experiencing a workday, or a meeting with friends or relatives. But you might also imagine life-changing medical news, a promotion, a surprise party, a lottery win, a breakup, or various iterations of fifteen minutes of fame. Ordinary life is ongoing. Ordinary life keeps moving.

In a traditional still life, there is often the sense that something just happened or will happen. Though still life is usually thought of as being outside narrative, a human being placed the objects on the table and arranged the roses and lilies in a vase, and a *felt* someone is potentially just outside the frame. Often there is the feeling that the precarious objects will topple, or that someone will come in and move, rearrange, or withdraw one of the objects. The bread will be taken away to be eaten, a flower petal will drop, a bee or fly will buzz in, the fruit will rot and decay. If a still life is outside of narrative, then it's only just barely removed from it. And yet it's a moment in time where things seem quietly certain, and where the forces of the everyday may gather. If we feel things as we stand in front of a still life painting, this has to do with the temporary cessation of the surging discrepancies of our everyday life, which is sometimes monotonous, repetitive, but also busy, and filled with emotions. We might be worried about our children, aging parents, coworkers, friends. We are constantly navigating relationships, trying to pay our bills, get groceries, figure out what's for dinner, and remembering to say happy birthday, or that today is the day to pick up the dry cleaning.

What does ordinary life have to say about still life and what does still life have to say about ordinary life? What even is ordinary life? If I wrote an essay even a decade ago (and I did), about how my own ordinary life intersected with still life, how would it be different now and why? Obviously, the prevalence of social media is at the core of how things are different. I used to think of ordinary life as life pared down to something pure and real, like an uncut diamond, no need, as Virginia Woolf said, to sparkle—"No need to be anybody but oneself." I believed that a life had value because of its very ordinariness. I imagined ordinary life as an existence that had sporadic but somehow reliable moments of grace even though it was humble and rhythmic and dull. My descriptions of my own ordinary life would be slightly humorous, slightly self-deprecating. Back then, I reckoned that if we could agree on the monotony of the ordinary life, we could also agree upon the potential for moments of annunciation or clarity or dazzling unexpected beauty that we all deserved and could all obtain if we wished it. I didn't quite have a mathematical formula but there seemed to be patterns, and one could, I believed, become adept at not only predicting them but also gaming them to some extent. A life in pursuit of these moments would necessarily propagate them. That was the payoff to the everyday: profound moments of poetry when you least expected it. But I did expect it.

Was I naïve? I continue to think that the beauty of ordinary life is that it is and is not ordinary simultaneously. This is a consolation, but is it also a kind of built-in placation? You know, your life is drudgery but if you hold it up to the light once in a while and squint, it becomes suddenly a miracle, a joyous unexpected moment of grace. And is that enough?

A large part of my everyday life is working at the public library, which I do half-time. I'm reluctant to thread my work life into this essay about ordinary life partly because the stories I hear and the things I witness are protected by the same type of confidentiality that a doctor has for a patient, and also partly because what interests me are details of stories and these are too revealing. I can't ethically talk about people in any identifiable way. But the ordinary lives of those who come into the library affect my ordinary life. I see the world in a different way because I have worked in the public library for over ten years. Some days I come home from work wired or sad or angry or running on adrenaline. Working at a library is one part performance, one part rules encouragement, one part deep listening, and one part channelling the King of Kensington. But what happens at the library stays at the library. Due to the nature of the job, we do more referring than anything else, and I'm often left wondering, what happened next? Did the woman we talked to about the shelter get there and is she okay now? Did the person we helped with the resume get the job? Did the man sleeping outside in -30 Celsius winter who didn't want to go to a shelter make it through the night? I have felt that my own life has been punctuated by moments of profound beauty, but have theirs?

The stories of ordinary life are enlivened by the details, but I have to leave the details out of any library stories I tell. And wow, I wish I could describe certain gestures to you, things people have said to me, faces, hands stuffed into pockets, hair brushed off a forehead, the colour of someone's eyes and the way they changed, softening, as we talked to each other. When we look at the details of our interactions, just as we look at a still life, sometimes the light will metaphorically swing in and a person will be profoundly illuminated, as in a Vermeer painting. If I could paint you such a picture, I think you would fall in love with these people just as I have. Ordinary life, I go on learning, is intimate gestures, raw admissions of fear, rigorous dissembling, small moments of joy and anguish and anxiety. Ordinary life is repetitive and monotonous but sometimes it is heightened by an experience. Ordinary life is a web of things gone right and things that go wrong, things that we make happen, and things that happen to us. Ordinary life is despair and hope and just trying to get by, trying to figure things out and how to make things better.

In my own ordinary life, I often feel as though I'm occupying multiple registers; I'm several people at once. And I think this is how many people feel to some extent. At the library, I might go from speaking to a woman with a black eye escaping domestic violence, to chatting with a homeless customer, to helping a child find a book to read on the subject of dragons. I love my work and I love, honestly, those trickier aspects of it. But it's a lot to hold. So, I go from talking to people who live rough or in precarious living arrangements, to speaking with those who are worried and afraid or have lived through unimaginable trauma. Yet when I returned from my three-week holiday in Rome, these very same people asked me how it was and genuinely listened and responded without bitterness. One person noticed I was wearing new shoes and mentioned how much they like them.

Then I go back to my warm cozy home, and it feels weird. It just does. There I resume the roles of wife and mom and friend, writer and photographer. In my sphere, I know people who have serious health concerns, money issues, and family turmoil. Meanwhile, Rob, my artist husband, and I have that ever-pervasive worry about art sales, and we worry about how the economy will affect us personally, which is relative to all the stories I hear of people with immediate and super scary concerns about their daily existence. I mean, probably we'll be okay? We always have been, lord knows how sometimes, but here we are. The thing is, I take strength and draw courage from the resilience of the people I meet at the library even as I simultaneously feel guilty for taking anything from an individual whose needs aren't being met because of a broken system.

These days it seems as though ordinary life is in opposition to celebrity life, or the lives of the rich and famous. When I post a photo of my coffee cup beside a writing journal on Instagram, quite a few people might "like" it and comment on it, but when a celebrity does the same, they receive a phenomenal amount of attention for a similar image. Maybe ordinary life is the thing you give up to star in a reality TV show, or if you win the lottery, or win an Oscar for best performance. Ordinary life is what you ditch to "make it." When Hozier posted an impressively grainy photo on Twitter on August 18, 2019, of a scene outside his hotel window, his followers good-naturedly teased him for it, asking him if he took the photo with a potato or a piece of bread or wondering if it was painted by Van Gogh. He responded "I swear to god its worth using an android phone just to read you guys roast me for it." To Hozier's credit, he took it in stride and seemed to have sheepish and genuine fun with it, which makes him seem more lovely and more special. He is actually sort of just like us, but obviously not at all like us.

The popular column in *Us* magazine began in 2002 with a photograph of Drew Barrymore picking up a penny. At an editorial meeting, paparazzi photos were spread out on a table, and seeing the Barrymore photo, Bonnie Fuller came up with the idea for the now well-known column, "Stars— They're Just Like *Us*." Kate Lee writes, in an article on

Medium, that "At that moment, the direction of the magazine—and, arguably, the nature of all celebrity coverage—shifted on its axis." The beauty of the schtick, the column, which plays on the name of the magazine, is that celebrities can never be seen as ordinary, because when we pick up a penny, no one really cares. Perhaps they are ordinary to themselves and those who know them well, but to the rest of us, they're always outside or beyond ordinary. Sure, we post grainy or terrible photos, but we don't get thousands of responses when we post them.

Let's imagine a still life from the seventeenth century. Maybe there's a black background, an intricately woven carpet on a table, a silver plate of fruit—lemons, oranges, grapes, a melon, a pomegranate. There is an ornate drinking vessel made from a nautilus shell, a wedge of ripe cheese, some decadent sweets, a loaf of bread, maybe some game birds waiting to be plucked. Perhaps there is a skull, an hourglass, a mirror, a bouquet of pink carnations, a butterfly, some coins. While the viewer gapes at the skill of the realistically painted objects, their lifelikeness, they also crave and covet the riches, the abundance. But the message of the painting, and maybe this arrives later for the viewer, is that all of these things in real life are fleeting. The skull most obviously points to the theme memento mori. But still lifes are always subtly pointing out the transience of existence. An apple will have a spot of decay, flies will alight on some sugar cookies to remind us of what happens to us when we perish, a flower will droop and have faded petals.

The overlapping theme of *vanitas,* from the Latin meaning "empty," could also be one of the painting's messages. Christians believed that worldly goods are worthless, futile. Possessions are merely possessions. Which is easy to say if you're the full-bellied chap hanging a painting on the wall of your well-appointed seventeenth-century home. These paintings always seem to me like an interesting combination of bragging and chastising, showing off and being humble.

Scholars have identified various streams or sub-genres of still life. Pronkstilleven is Dutch for ostentatious still life, and the bodegón is a Spanish still life that depicted food and drink in a kitchen scene, often quite austere and humble. There are breakfast still lifes, floral still lifes, and monumental still lifes. For a genre at the bottom of the so-called hierarchy of painting, the subject matter seems limitless, keeps evolving, and continues to speak to viewers and creators. Still life says something about who we are in intimate and relatable ways. The objects depicted are ones we, too, have held, eaten, or wished for.

When I look at a still life it reminds me to look at everyday objects in my own life more carefully. It reminds me that there is beauty often right under my nose. Beauty enlivens, raises the eyebrows, widens the eyes, makes the heart skip a beat, takes the breath away. Wow! It reminds us that we must do more than just get through our ordinary days.

Why did someone in the seventeenth-century commission or purchase a still life, though? They were hung in the homes of the wealthy to telegraph to their guests their prowess at trade and how well off and successful they were. The still lifes might showcase curiosities or delicacies, things that were quite extraordinary—exotic fruit, unique shells, hothouse flowers. In the age of the internet, we've seen it all, but hundreds of years ago, to see a pineapple when you hadn't seen one before would have been mind-blowing. In addition to the opulence of a vessel or bowl, there might also be an abundance of decadent food. In scholarly articles about still life of this time period, you will often see words like desire, appetite, and power. I'm not an art historian, but I have tended to think of still life in a broad way, as the genre that reminds us that we're all the same, we all eat apples, we're all connected in these humble ways. I'm thinking Chardin or Cezanne. But still life didn't always function that way. Still life as a genre had intervals where the message was: Super rich people, we're so *not* like you!

And so, still life has always been in conversation with who we are and who we are not, in terms of class and wealth, in terms of what we have and what we don't have, and also in terms of what we see as important and beautiful. Still life has at times been a not-so-humble-brag. Sure, it was the overlooked genre, but it also quietly speaks of personal refinement, taste, and affluence. It speaks to the need to share beauty, to convey that the world is a beautiful place even amid the commerce and the consumption. It's people who have stuff trying to keep their stuff by appearing enviable in a dog-eat-dog world. Not so different from what all the Instagram influencers posing in restaurants and cafes with coffee, croissants, and luxury goods in paid promotional posts are up to today. One Instagram account that I enjoy is "Follow the Nap," which is devoted to, as you might guess, to napping. Alex Shannon's tagline is "the world's first sleep influencer." If you follow along, you'll see him napping in luxury hotels on comfy beds or in posh window seats with an amazing view, or poolside, in swish locales. And, of course, there is quite often room service, arrayed on the bed, a splendid still life. Using still life to sell you on something that you'll never be able to afford is not a new tactic at all.

I've kept a blog in various incarnations for over a decade. The kind of writing and gathering and noticing that one does when one keeps a blog is comparable to how commonplace books were assembled in the eighteenth and nineteenth centuries. These commonplace books acted as repositories for copied out poems and prose of others as well as personal ruminations, quotations, recipes, and sketches. In blogging, one is always keeping a sharp eye out for something to share. An idea, a quotation, a poem. Part of my process is to take photographs with a digital camera. And so in tandem with mining the everyday, both digitally and in real life, in books, on television, and on my kitchen table, I'm stilling with my camera: snow on a leaf, a teacup, a stack of books, some flowers. Most of the images are in a certain way, still lifes. And this has given shape to my days, to my weeks.

I have spent a great deal of my life sitting in the ordinariness of existence, in the drab light, waiting for the sunlight to swing in through my window and make a thing seem as though it's stepping out of its dress of rags and into a sequined number, ta-da! Maybe it doesn't happen every time, or every day, but though it is variable, it is also a certainty. Even so, I continue to be surprised by the intensity, by the very gift of such a moment.

I have worked an evening shift in the middle of winter at the library, where we helped someone in distress find shelter for the night. We didn't really do anything other than find out information from the person in need and arrange for one agency to pick them up and deliver them to another. It's a lot of legwork, and it's careful work, because the goal is to have the person you are helping retain their dignity. But there are also a lot of emotions. The distressed person is often *very* distressed and exhausted. Or hungry. Sometimes crying. A lot of one's time is spent carefully trying to discern if the person is physically or mentally unwell. To what degree? What service would best fit this circumstance? How to advocate for a person in distress with the person on the other end of the phone? How dire is the situation? What small bits of comfort are we able to offer? A glass of water? A cookie? Is an ambulance required or just a warm mode of transport? Bus or warming van?

The next day at home I'm back to mining my life for what Kathleen Stewart has called "shocks of beauty." I move from my study to the kitchen, waiting for the light to strike the bowl of oranges on the table just so. The pink roses I brought home from the grocery store might inhabit a circle of calm when the sun hits them and seem to be aglow from within. I get out my camera and take a few shots. I wait. I bide my time. I know what I'm waiting for. It's a combination of what's happening on the table and what's happening in me. There's a feeling of creative shock or a feeling of being in the zone, and that's when "the" photo transpires. I crave this photo; I need it like some people need a drug.

It's not a work of art, but a photo that goes into my commonplace book, onto my blog. And maybe it's there to illustrate something specific, or something I can riff on, but mainly the photo acts as a marker of those small moments of beauty in my everyday life. Leonard Cohen once said that "Poetry is just the evidence of life. If your life is burning well, poetry is just the ash." These photos are the evidence that my life is burning well.

I sometimes wonder if I'd never met and married Rob, would I have been drawn to the subject of still life anyway? Or was I drawn to him because of his art? Probably the most common comment he gets about his work is: I don't know how you do what you do. I don't know how he does it either and I've watched him paint for thirty years. What does it mean to want to translate everyday objects and flowers into paint and to reference both all the art that has been made in the past as well as the way we use and admire things today?

When we were in Rome this past November, there was a still life show on at the Corsini Gallery which we visited twice because it hit us in all the right ways. We spent hours there, looking at the paintings of lemons and pomegranates, oranges and game birds, quinces and cookies. There were paintings of meats and cheeses and bread. But it was the lemons that drew me, and I kept circling back to a few of the paintings that had lemons in them, all by unknown Roman, Caravaggesque artists.

After looking at art, most days we'd walk through the Campo de'Fiori, which was right by our apartment. And there I'd take photos of the crates of fruit and vegetables, the flowers. There were all these connections, of course there were. We brought lemons back to our apartment, much like the ones we'd seen on trees in the garden of the Villa Farnesina that was across the river from the apartment we'd

rented, and of course in the paintings. On many late afternoons Rob would sit in the corner of our living room and
do watercolour sketches based on paintings we'd seen, or
of fruit and flowers we'd bought at the market. One of the
sketches was of lemons and we propped it up on the stone
mantle in our Rome apartment. And now it's propped up
on a table at our home in Edmonton.

After a day of looking at art, and then making art in the
late afternoons, we would often have a dinner of bread and
meat, cheeses, nuts and pickles, fruit—not unlike in the
still lifes that we had lavished our attention on earlier. I'd
slice a lemon and squeeze it into my glass of water. I don't
know what it was about the combination of the lemon
juice and the Roman water, but I drank it slowly and it was
a bit of a miracle.

What I'm interested in is how people lived then and how
we live now, and how the everyday objects in our ordinary/
not ordinary lives change and don't change. How these still
life paintings we saw speak to our relationship with our own
mortality, our fears, our loves, our needs. How they reveal
things that we don't mean to reveal, about class, and wealth,
and privilege, and exclusion, and maybe exhaustion. They
talk about beauty and hunger and nourishment, order and
chaos, quiet and calm and daydreaming. They say so much
and they hold my attention. They take me right into this
precise moment and remind me that everything in a still life
is a continuous right now.

Yet not everyone will be interested in still life, not everyone wants to look at paintings. Not everyone wants to
think about how much we all have in common. How when
it comes down to it, we'd most of us like to sit at a table with
a small repast, with some lemons and a tiny vase of flowers,
some cookies, a bowl of fruit. Maybe we'd like to order in
a pizza, or some Chinese takeout. We'd like to eat a meal,
some toast, have some hot cocoa. How ordinary we all really
are. How meaningful it is, to be just that: ordinary.

When interacting with people at the library, people who are forced to endure a rough living, especially in the winter in this brutal Edmonton climate, I have often had the response, sometimes jokingly, sometimes with sincerity, that what they most desire is to sleep in a bed in a five-star hotel. To use the remote control, and to eat pizza or lasagne or french fries, or some other favourite food in bed. I've heard this on more than one occasion over the years. And it doesn't seem like too much to ask: to be somewhere safe and comfortable, somewhere a bit decadent and fancy, and to eat something delicious. I completely relate to the desire. Don't we all? I too would love to sprawl out on a pillowy soft bed, a pizza box still life on the side table with remote, glass of wine. The bedspread would be rumpled and half drawn back, and there would be plates of pie and sticky toffee pudding and cheesecake with raspberry coulis. Bags of chips open and spilling out. I would watch *Bridget Jones's Diary* or an adaptation of *Pride and Prejudice* or *Persuasion*. I would love to escape into a favourite movie where I know that the ending is a happy one.

In our real lives, we have no idea if the ending is a happy one. The thing most of us have in common is wondering what will happen next. And some people have to constantly worry about what's going to immediately happen next, because it means the difference between staying alive or possibly, perishing.

Mark Strand said in a poem, "Our masterpiece is the private life." I think this is true. But not everyone is able to write out their masterpiece in a poem, or in prose, and this changes our relationship to our masterpiece. Anne Bogart, in a book about storytelling, says that "speaking a story can be an act of letting in light." She speaks of our collective hunger as human beings for stories. We have often heard it said that everyone has a story to tell, and I've lately been reminded of David Foster Wallace's commencement speech, "This is Water" in an essay by Leslie Jamison. Wallace, she says, "talks about the tedium of standing at supermarket check-out counter, irritated by the other people in line." Wallace says you can see them as "stupid and cow-like and dead-eyed and non-human" or you can choose to see them differently. You can imagine their story; you can have empathy. And then, says Wallace, "it will actually be within your power to experience a crowded, hot, slow, consumer-hell type situation as not only meaningful, but sacred, on fire with the same force that lit the stars." It's Jamison who says, referring to a stranger, that "I forgot, for a moment, that his life—like everyone else's—holds more than I could ever possibly see." And I think about these three things when I work at the library, the way stories can become light, the way empathy can change your life, and that much of one's private and inner life is invisible to others.

When we were in Rome looking at the still life exhibition at the Corsini Gallery, it was such a heartwarming feeling to have the paintings grouped together. Rob has been making still lifes in one form or another for his entire life, though he is not particularly well-known and certainly not famous. When we travel, it has almost always included visiting museums and art galleries. Not surprisingly, we always gravitate toward the still life paintings. They're usually in little corridors, or smaller rooms, or quietly occupying an unobtrusive space. Many people seem to walk right by them. Generally, the larger paintings dominate—the depictions of myths, the annunciations, the beheadings, saints and the sinners. So, it was actually quite gratifying and soul-lifting to see a collection like this given such prominence. Many of the artists are not known and are designated as "Tuscan Painter," "Caravaggesque Painter," or "Painter Working in Rome." This made the work all the more poignant.

One of the things I like about looking at art in person, and specifically at still life, is that there are layers of meaning, and there are details that are not always apparent upon first viewing the work. In one painting, there was a

fly perched on some cookies. As people strolled by, I wanted to stop them, and say, but did you notice the housefly?
A fly on cookies is a thing that happens. You've seen it;
I've seen it. But it's also a religious symbol connoting our
eventual decay, our sin, and reminds the viewer of Satan's
assistant, Beelzebub, "Lord of the Flies." A painter who
could realistically paint a fly deserves serious props and
there are many stories out there about how a patron tried
to flick one away from a canvas. These days a fly might remind us of surveillance, that we're being watched, or have
been "bugged." But even a modern spying device will only
ever be able to record part of a story. Ultimately, the objects on a table are inscrutably silent. Ultimately, we are
given fragments.

The fly in a still life also reminds the viewer that something is happening, even if very slowly. It reminds us to look
closely. It reminds us that things are not necessarily what
they first seemed. I am reminded about the nature of surfaces and how lightly we touch them. We alight, spend a little
time, and often come away knowing less than we might like
to know. We must put a bit of faith in our powers of empathy, in our power to make a story out of what we've been
given. The story we make up might be completely wrong or
based on outcomes that we wish for rather than what really
is. There is an unknowability about still life. The before and
after of a still life, while imaginable, are not secure, and we
can never access them with any precision, any certainty. And
we remember that the story around these objects arrayed on
a table is not really ours.

I wish to work through the connections between the ordinary life, yours and mine, the still life from art history and
contemporary art, and the ones that arise in your home,
maybe without ever being thought of as still lifes. How do
still lifes act as prompts for the rest of your life? I've always
thought of the everyday as something humble, something
for everyone, but now I know that not everyone has access

to "ordinary" life. The way we talk about ordinary life is very much a middle-class (and above) conversation.

I always find it tricky to talk about my library life, but then we've never been able to talk about still life without also thinking about privilege, about all those things outside of the frame, the myriad kinds of silences that a bowl of peaches might rest within. There is a profound and patient unknowability that we come upon as we stand before painted things. And it's a good humble place to inhabit, though not everyone is able to make it there.

In *Affect Theory*, a book that has influenced a lot of my recent thinking on still life, Kathleen Stewart talks about the unfinished quality of the ordinary life. There's an ongoingness to it. She reminds us of "the vagueness or the unfinished quality of the ordinary" which is "not so much a deficiency as a resource, like a fog of immanent forces still moving even though so much has already happened and there seems to be plenty that's set in stone." She talks about the ordinary as "a mode of attunement" and "a continuous responding to something not quite already given and yet somehow happening."

When we look at a still life, we know it is only just one permutation of how things could be. We might wonder, what will happen next? What forces are at play? What are the resources that can be mined from the moment that will enlighten us and deepen our knowledge of the human condition? We also know that there are possibilities, permutations. Another way to arrange things. The table holds an ongoing and inconceivable future of endless still lifes. A still life statically hums and vibrates at the same time as it allows us to pause, to ask the question, to loft it in the air, to look around us while it is aloft: what has happened and what will happen next?

Still Life Musings

If I could become an expert at still life photography, maybe this would be the key to also figuring out life.

As soon as I consider becoming an expert at still life photography, I remember that my project has been about the practice more than the result. Yes, I'm invested in the results. There's a joy in seeing my arrangements make some sort of visual sense. I have no great audience. But when I've made a photograph that I find to be aesthetically pleasing, it's a surprising pleasure. A different pleasure than I get from writing. It's immediate. It's joyful. The process of setting up and photographing a still life is a delight that I haven't found anywhere else, and yet the possibility is there every day, right in front of almost anyone.

I wonder how many photographs I've taken in my life? With film cameras, this could be measured out, but with digital cameras so much disappears into the ether. I'm not a technical photographer. I proceed error by error and the delete button is part of my process. I delete some images in camera, and many more when I import them to my computer. At each stage, there is deletion.

I think of what Hélène Cixous says about errors in her essay on the ecstasies of the artist's atelier. She says, "I advance error by error, with erring steps, by the force of error. It's suffering, but it's joy."

With digital photography, the errors disappear into the ether too. But they're still there. In every digital photo there's an invisible trace of the trial and error that goes into producing a final photo. In Lightroom, the Adobe photo processing program that I use, there is a log of all the changes that you make as you edit. When I think of all of the choices that are made before that final photo is given its big reveal on say, Instagram, I'm a bit agog. For users of Photoshop the choices are even more extensive. The tracery behind one photo is a bit of a tangled frenzy, even if it's not the beautiful instantaneous feeling one finds in the expressive drawings or studies for paintings by Degas or Picasso.

The process of making a photo or making a painting has this in common: the moving forward, choice by choice, and yes, error by error. In a photograph you're adjusting clarity, contrast, darks and lights. You're choosing which parts you want to stand out, how crisp you'd like the overall image, and how poetic. I've always been drawn to the term (and the effect) "bokeh," which refers to the creamy or sometimes bubbly background in a photo.

As someone who has worn glasses from a young age, I'm drawn to photographs that reflect the world that I see when I remove my spectacles. Which is to say: I enjoy a lot of bokeh, that bubbly or blurred background.

Painters have always made choices in a similar fashion, and contemporary painters are influenced by the effects visible in photographs. When you are aware of these effects, the lens distortions, the way one adjusts the focal point, you can trace them in paintings where the artist uses a photograph as a reference point or has adjusted their seeing based on the experience of viewing photographs.

Occasionally I like to take a behind-the-scenes picture of a still life shoot. I most often use the coffee table in our living room, propping a trifold black screen behind the tableau of books and flowers and objects. The working area is comparatively tiny even though in the photos produced there is the illusion of expansiveness. The staged scene is articulated in one way, and the room contains a chaos or mundanity inconsistent or surprising when compared with the finished product. The framing of a scene isn't a lie, but it is a narrowing.

It feels important, more than ever, just to show these small truths. To document how things look from further back. To show that this kind of perspective too, is a kind of beauty.

You don't need much room to open things up. You don't need a warehouse to make a beautiful image. With a macro lens you can get in close, and a small flower can feel so expansive. One day I'd like to blow up one of my flower images to 40" x 60". But I know that that's a risk. Was I able to capture the correct amount of detail? This is where the edits I make will be crucial. Do they stand up at this scale, with this level of scrutiny? I'm thinking about Georgia O'Keeffe and her large-scale flower pictures—her interpretation of what she saw represented so expansively. Maybe this is an instance (one of many really) where a photograph can't come close to doing what a painting can do.

When I first started playing around with digital photography, I bought a 50mm 1.4 lens. I'd looked at other peoples' photos on Flickr and the images I tended to like best were made with that lens. That's when I became really addicted to taking photos. It became part of my writing practice, part of my daily practice. I've never thought of myself as a photographer, just someone who captures a few images every day. The 50mm lens works for portraits and for still life. My vision, how I wanted to see things, aligned with the way this lens allowed me to frame the world.

More recently I bought a 100mm lens, a macro, and that's what I shoot most of my still lifes with now. I can go closer in, and there's a clarity that I'm after that the lens can give to me. Whatever lens you use comes with restraints of some sort. The trick is to have that restraint match up with how you see without the lens. With how you envision that slice of existence showing up in a rectangle of space.

Everyone's home is full of still lifes. We make still lifes inadvertently all day long. At breakfast we set the cereal box on the table by the jug of milk. The jam is set out, a knife, some butter. We shower and assemble our makeup on the vanity. Lipstick, compact, brush. Before we leave, we place our lunch bag on the counter beside briefcase or satchel and car keys. In the evening our book is on a side table, along with a glass of water, our spectacles. It goes on like this.

Does it matter? I think it does. When we look to the past to try and understand humanity, why humans did what they did in difficult times, we often look at objects. We want to know what food was eaten in ancient civilizations. We want to look at the patterns of bowls and imagine the heft of them in our hands. We are looking for a human connection. Your cornflakes, yellow cereal bowl, the carton of milk, the book you're reading, the coffee steaming beside the book—I remember you there, I know you there.

The inexhaustibility of still life isn't remarked upon often enough. But it's part of why still life is a balm. Not only does it continue through time, it persists and can be recreated in endless permutations. The same object turned 30 degrees is new again. A single vessel can be transformed in myriad ways, as we know from viewing the work of Morandi. The addition and subtraction of a number of vessels is an inexhaustible experiment. The practice of assembling a still life need not be elaborate.

Before the digital age, and since painting has been studied, artists have used still life as studio practice. Students reproduce an object study as part of their art training. When I first started taking digital photographs, I set up a few red peppers in a patterned bowl and tried out all the settings. The patience of the objects was valued.

Because there is an abundance of still lifes produced, both paintings and photographs, there are likely more poorly executed examples than of any other genre. What makes a still life rise to the level of art? Will time eventually cause all the images to sift through, separating the stellar from the ill-designed or ill-conceived? Because there is so much to sift through, what ends up getting lost? Does that matter? While I believe in the importance of the process, the practice, not everything is art. Not everyone is an artist. But that doesn't mean we shouldn't all try.

What are the ineffable qualities of a still life as a true (whatever that means) work of art? What will be valued in the future? How to define a successful still life? The feeling of time stopped, an elusive magic, the light, the skill or technique, the poetic? What are the ingredients?

Waiting for the light is a bit like waiting for inspiration. You have to put yourself in the way of it, bring the bowl of oranges to the table near the window. You can check your phone for the weather report and you can keep an eye out the window. You can look at the clouds and gauge the breeze. How fast are things moving higher up in the sky? You have to accept the unpredictable and you have to accept the gray and rainy days. You can also have faith that the sun will swing back in, screech on the breaks when it arrives at your house. You have to believe in the slicing dive, the low slide, the athleticism of the light. Even the dim days contain light, just softer, gentler. You have to love it too. Maybe more.

The line by Virginia Woolf from *A Room of One's Own*, "For interruptions there will always be" runs through my head a lot. A still life exists in spite of interruptions. It is between the interruptions. It is a beacon, a still point, a rest between the notes. But you can still hear the notes… what are they? The notes of hope or despair? The notes of calm or frenzy?

An object must be lived with for a while before it can properly take up space in a still life. Perhaps it also needs to be dreamed, to appear in dreams. A magnetic field of cosmic vibrations develops between object and viewer, the contemplated and the contemplator. Gaston Bachelard talks about the "painter who likes to live the object in its ever-particular appearances..." He speaks of the need for familiarity with an object, to faithfulness to an object. Only then will the conditions be met for an "intimate reverie." An object with which we commune will enhance our dreams. And when we dream good dreams, we will find an inner calm. The object leads us to reverie, which leads us to tranquility. Which leads us, as Bachelard says, to being "at peace with ourselves." Reverie, he also says, is "an original peace. Poets know it. Poets tell it to us."

Maybe a still life will appear in one of your dreams because it has been well-dreamed ahead of your viewing of it. The original dreamer/artist kept faith with the object, kept it company, let it seep into their subconscious, so that it may at some future point commune in yours. Perhaps this sounds flaky or too new age-y. But don't we all have a memory of a still life that arrives in our dreams, deep in our subconscious? Maybe it's a still life from your childhood. I will always remember the strange arrangement of things on my grandmother's bureau when I gave her a last kiss goodbye, though I might not have known that's what it was at the time. I had bought what I thought was a gumball from a machine but it turned out to be a jawbreaker. The candy turned my lips black, and I remember looking at the mirror over the chest of drawers and seeing my lips, and then looking down and seeing the jar with raised purple flowers on it filled with loose change, a comb, and a handheld mirror, and a rectangular wooden box.

A still life painting that often appears in my dreams is Chardin's *Basket of Wild Strawberries*. In the catalogue to accompany the Chardin exhibition that travelled to Paris, Dusseldorf, London, and New York at the end of 1999 and the beginning of 2000, the entry to this painting says, "Nothing could be more natural or more free, more composed or more carefully considered, nothing more tender or more moving. Indeed, 'this magic defies understanding.'" When talking about this painting, critics use the word "miracle." In my dream, I am reaching in for a strawberry from that miraculous pyramid of berries. I know this will alter everything in the dream that follows. I know also that I am thirsty, and the glass of water lets me know it waits. The two white carnations know that I will choose one of them. These things are as inevitable as the two cherries and the peach, which I will leave behind.

I've seen a lot of art in person, but not enough. Living in what we like to refer to as the boondocks, it's just not possible. We've travelled when we could. We've seen quite a few of the great museums. But I want to see more. I'm 53 writing this, in the middle, or for all I know, the beginning of the COVID-19 pandemic. It's April 13, 2020. And I can't help but feel that travel will never be the same again. There is so much art I haven't seen. It's upsetting.

If there is one painting that I would like to be magically transported in front of it is Willem Kalf's *Still Life with a Nautilus Cup* which resides in Madrid at The Museo Thyssen-Bornemisza. I've never been to Spain, never been to Madrid. I'm grateful that I can look at it in reproduction. In an essay titled "Contemplating Kalf," Anne W. Lowenthal gives a wonderful description and analysis of the painting which I won't attempt to replicate. She describes the nautilus cup, the unwinding lemon, the Chinese bowl with the eight Taoist immortals in high relief on its sides, with utmost care and she thoroughly traces the objects and the symbolism of their entwined presences. She also makes clear that there is "no set 'meaning' for any given thing, no single message, like vanitas or temperance. Rather, a web of resonances engages the viewer's imagination, eliciting active participation."

When I first saw a reproduction of the painting, I was drawn to it, and I continue to feel its pull. What is it about one image that has that particular power to captivate and insert itself into your visual memory bank with such force? The wild opulence of the objects is part of the allure. But the colours draw me back again and again. The way the eye is drawn from the glowing orb of the nautilus cup, to the glow of the peeled lemon. And then the triangle of orange-y reds—my gaze begins with one of the Taoist figures on the covered bowl, moves right to the Seville orange, and then up and over to the glass of wine behind and to the left of the nautilus cup. After this my eyes drop down to the left-hand corner of the table where there are some cracked nuts, and back up to the blue design in the bowl. Saying this, I realize, it's not even so much the colours, but the light that illuminates these colour points. It's the light drawing me to each object, each colour. The subject is light. As always. There's light, as has been said, and there's light.

I asked Rob if he could pick any still life from the history of art to take home and keep which would it be. He told me that it would be Francisco de Zurbarán's *Still Life with Lemons, Oranges and a Rose*, from the Norton Simon Museum in California. He once painted a version of this painting in a series called *The History of Still Life*. And in fact, we saw this painting in person when it was on loan to The Frick in New York City. I can't say how lucky we felt when our trip there coincided with the loan.

When I asked him why this painting, though, his answer was this: "It's austere, not flashily painted, but poetic with the rose resting on the plate by the cup, the gleam and geometry of the pewter plates. Both intimate and monumental, it evokes an altar with its offerings, a strong image from my Catholic upbringing. There are still lifes with more panache, more garish overflowing abundance. There are still lifes with fancier gold and silver and crystal objects. I'm drawn to the humble citrus fruit of Spain, the strong Mediterranean light piercing the darkness, the light describing the surfaces of the fruit and unadorned cup."

There's a black-and-white photograph by Irving Penn that I love titled, *The Empty Plate*. As soon as I saw it, my heart went out to this photo. My heart was this photo. I've tried to photograph my own version of it a few times. And I just gave it another try. As an exercise this is a great thing to do because you realize how nuanced the thing that you're riffing on really is. The artfully crumpled napkin with all its planes and folds touches the plate but only in one spot. It reminds me of two lovers on a bed, tentatively touching each other after a fight. Are we okay? Can we embrace? Not yet. The food residue on the plate is an abstract painting. When I attempted the same setup myself it took me a few tries before I was satisfied with the placement of the knife and fork. In the Penn photo, there is a shadow coming in from the left side. Is it the shadow of a glass of water? A coffee cup? I decided for my version to use a glass of water. However, the light in my photograph ends up being nothing like his. I go with what I have. There are crumbs on his tablecloth and rumples and some kind of bubbled areas. I had taken my tablecloth out of the hall closet and there are creases from where it was folded and quite a lot of rumples. I put some food on the plate and then I scraped it off and put it back in the fridge with the rest of the leftovers. I wasn't hungry. It's a lie but it's the truth also.

The exercise isn't to make an exact replica but to try to capture a feeling and to try to more deeply understand where the greatness of the original resides. A thousand little accidents and quite a bit of intention. Did he place each crumb around the plate or were they all just happy accidents? Was the plate smeared just so after an actual meal, or was it a combination of that and some manipulation? Did anyone eat what was on Penn's plate? The answers to these questions don't really matter. It's good to ask them though.

The beauty of still life is that it might by its presence ask the question who was there before and who will be there after? Is this a restaurant? Who ate the meal? And who will clear the plate? But we might also wonder, is this an imaginary scene, a constructed one, or a natural one? Again, I don't think the answers matter so much as the wondering. A still life is a site for wondering, imagining possibilities for flights of fancy. How does ordinary life transpire, in what small gestures, and in what tiny spheres? What residue do we leave? What is it to be so done, so empty? If the plate is empty, has someone been sated?

The thing that I've not mentioned and part of what draws me to the Penn photograph has nothing to do with the image. It's a quotation from *The Waves* by Virginia Woolf. I'm not the only one who loves it; it's widely quoted.

> "How much better is silence; the coffee-cup, the table. How much better to sit by myself like the solitary sea-bird that opens its wings on the stake. Let me sit here for ever with bare things, this coffee-cup, this knife, this fork, things in themselves, myself being myself."

When I'm looking at Penn's photo, I'm feeling also Woolf's words. I'm looking at the objects and thinking about silence, the solitary sitting, bare things. I am myself being myself.

Still life is about making connections both internally within the composition but also externally. There is a way that things will rhyme and half-rhyme. A colour and shape together will echo another one though their meanings and connotations are quite different. An object will set off a memory, remind one of a scent, recall a dream, or a hint of a forgotten moment.

Because I have made beauty the overall subject of my writing, maybe some readers would be surprised to know how much I love Irving Penn's series of cigarette butt photographs. He was obsessed by them, saying "I am possessed, possessed by these cigarettes." Apparently, he sent out his assistants to collect them from the streets, from the gutters. This is often mentioned as though maybe he was above going out treasure hunting for street detritus.

In every article you read about the cigarette series, the typography is mentioned, the way that the butts can be compared to the ruins of stone columns. At the time, some critics thought the images were boring or maybe trying too hard to be arty. Penn, it is noted, lost a friend to smoking-related cancer and was privately against smoking. These are all fine things to know when looking at the photos. I don't care that critics found them disgusting or eloquent or symbolic of the contemporary condition. They are all these things. I shouldn't say I don't care, which is a lie. This sort of shrugging, "I don't care, fuck it," attitude resides in the images. Someone sucked the smoke into their lungs knowing it was killing them, feeling good for a short interval, and then flicked the object of all this into the gutter, littering the street where they lived or worked.

When I see these images, I remember coming of age in the 80s and how my mother smoked all my life. I remember the ashtrays and the lipstick on the ends of the butts, eating breakfast with the ashtray on the table. I remember trying to smoke in high school, and how I never could, how I coughed uncontrollably. I'm thankful I didn't persist. My mother is 81 and still smokes. She never stopped smoking. I wanted to smoke though, because I was angry and wanted to express how mad I was at the world and at my helplessness and how my place in it was largely dictated by society.

I admire Wayne Thiebaud's cakes and pies. The impasto on the cakes that replicates the icing seems so clever and obvious at the same time. There's a melancholy about the cakes—as though they're at a birthday party where no one shows up. Whenever I look at images of them, I remember seeing one in person in Washington D.C. at the National Gallery on a family vacation. Why didn't a woman paint something like this first, I remember thinking, standing before it with my daughter. I didn't voice it then but it's always there, this sort of disappointment when I look at the cakes of Wayne Thiebaud. A woman didn't have time to paint cakes because she was too busy making them. Then I'm able to go back to loving the paintings, because the love and admiration for the cake maker is there, in the way they're painted.

Many writers on still life have compared the objects depicted in a painting with the actual objects themselves. Sometimes a museum will have the objects in a case in the same room as the painting hangs. In her book, *What's the Story*, Anne Bogart speaks about just such a thing. She is in Amsterdam looking at a Rembrandt painting and comparing it to the objects in a case. She says,

I had been thinking about the power of art to transform the frustrations and irritations of daily life into a realm of grace and to embody, through arrangement, composition, light, color, and shade, nothing less than the secret elixir of life itself. We encounter daily frustrations, irritations and obstacles. Perhaps we feel hampered and limited by our hit and miss upbringing, our apparent limitations and our imperfect ongoing circumstances.

Bogart speaks to the power of the artist to transform a random collection of mundane objects into something transcendent, into "grace and poetry." Maybe this is the most profound function of a still life: to remind us that however messed up our lives are and have been, we can find order and harmony and calm out of the at times ridiculous horridness and tawdriness of daily existence. We can spin some gold out of the poverty, we can transform the imperfections and neglect into something beautiful and substantial. We can bring forward the weight and heaviness that we have carried throughout our lives and bring it into the light.

What if every single day, we could transform our troubles, our worries, our humiliations, disappointments, petty grievances, larger slights, deep pain, into a still life? If we could just deposit all these feelings into an arrangement of things on a table, set in such a way that the objects cast shadows, absorb light, reveal the secret elixir of life? What if were able to come to a moment of grace in this way?

"There aren't enough flowers." Thus begins a review by Peter Schjeldahl of Andy Warhol's retrospective at the Museum of Modern Art. He quotes Warhol, who said that Pop Art was "about liking things." And Schjeldahl likes Warhol's work. He likes the show a lot. He had met Warhol, and Warhol had written in his diary about him: "Peter Schjeldahl who I know hates me" and which he, Schjeldahl, felt remorse over and to which he attributed "to my way of dissembling nervousness. What looked like hostility was terrified respect." But he bemoans the lack of flowers in the retrospective.

Referring to his flower series, Warhol said, "My fascination with letting images repeat and repeat—or in film's case, "run on"—manifests my belief that we spend much of our lives seeing without observing." Compare this to Georgia O'Keeffe's line about flowers: "Nobody sees a flower really; it is so small. We haven't time, and to see takes time—like to have a friend takes time."

I wish that Warhol had seen that Schjeldahl was terrified rather than imagining dislike. Looking at flowers is hard and looking at humans is also difficult. It's hard to get things right. Adam Zagajewski, the poet, said in another context, "It's not time we lack, but concentration." The question of how we can see more deeply with greater concentration is increasingly pertinent for the digital age.

There are a number of books about "things." A lot of them are about the human truths to be found in the things that people keep, collect, can't give away. In his book, *The Thing Itself*, Richard Todd says, "Art is to objects as sainthood is to people. Most people can't be saints, and most objects can't be art, but in each case the extent to which they are marked by an impulse toward grace is a measure of their worth." When we see things or objects represented in a still life, in art, we go back to our own life, our own bric-a-brac, and see it anew. We look at those everyday objects, the made things from our "tangible, perishable world" and our eye is sharpened, says Todd.

The books I have on my shelf on the subject of "things" came before the Marie Kondo movement to organize and declutter. Her now famous question (to ask ourselves about objects in our homes) is, "Does it spark joy?" Some might find her methods a bit excessive, but at the same time, you never hear anyone disputing that some objects spark joy while others do not.

My favourite writer, Clarice Lispector, said this in her book *A Breath of Life*: "The spirit of the thing is the aura that surrounds the shape of its body. It is a halo. It is a breath. It is a breathing. It is a manifestation. It is the freed movement of the thing." And it feels right to me, that a thing potentially has a halo, that it has a spirit or aura.

When we're looking at a still life, we're bringing a lifetime of experiencing the sparks of joy, the auras, the "impulse toward grace" that an object might have.

Still lifes engender poetry. Of course, there are reams of poems about particular still life paintings. I'm fond of Charles Wright's takes on Morandi, for example. One could compile a substantial anthology of ekphrastic still life poems on Chardin's paintings alone. But it's not just the poets who are moved by still life to wax poetically—there are sentences written by art historians and critics on still life that are like found poems. Peter Schjeldahl on Chardin: "A smear of orange tells everything knowable about light when it collides with the bottom of a copper pot." He goes on to say: "If you won't wholeheartedly contemplate it, it will have nothing to do with you. You must relax and gaze. No special effort or acuity is required, but patience is not optional. Gradually you are engulfed in the mysteries of painting and of something else, supremely indelicate—something about existence." Still life is succinct. It can say much with little. If you take the time to parse the meaning not just of an individual painting, but of the genre, the depth of still life is surprising. A single work can talk about paint itself, the practice of painting, while allowing us to think about the mysteries of existence. It's not necessary to come to a painting with a great knowledge of art history. Patience is what is required.

Schjeldahl remarks on how Chardin's work takes his breath away and then asks: "How does Chardin do it? He paints. He keeps reaping epiphanies that are within the reach of painting…" And maybe that's why still life paintings

continue to draw viewers, even if it is an increasingly se-
lect group. There is a hope, there is the possibility that we
could be thrown into a state of epiphany. That not only will
we awaken in some Rilkean fashion to "you must change
your life," but that we'll also receive some direction in this
realization.

Frida Kahlo's still lifes are wonderfully unsubtle. She was
commissioned to paint two round canvases, one of fruit
and one of flowers, for the president and his wife for their
dining room in 1942, but they were returned because they
were thought to be indecent. Before she sent them, friends
viewed them at a dinner party, and Guadalupe Rivera said of
them, "The sexual connotations of these flowers and fruits
were so strong that, arranged as they were side by side, they
seemed to be making love."

An article about the Georgia O'Keeffe retrospective at
The Tate in 2016 opens, "There are few artists in history
whose work is consistently reduced to the single question:
flowers or vaginas?" The exhibit purports to redress this
simplification of her work, and the director of exhibitions
says, "Many of the white male artists across the 20th century have the privilege of being read on multiple levels, while
others—be they women or artists from other parts of the
world—tend to be reduced to one conservative reading. It's
high time that galleries and museums challenge this."

Why do I feel as though we're going to be saying "it's
high time" for some time?

I've never read anything about Warhol's flowers or Penn's
that mentioned their sexual connotations. Maybe someone
has written about this, but I've not come across anything.

The theme of memento mori is common in still life but
that's not the first thing people want to talk about either.
Every flower says "time is fleeting" but we can ignore that
and look at their beauty. Why shouldn't we? We must.
Frida Kahlo said, "I paint flowers, so they will not die."
But we all know they're already dead when they're in the

vase. The flowers go on, oblivious. Or if not obliviously, at least valiantly.

There are all sorts of deaths, though. In her painting, *Pitahaya* Kahlo initially painted the tiny skeleton figure perched behind the dragon fruit with a smile. The painting was exhibited in a surrealist show in Paris in 1939. Kahlo returned to her home in Mexico with the painting unsold, upon which she found out her husband, Diego Rivera, wanted a divorce. At this point she repainted the skeleton with a frown. This particular still life has been written about as a portrait of Kahlo and I suspect the tiny skeleton is a symbol of a psychic death and a reminder of all the small losses that might occur through a life.

Today (though tomorrow it might be different), if I could pick one still life painting from the history of art to hang in my home it would be one I've never seen in person, Juan Sánchez Cotán's *Quince, Cabbage, Melon and Cucumber* which is at The San Diego Museum of Art. The arc of the composition, the surprising combination of the fruits and vegetables, the beautiful and mysterious light, the silence that emanates from the picture, which I imagine must be resounding in person, and the way the quince and cabbage hang from string so that you feel your heart is there in the painting, too—I would love to gaze upon all of these things together every day. How would one's life change with that experience every morning with coffee?

The objects in the painting are suspended so perfectly. The cucumber is close to the edge, but it's firmly placed, not teetering. The melon is some distance back from the abyss beyond the edge of the niche. The viewer can take in the quiet scene for some time, being utterly present, before even vaguely drifting into thoughts of how the objects came to be placed there, and for how long they would last in real life before succumbing to gravity or whisked away to be consumed. One's faith in the world is renewed a little in looking at the firm hold these painted objects have in the space they inhabit. Look at what's possible, it seems to say. Beauty, balance, and the sweetest bit of light.

I wonder how or to what degree our attitude to still life has changed since Norman Bryson wrote *Looking at the Overlooked* in 1990. There's an essay in Peter Schjeldahl's *Let's See*, where he talks about going to an exhibition, "Still Life Paintings from the Netherlands 1550-1720," at the Cleveland Museum of Art. He says, "All my museum-going life, I've walked past Dutch and Flemish still lifes on my way from one to another of the portraits, interiors, landscapes, and so on—every kind of picture…" And he talks to his friends and finds he's not alone in this behaviour. But in this article, he chronicles his change of heart, his conversion. He realizes the artists paint "like angels" and he notes that they made "god-like renderings of light." He finds in the work a mystery, a sorcery, a finesse that he had hitherto passed by.

Is that part of the allure of still life for some? That many people pass it by on the way to other more well-known works of art? Anyone who has been to The Louvre has seen someone dashing by a great many wonderful paintings to get a glimpse of the Mona Lisa. The still life is the underdog genre, always has been, always will be. If there is mystery to the paintings of things, and there is the fact that you have to go looking for it, that you have to know not to pass by it, means that you're part of a smaller art-loving club. And who doesn't want to feel special in that way?

Keats said in a letter dated February 3, 1818, "Poetry should be great and unobtrusive, a thing which enters into one's soul, and does not startle it or amaze it with itself but with its subject." I like that still life is unobtrusive because when I'm in the presence, I hope to be alone with it for a while, that it might enter into my soul.

My photography practice of arranging still lifes with a stack of books on the subject as the centre of the image has taught me a lot about looking at this genre. I find myself thinking about still lifes from the past as I arrange them.

They pop into my head as I'm arranging the objects I happen to have. If I have strawberries, Chardin is right there. Apples, it's Cezanne. Shells, it's Anne Vallayer-Coster, jam it's Mary Pratt, a melon it's Cotán, a basket of fruit it's Caravaggio. And so not only is one trying to understand composition and which colours are pleasing together, but one is in a deep conversation with all those who portrayed plums or peaches before you. Who set them just so, nudging them, propping them one against another, waiting for the light to strike them, noticing the shadows they cast on the table.

What is Ordinary Life, now? Or, Still Life in the Time of COVID-19

April 3, 2020

For the second time, Rob phoned in a flower order to our local preferred florist and picked them up at the curb, which is what people are doing now to maintain physical distance. It seems decadent to have flowers at this time, though maybe it's always decadent. But this is our livelihood currently. Flower paintings. And so, what seems decadent is actually necessary. How long will this be possible? With any luck we'll be able to always get flowers until this thing is over, and our own peonies will bloom. Peonies are perennials, but even perennials don't last forever.

But right now, there is snow and more in the forecast.

Ordinary life is finding a way to get flowers and arranging them in a vase and putting them on a table, remembering the lines I love by Anne Morrow Lindbergh in *Gift from the Sea,* "Arranging a bowl of flowers in the morning can give a sense of quiet in a crowded day—like writing a poem or saying a prayer." Buying flowers is such a privileged act, but also, they're part of our life, our livelihood. And the florist's, too. We've gotten to know the people at the store we frequent, and they're trying to keep going as well.

April 6, 2020

I've spent the last year writing essays mainly about still life and thinking about its intersection with ordinary life. I've thought about attention being akin to prayer and wondered about what it is to depict humble things, real things. I've thought about everyday photography projects, and about dailiness, the quotidian. I've read a ton of books on still life, and I've worked on my photography practice. I've read the Andrew Epstein book, *Attention Equals Life*. I am a fan of what we would ordinarily call the ordinary life.

But what is ordinary life, now? Life seems anything but ordinary right now and our attention has been shattered. At the same time, we are all smack-dab focussed on the ordinary life. Our attention on everyday details is almost overwhelming. Our sharing of the details of our daily life is exhausting to try to keep up with. It's also pretty freaking wonderful. I mean wow! I'm seriously in awe. I think I love the bread makers the best. Not kidding. Serious admiration. As for me, I have been encouraging people to #groundyourselfwithaneverydayproject

Another thing that I've been thinking about this past year is ordinary life versus celebrity life, and obviously this has been a pressure cooker of revelation in this category. COMPLETELY FASCINATING. And at times horrifying, but also: FASCINATING. What is it to be relatable? Or real? The thing is that the so-called "ordinary" people are the ones carrying us right now.

I've been temporarily laid off from my job. We're lucky in Canada as we have funds we can apply for, and I'm confident that I'll be back at the library before too long. Of course, when your partner is an artist, it's impossible not to think about how uncertain the art world is right now. We'll get through. We always have. But it's going to be, shall we say, interesting?

I keep returning to the Anne Bogart book, *What's the Story*. Essential reading as far as I'm concerned right now—for creatives, but also for anyone interested in storytelling. And we're all in this rather massive story right now, aren't we? There is a chapter, "Heat" which was written after 9/11 but seems appropriate for this moment. She says, "In challenging times, spectacle takes the back seat in favour of the human need for intimacy and exchange." What one craves at these terrible times is "aliveness." We crave "realness" and "authentic encounters." I think this is why I like that Patrick Stewart is reading Shakespeare's sonnets on Twitter and Jennifer Ehle is reading *Pride and Prejudice* on Instagram. These things align with where they've been, who they are. Their offerings seem real and authentic.

Bogart talks about the Polish theatre director Jerzy Grotowski and his manifesto "Holiday." He wants to "transcend the separation between audience and actors. Rather than spectacle, he was interested in the potential for human co-presence…" The word, "holiday," Bogart notes, is "a translation of the Polish 'swieto.' Rather than vacation or time off work, 'swieto' refers to the notion of the exceptional, the holy, the sacred or special. Perhaps, closer to 'holy day.'" Grotowski's vision is one of "collective effervescence." Is it possible to think of the time right now in some ways as holy or sacred? Where can we locate our "collective effervescence?"

So maybe I'm taking this off in wild directions, but these are clearly extraordinary times. Those of us who are ordinary, and who work with everyday ordinary people in our usual jobs, well, we have always been both ordinary and not. It may take a long while after the pandemic to make sense of things, if we can make sense of things, but I feel like the truth is going to reside in the ordinary. In the ordinary lives, the ordinary moments, the authentic encounters, and in the attention to the everyday.

What will our everyday lives say about what is going on in the world politically? Is the ordinary where the most profound truths will be found in the future? I do not know. There is so much that we can't know right now. Yes, we have numbers, and yes, we know what we have to do to flatten the curve[21]. What will this end up saying about humans? About connections? About how our society really works? About who is valued and who is not and why?

April 7, 2020

The skull in the time of COVID-19. I keep looking at the replica skull that is sitting on the shelf in Chloe's room. I've photographed it many times in the past—on the stack of still life books, with flowers, with fruit, with various objects. When I post the photos, some people like them and some, I know, find them perhaps a little disturbing. The skull is the best reminder of our mortality. It still shocks us. I don't know that I could post a photograph of a skull right now. I don't want to remind people of their mortality any more than they're being reminded on a daily basis. Every day, in every part of the world, every country, province, a medical person stands up and says how many deaths there have been in each region. And it seems unfathomable. There's nothing to compare it to, other than plagues. Bodies are currently being buried in Potter's Field in New York. Bodies with no relatives to claim them. Just stacked up. But then, it's easy enough to forget this and go on with one's day. Go for a walk in the neighbourhood, decide what to make for dinner. Sit outside on a chair in the sun.

---

21 At the beginning of the COVID-19 pandemic, health experts sought to slow down the spread among those infected. This strategy was known as flattening the curve. The numbers constantly referred to at this time were the total number of deaths, the percentage of positivity, hospitalizations, and other related data.

April 9, 2020

The Edmonton gallery informed Rob they were closing. Yesterday, he rented a white cargo van and retrieved thirty of his paintings. He brought them inside and at first, we stacked them in the living room. After talking with friends in the same predicament on the phone, he decided he couldn't look at them and so moved them to the basement.

After he loaded them into the house and drove off to return the van, I was alone with the paintings, stacked and facing the walls. I started to shake like a leaf. I didn't cry. I couldn't stop shaking. Fortunately, I did stop before he came home. It felt like a death and a welcoming at the same time.

I am tempted to order more flowers from our favourite florist. They posted some beautiful peach, coral, and pink ranunculus, which is pretty much my dream bouquet. But with all the paintings in the house, and an ever more uncertain future, I refrain. I am afraid, suddenly, in a more tangible way. Before this I focussed on the thought that this would be over in a month or so, that we'll get through, we'll be resilient. We always have been. But this, it suddenly strikes me, is different. When you're in something, and we all know this, it's difficult to know how we'll be affected. There are waves of acceptance. Oh, this is how it is now. And now this. The way we have always felt—the rug being pulled out. Now here we are, and, in some ways, it has been a revelation. Whoosh! The rug is gone but we're still here. Still standing.

I'm fine and then not fine. And so, this leads me to believe that there will be other not-fine or less-than-optimal moments of not-fineness.

The ever-shifting ground is disturbing, but also familiar. Isn't this how we always live? It's not that unusual for us. Artists lives are always uncertain, fraught, filled with equal amounts of despair and hope. We've been training for this moment in time. We don't have to like it, we just have to live it, move through it. Dance on that shifting ground.

April 11, 2020

Let's continue to play that game of existing.

> "In the closed up house
> he focuses on an object in the evening
> and plays that game of existing."
>
> — Jean Follain
> (found in Bachelard's *Poetics of Reverie*)

I've been posting photos of my breakfast table in the morning on Twitter and Instagram. I begin each post with the words: "It's useful to ground yourself with an everyday practice in difficult times." I don't know what it will mean in the end. I don't think anything. But it's true that it does ground me. It says something about our days. Perhaps eventually the food will be less appealing. The flowers less likely. I've just been playing at it, but this morning it feels like something solid. Something that I'd like to carry on with. Hold on to.

All day I've been fine, but now it's 6:30 and we've had walks in the sunshine and video calls with family. I drank two glasses of wine and maybe I should not have. But now I feel like crying. Now I feel I'm in mourning.

April 15, 2020

I'm standing on a chair. On the table is an orange cut up into quarters, a small dish of blackberries, a cut crystal bowl containing our last two apples, a glass of cranberry juice, an open jar of Smucker's seedless strawberry jam, two slices of toast—one with jam.

The table is shoved way over into the light. I'm thinking of Mary Pratt and how I should probably be writing instead of taking photos. I'm thinking of art and the art market and how our lives will be going forward. I'm thinking of toast, just toast, and how I'm hungry but not really hungry. I'm thinking about hunger. I'm thinking about the light in the jam jar. The way light loves jam and not just snow. The light loves strawberry jam the way, as Lewis Carroll once said, snow loves the trees.

April 25, 2020

So-called ordinary life is still in the details. That's what I'm thinking about today. Bread has become the still life of choice. Sourdough starters. But maybe that's going to wane now too. That excitement has passed. And with the increase of yeast sales and now a shortage, only the hard-core bakers will continue. Maybe not. There have been a lot of baking posts on Instagram of late. Fancy whipped coffee is another big trend. I want to say something intelligent about it, but it's nice that people are finding a way to spend their time that is cozy and homey.

I'm thinking about bread in still life, especially Dali's bread. We think of his melting clocks and surreal imagery, but he said of bread that it "has always been one of the oldest fetishistic and obsessive subjects in my work, the one to which I have remained the most faithful." Bread is a trope throughout Dali's work used to comment on consumerism, mass consumption, capitalism, moral hunger, et cetera. Bread has the ability to hold so many meanings at once and to resonate through time and take on new connotations and historical moments. Bread is always with us.

When I think of bread I also think of the words of Gaston Bachelard. On bread in poetry and its place in the memories from childhood he says, "In days of happiness, the world is edible." And "I am taken by the urge to collect all the warm bread to be found in poetry." And then, "How they would help me give to memory the great odors of the celebration begun again, or a life which one would take up again, swearing gratitude for the original joys."

What will this time smell like, when we look back upon it? Will we remember it for the original joys? Will we place those memories beside those of the body count? Will future historians wonder how we so easily let those two things live side by side? The sorrows and the joys?

April 28, 2020

Today's photo is a bowl of lemons in my mother-in-law's cut crystal bowl on our kitchen table. You can see the bowl reflected in the wood, an abstraction. I pair it with these words by Mary Pratt: "My only strength is finding something where most people would find nothing." There are more people than ever finding something in nothing. Maybe especially now that we all have time. We are noticing the light in our houses, our workspaces. We are noting the light on the kitchen table, as it illuminates the fruit bowl. We are taking note of the fruit, the way it reflects on the table. Those of us who are noticers are no longer quite so special. There is a community of noticers. It's both comforting and disconcerting.

April 30, 2020

> ... and our effects,
> shrugged and settled
> in the sort of light
> jugs and kettles
> grow important by.
>
> – Eavan Boland

On April 28, Eavan Boland died. I post a photo of tea, a croissant, jam, and butter on the kitchen counter near the sink. I have loved her poetry since I was an undergrad and wrote an essay on her book *Outside History*. It was the first collection of poetry that I really sat with and read and reread. I remember questioning quite heavily what a poem is, what makes a book of poetry. Before that, I had no idea. Like still lifes, there are poems that have a sort of light, books that emanate light, and if you carry them with you through life, you see how they become important in one way, and then in another. They keep sinking into a greater weight, a lighter light. The glow becomes quite a comfort. I suppose this is why I have always had a particular fondness for still lifes that include books.

May 3, 2020

"When I get in front of the easel and begin to paint, I sometimes burst into tears because I am so happy to be here. I am so glad it is just me, the canvas, the paint, and this dear little brush."—Mary Pratt

The cut glass crystal bowl again. Full of strawberries. The shadow on the lace tablecloth is what I am most interested in. What I have is my dear camera, these dear words. They are something. I don't take them for granted.

I also have this photograph: some toast, coffee, the bowl of strawberries. And this, also, from Mary Pratt: "I have found life very emotional and difficult to stay even. And I think that perhaps that comes out in the paintings—certainly I would never paint anything that didn't strike me emotionally, something that didn't physically bother me." What is it that bothers one about toast and strawberries on a lace tablecloth at this point? The unsettling privilege of it all, I suppose. It's not like we're all that rich. Though we've lived a precarious life, financially, we're further ahead than many, and we know that comes down to luck, circumstance, skin colour, address, et cetera. But nor are we in the 1%. Not even close.

I've been Facebook messaging a houseless person I know. He's worried about his disability money drying up. He lives in a stand of trees in an undisclosed location, never coming in, even in the -40 weather. He's done this for years. I'll write to him, and then go eat my toast.

May 6, 2020

On my birthday, two days ago, my coworker from the library, Angie, had brought over a box of chocolates that looked like jewels from a boutique chocolatier. We stay two metres apart as she comes in to look at Rob's recent flower paintings, all hung on one wall, salon style. The chocolates complement the wall somehow, I later think. Perfect bites, perfect moments of joy to savour. I hope chocolates and paintings never disappear from this earth. What are we without them? I photograph both the wall and the chocolates. It's not long before the chocolates are eaten and Rob takes the paintings down, reconfigures the wall, pushes our couch back where it belongs.

May 8, 2020

Today's photo is a bowl of oranges. Same bowl, different fruit. In *Mysteries of the Rectangle*, Siri Hustvedt says, "Our eyes continually roam over the world of things, and we notice things more when we are alone. A human face will always draw our attention away from objects, but in solitude objects are the company we keep."

Will we feel differently about the objects in our life now that we have all spent so much more time with them? Will we wish we had more or better objects? Ones worthy of a longer, lonelier gaze? Which objects, I wonder, have been the best company, in our isolation? What consolation have we found there? What have the objects expressed that we could not?

May 9, 2020

I'm searching for ordinary life in my own ordinary life.

Still life is composed of things we have held on to, perishable things, fleeting small things, that come together for a short moment and then are again dispersed. It's an array unique to you but they're also things that a lot of people have. They're not special, until for a moment they are.

I post a photo of the stone bowl that we have had for upwards of twenty years. The bowl is full of dried flowers, many of them collected from our backyard at the end of last fall, before it snowed. There are also flowers from various bouquets over the winter. Some I kept because of the colour or the way they dried out. The bowl is heaped up by now. And usually when summer arrives, when there are fresh flowers to float in water, I'll toss out this present compilation.

The sun comes into the kitchen window in the morning, a little higher now than last month. The quality of the light is different. The shadows a bit less dramatic. But the light on the dried flowers is still the same kind of miracle it always is. The bowl holds all these bits of dried life, colour, and light, in the same way it always does. The bits and pieces resemble our lives.

Still life is an articulation of the faith that things hold and come apart and can be brought back together again to mean something, even intermittently, seasonally.

May 11, 2020

A purple-blue hydrangea suspended in a water-filled glass ball is today's photo. As I usually do in the spring, I've dusted off my aquarium ball which reminds me of a crystal ball. And so, I think about telling flower fortunes. Everything is coming up flowers in the near future, I'd say. I wish this could be true for everyone. I'm trying not to look too far ahead. But I do see flowers there, they'll grow with or without us.

I also post a photo of me holding the crystal ball, my blue hydrangea. I joke about being a regular Madame Marie, wondering who will know the Springsteen song.

There's a new song I've been listening to—out for a few days only—by Ray LaMontagne, titled "We'll Make it Through." I feel as though I knew this song by heart before I heard it. Like it was in some huge rock and Ray chipped it out but it was always there. Or, it was in my bones and this song seeped out. Or, I heard it in a dream and then woke up and here it is. That's how art works. And honestly, I don't know that we'll all be alright, as he says. We probably won't. But we'll make it through. In fact, I've often said this to Rob, we always do. I'm also realistic. And I know, too, that my chances of being okay are not the same as it is for others. My chances are quite good, I tell myself, but we never know for sure.

The flower will last a bit longer than usual, suspended in water. In fact, when I put it in, it had been wilting a little, but rehydrated when submerged. Even so, it won't last forever. It can't. Is this year any different than any year? In many ways yes. Yes. A resounding and holy and shocking yes. But in other ways, the future is always this: uncertainty. We are all craving ordinary uncertainty and I have to believe we will have that again.

May 12, 2020

In *A Breath of Life* by Clarice Lispector, the character Angela wishes to "write a book studying things and objects and their aura." But the narrator says, "But I doubt she's up to it." Then Angela says, "I'd really like to describe still lifes." She wants to look at things, make use of them in that way. It's not an essay she wants to write, it's a novel, a "novel of things." Things have a fictional life because they're alive. She says, "I can't look at an object too much or it sets me on fire. More mysterious than the soul is matter. More enigmatic than the thought, is the 'thing.' The thing that is miraculously concrete in your hands. Furthermore, the thing is great proof of the spirit."

This morning's photo is of breakfast. Jar of jelly, toast, oranges, a purple-blue hydrangea in a green Buddha Beer bottle. The green of the bottle and the red-purple of the grape jelly are cast in the shadow that falls on the white lace tablecloth. And that is perhaps where the spirit lies. That is what sets me on fire. The objects speaking in tandem with light. The spirit of the thing.

It's a radical thought, but Clarice Lispector has always been radical. To consider that a thing, an object, might be the subject of a novel, that it has a story to tell, to reveal in layers. The story of a beer bottle and a jar of jelly might hold the same possibility for story as two humans sitting at a kitchen table. When we really see a thing, perhaps we also find ourselves "discovering a new way to live." What if we see ourselves, too, as things? Where do we fit into the order of the cosmos, and can knowing that we are mere things change the way we live each day? That is the question, darlings.

May 16, 2020

Our lives haven't changed that much in terms of the still lifes on the table. Or, perhaps we've not physically changed, but emotionally. We can still buy lemons, tomatoes, and so on, but we think more about where they're from. How are people doing where oranges are grown? When will we be able to grow tomatoes here outdoors? Food holds meaning in a different way. All people talk about these days it seems are groceries, going to the store, ordering food online, baking, cooking, trying new recipes. Today I learned that mangoes as grown in India are "interrupted." The work force is under lockdown, and the prices have fallen. Export is down, prices reduced, the supply chain has been affected. Mangoes are grown in Mexico, also, and there are similar issues there. Next time I'm at the grocery store, I'll take a look and see if mangoes are available.

May 20, 2020

A capture of an everyday moment can feel revealing, even embarrassing, maybe because the ordinary is such a privileged space. Today I post a photograph of toast with peanut butter and honey. Comfort food. I took the photo several days ago and just didn't have the heart to post it. Today I still didn't really have the heart, but I forced myself to put it out there.

May 21, 2020

They're not still lifes, but I've been drawing scribble angels. I've been posting them at times on Instagram, though I know they're probably meaningless to anyone but me. I draw the angels and then I have them say something. They are angels of Annunciation. In other words, they bring a message. Sometimes they use song lyrics as a vehicle to convey their messages. Sometimes they say things like, Oof! Or, FFS. Or, No. The messages of these times are not the news of an immaculate conception but of how we are confounded, living in a time of contradiction, uncertainty, brain fog.

June 1, 2020

On my blog today, I put beauty on hold. Beauty can wait, I said. I never thought I would say this with conviction—that there would be a moment in time in my lifetime that would provoke such a statement. I was stupid and naïve. It's a truth that a single human life will always be worth more than any beautiful thing. Violence against any human being is not tolerable. I would not trade my daughter's life for any object, not the *Mona Lisa*, not a Bernini sculpture. The brutal loss of George Floyd's life by police violence has started an uprising and the effects of systemic racism are all that can be thought of at present.

And so, the table is empty…it can wait.

June 8, 2020

I want to investigate further and think more about the way that COVID-19 and the pandemic intersects with and reveals systemic racism. In an article published in May, about the history of pandemics, in the context of the 1918 flu, Lizzie Wade says,

> In the United States, that pandemic did nothing to
> blunt structural racism. "The 1918 pandemic revealed

the racial inequalities and fault lines in health care," Gamble says. At the time, black doctors and nurses hoped it would prompt improvements. "But nothing changed. After the pandemic there were no major public health efforts to address the health care of African Americans."

Could the COVID-19 pandemic, by revealing similar fault lines in countries around the world, lead to the kinds of lasting societal transformations the 1918 flu did not? "I want to be optimistic," Bristow says. "It's up to all of us to decide what happens next."

So yes, we are now in the stage where things have gotten real. I keep thinking of the scene in the series, *Sanditon* (based on the Jane Austen fragment) where the pineapple is found to be rotten to the core, and is quite obviously, as Jasmin Malik Chua says in *The Daily Beast*, a symbol of "Britain's colonial legacy" and tied to "a history that is intrinsically tied to the theft and exploitation of indigenous land and enslavement of African people." Still life is an interesting site to look at inequities because it's a site of our capitalist consumerist society. It might at first glance seem like quite an innocuous study, a slight one, in light of the real danger that people face every day in our time, and comparatively it is. But when we start to think about who has access to the food on a table, how the food gets there, who delivers the food, produces the fruit, who can afford to eat what, and who labours in the fields, it starts to get stickier.

In the book, *Still Life and Trade*, Julie Berger Hochstrasser traces the connections of slavery to the Golden Age of still life painting in the preface. She says,

> ... it is not just the abominations of slavery and colonialism per se but rather the larger workings of capitalism that have brought us to this point where inhuman inequities of many kinds can continue to

generate such proportionate profit in the world: distant markets and unseen sweatshops are too much with us still.

As in still lifes, we have always known there is a dark and sinister side to the objects and food on our table. In an article titled, "In Dutch Still Lifes, Dark Secrets Hide behind Exotic Delicacies," Julia Fiore remarks on the presence of the sugar bowl in seventeenth-century paintings: "The sugar obliquely references one of the most barbaric elements of the global Dutch empire: the horrific, widely documented treatment of slaves on South American plantations." And that's just one example.

Once we know the metaphorical pineapple is rotten, once it's been cracked open and looked inside, then what? We can't go back to thinking about it in the same way and we certainly can't consume it any longer. We need to stop glossing over the troubling details. We must change how we live our lives, on so many fronts.

June 11, 2020

I seem to have given up on the centering, grounding, process of making a still life. Almost as if I don't want to be centred or grounded. It seems too comfortable. Too safe when the world is chaos, and when all we can think about, and rightly so, is the BLM uprising and all of these new health and safety concerns.

June 27, 2020

Skull with an abundance of roses, ranunculus et cetera from the florist—soft pinks, peaches, yellow. My favourite palette. Flowers in the eye sockets and Scotch-taped to the crown.

I took these photos back in April and it seemed too much to post them, then. Death was just too frightening, too real. It's still real and more prevalent. We become desensitized to the numbers. (Notice I say numbers). But maybe if we all contemplated the theme memento mori we'd be a little kinder, a little more mindful. We're here so briefly, so beautifully.

Also, scotch tape is one of the secrets of still life construction.

June 30, 2020

Sandwich and skull. I bought big thick Dagwood sandwiches at Safeway. I'm not sure why I find this such an amusing pairing: giant mass-produced sandwich and skull. And then of course I'm going to think of Samuel Beckett. "I can't go on. I'll go on." Which is the last line of *The Unnamable*. Because of course we go on. Of course, we need big-ass sandwiches. It's brutal out there right now and the world is on fire but there are sandwiches.

July 6, 2020

KD.

Today's photo is of a glass bowl filled with Kraft Dinner. I tried to squirt the ketchup on it so that it resembles a sundae. I think I'm the only one who might see that. Which is actually quite fine. I love this image more than anyone else could possibly love it. Sometimes you just have to photograph what's in your heart to photograph.

July 7, 2020

Big peach roses from the florist and peonies from our garden.

"I would like to be able to take a photo of a dream," says Hélène Cixous. This would be it then. These big pillowy fluffy puffy poufs. If this ain't a dream, I don't know what is, baby.

July 8, 2020

Photos of roses and peonies with yellow poppies from the garden. The yellow poppies don't really go. But they make the bouquet stand out. They are gangly and have flare and panache. They sing out. Which reminds me of the lines from Elizabeth Smart in *The Assumption of the Rogues and Rascals*. "Isn't there some statement you'd like to make? Anything noted while alive? Anything felt, seen, heard, done? You are here. You're having your turn. Isn't there something you know and nobody else does? What if nobody listens? Is it all to be wasted?" From these lines I jumped to Mahmoud Darwish's poem and the way my roses rhyme with the peonies. The poppies are additional.

> "This rhyme was not
> necessary, not for melody
> or for the economy of pain
> it is additional
> like flies at the dining table"

July 12, 2020

A still life says things about the time in which it's constructed, that won't be evident until another century. (Today's still life is of a Diet Coke can with a withered rose in it, porcelain cat, skull with dried flowers in the eye sockets, and a plastic wrapped tin of Sardines).

July 13, 2020

There has long been a photo I've wanted to take after the Van Gogh image from 1886: *Head of a Skeleton with a Burning Cigarette*. The Van Gogh painting is held at the museum named for him in Amsterdam. The entry on their website says it was painted after or between his lessons when he was a student at the art academy in Antwerp. It's a "juvenile joke," they say.[22] The painting is described elsewhere as macabre and disturbing. In his diary of that time he says, "the doctor tells me I absolutely have to keep my strength up . . . and until I have built it up I am to take it easy with my work. But now I have made things worse by smoking, which I did because one doesn't feel the emptiness of one's stomach then." He'd had dental work and was self-conscious about his teeth, and the gap that he had and which the dentist apparently fixed.

I've had the Van Gogh image in the back of my mind for some time now, so I no longer find it shocking. The first time I saw it, it was quite a surprise. Is my photograph also a surprise? I don't know. One can never really experience one's work, one's images, in the same way someone else will, just because you've spent so much preparing for it, looking at it, and then living with it afterward.

July 27, 2020

I've been slowly crossing things off my photo bucket list in this strange time we now live in. I think most photographers have a list something like this, whether they write it down or not. For my still life series, I've had "dahlias like Henri Fantin-Latour" sitting there for some time. And finally, we got some from our florist in the shades I was hoping for, pinks and peaches. I want more, of course. That's the way one proceeds into one's obsessions.

I love dahlias. I love their sturdy goofiness, their uniformity and pizzazz. And I love Fantin-Latour's paintings of flowers. He's not a household name but neither is he completely obscure. Or maybe he is obscure? If you're a fan of New Order you might remember the album cover for *Power, Corruption and Lies*. Originally another image had been hoped for—a dark portrait—but the perfect one couldn't be found. Peter

---

22 My jokes would have been 9% funnier in the nineteenth century. Still life jokes really are quite timeless.

Saville, the designer of the cover, said, the painting of flowers "suggested the means by which power, corruption and lies infiltrate our lives. They're seductive." I guess parents would have thought their kids were listening to some sort of classical music in this packaging. Things aren't always what they seem as we know all too well these days.

I love the process of starting small with a still life and enlarging upon the themes, adding and adding, and at the end slowly taking away each object. I started with just the vase of dahlias on my usual stack of books and built upon it from there. Which is better, the more minimalist version with just the one vase, or the addition of shells, flowers from our garden, lemons, the skull? For me it doesn't really matter, it's the process that's the thing. These small gestures. Standing up on the sofa with my camera and then jumping down to nudge a shell, turn the vase, heading to the kitchen to peel the lemon, wondering if the skull is too much, pulling the one broken bloom out to dangle its head, turning the nautilus shell so you can't see the broken-off part, turning it back so you can. As I work, I'm blessing the still life, all still lifes, their quiet, their infinite nature. I'm blessing the held breath of the photographer, the perfect blooms and the more ragged ones. I'm loving the way that all the time I'm shooting, Fantin-Latour is in the back of my mind and how art and loving art and objects and flowers connects us through time. It's a small thing to love, but it helps.

July 30, 2020

"Current existence, the ultimate astonisher …"
—Dorothy Richardson

"I think everything in life is art. What you do. How you dress. The way you love someone, and how you talk. Your smile and your personality. What you believe in, and all your dreams. The way you drink your tea. How you decorate your home. Or party. Your grocery list. The food you make. How your writing looks. And the way you feel. Life is art."

—Helena Bonham Carter

There are pastel dahlias in our living room with the painting Rob did of my birthday bouquet in the background.

In difficult times—pandemics, natural disasters, in Pompeii—the still lifes on the wall tell us how people lived. They remind us, also, to live. This is why these still lifes from history are so poignant. We know that the people who drank from that cup or gazed upon those flowers perished shortly thereafter. And we will, too. Maybe the Pompeiians gave little thought to the still lifes meaning something way off into the future. But maybe they understood. They had an inkling, or else why would they have painted them in the first place?

August 3, 2020

The photographer Ernst Haas said, "A picture is the expression of an impression. If the beautiful were not in us, how would we ever recognize it?" In a practice of photography, one cultivates an inner light. I don't suppose I can really prove that statement but it feels true to me. For the impression of a photograph to come through to the viewer, it's something the photographer had to wait for, to create, to seek out. If the light is not in us, how can we recognize it?

I have learned so much from observing and trying to capture the light. I've learned to wait for it. To move toward it. To run out of my house in my pyjamas if I have to, to capture it. To position my subject nearer a window, whether the subject is a person or an apple. To remember when the golden hour happens to be and to get out into it and bathe myself in its particular glitz. Sometimes I hold my camera above my head and shoot blind, hopeful. And at other times I kneel on the grass, elbows on the ground and meet the light there.

I try to remember to put my soul in the way of light. And I try to remember that it's possible to nudge an apple or plum from a shaded area of the table, into the true and steady beam of light that eases onto the table at certain intervals.

If nothing else, this still life experiment of mine is just that: a way to put my soul into the way of light.

August 3, 2020

"There are those who give shape to their everyday by mining it for something different or special."
—Kathleen Stewart

Flowers from my garden, junk food from the Sev down the street.

We might think of a still life as a lull in the narrative. A place to catch your breath before the story picks up again. Maybe it's just there for refreshment or palate cleansing. Or maybe it holds clues to what will happen next. It's always the convenience store that gets looted in movies about the apocalypse. Even in the apocalypse we like convenience store food. It is, after all, convenient.

August 11, 2020

When composing a still life, you're always pushing things to the edge, fixing objects there with tape or wedges of folded paper. Often things fall off, even so, causing you to begin again, try another composition. See what will hold, stay, cohere. What does it mean to compose a still life these days? A still life is said to hold a place outside narrative, but one trembles placing objects precariously near the edge. My nerves are frayed, the flowers know.

I begin with a vase of ruffled roses in pastel tones—peach, pink, soft yellow, cream. I pile dark plums on a small cake platter and slice a cantaloupe in half, the seeds spilling out.

I pick some Evan's cherries from the tree in the backyard. Still, I want more. I gather up some shells, including a paper nautilus, gifted long ago from a friend. Something is still missing. The floral porcelain cat from our daughter's room.

And then the "not enough" suddenly becomes "too much", so I start removing things, until at last, there is just a slice of cantaloupe perched like the moon on the corner of the book *The Magic of Things: Still Life Painting 1500-1800*. This is the one I feel the most, in the end. I post it to social media to no fanfare whatsoever. Which confirms to me that still life continues to be the overlooked genre, and good. Good, really. I can go on saying and feeling and contemplating things, magic and otherwise, quite contentedly with no one watching or caring. That's a gift, too.

Still life in a pandemic, though. We're past the hoarding stage right now. In my cupboard I still have a pretty good stock of canned goods. I can't stop buying tins of tomatoes when they're on sale, packages of spaghetti. I have yet to touch the lentils I stocked up on at the beginning of all this.

August 12, 2020

There's the line by the Canadian poet Phyllis Webb about how the proper response to a poem is another poem, and I can't help but think that applies to photographs, too. To still lifes. One of my experiments in still life led to another experiment. This one might quote something from the history of art, or maybe even one of Rob's paintings. And that composition will beget another one. They'll begin talking to each other. It's a way of entering a conversation you want to be part of.

August 14, 2020

When you bring your imagination and curiosity to ordinary life it becomes a meeting place, a possible site of vulnerability. A tin of flowers, coffee cup on the back porch, soul bird crying out, the sound of traffic from the nearby highway this morning, for example. Here I am.

In the photograph I take I'm able to capture that early morning light, about 7 a.m. Steam from my coffee rising up into the bokeh bubbles. When I make an image like this first thing in the day, I can carry it with me through the day; it fills me up. The light paused is a full meal. It's a breakfast for barbarians, as Gwendolyn MacEwen said.

August 20, 2020

A picture of a fork twirled into and stuck upright in a plate of spaghetti on a lace tablecloth with a white cloth napkin beside. There is a tin of Bravo tomato sauce that has been used to hold tea roses in pastel colours. There's a lot going on in this photo that no one will see but me. First, I want to nod in the direction of Irving Penn. This photo was inspired by his work though it's not a direct reference.

I was born in 1966 and growing up in the 70s, every dinner was meat and potatoes and vegetables grown in the huge garden. A spaghetti dinner was so rare I can pretty much remember each occasion. When I moved from home at eighteen to a crumby bachelor apartment downtown in the big city, I think I made myself spaghetti with jarred sauce five times a week. It felt very fancy to me. Jarred sauce was fancy then. I mean, sauce in a jar? Come on. What a delight.

Of course, nowadays, we are well-versed in Italian cheeses, and in particular Parmigiana Reggiano. On some grocery trips I will buy a hearty wedge of parmesan instead of meat. But for the photograph I have sprinkled on some grainy and distinctive Kraft parmesan. I guess it speaks to a certain kind of upbringing, and to another era altogether.

August 21, 2020

Spent most of the day thinking about Irving Penn, flowers from the history of art in general, and the not-quite collaboration (more like riffing?) I have with Rob. The flowers in most of my photos are for looking at from a distance, while with his painted flowers I imagine the viewer leaning in to breathe in the scent.

He's often asked if he paints from my photos and no, he doesn't. The information he needs from a photo to paint from is quite different from the effects I'm trying for.

Yesterday he went to our favourite florist and bought a combination of pink and coral zinnias, pink snapdragons, and pale purple dahlias. I first tried photographing them with a white backdrop, which I haven't done for a very long time. I guess both Rob and I have been fixated on the black background. Chiaroscuro. The darkness. But I like a lot of the Penn photos of flowers on white. I'll have to experiment a bit more. Perhaps it will lead me out of the darkness. Currently though, I find the images of the same blooms to be more interesting on the black background.

September 9, 2020

It's been a few weeks since I've had the time or inclination, I suppose, to shoot a still life. (I was not brought up nor have I ever gone to church, but it reminds me of the whole "forgive me father for I have sinned, it has been three weeks since my last confession" sort of thing that you hear in sitcoms).

Yesterday I was gifted some dinner plate dahlias by a coworker, and another coworker gave me a photograph of Frida Kahlo that she'd bought at the Kahlo museum years ago. They go well together from the point of view of palette, but the flowers also seem to be something Kahlo would enjoy. I arranged them with a cross, Rob's old rosaries, some seashells, and on top of the usual books.

My coworker and I had been speaking about Kahlo's persistence. And she knew that I liked her because of my early pandemic purchase of a dress with Kahlo printed on the front. When she gave me the photograph, which was printed on cotton paper and mounted on cloth, we laughed about how it pays to advertise what you love, and the world gives you more.

September 19, 2020

Rob brought home roses in the pink and peach tones I'm fond of. One of the varieties is called Mansfield Park. I'm chucking the kilometre-long to-do list in favour of communing with roses, having an emergency meeting with roses. Saying yes to impromptu appointments with bouquets.

Meanwhile the flower factory in the basement continues to hum. It feels strange that we would be "saved" ourselves personally, financially, by flowers, by beauty. But it seems so far to be true.

October 15, 2020

Self-Portrait. With whisky bottle, flowers, blue paper butterfly, skull, and lit cigarette.

It's a joke, but it holds some truth. That the still life is also a self-portrait. Maybe most still lifes are such. It's a portrait of the pandemic in a certain way too. We're doing all sorts of things we wouldn't ordinarily be doing. We've developed hobbies, rituals, and maybe a few bad habits. So while this illustrates the certainly bad habit of smoking, and the potentially but not assuredly bad habit of drinking, they're representative of whatever bad habits a person might have acquired during this strange and increasingly long time.

October 18, 2020

Things taste different now, don't they? Along with a bouquet of roses and dahlias in peaches and pinks and a burnt orange, I have photographed a Diet Coke and cheese-flavoured Ritz Crackers. Which are sometimes the only thing I feel like consuming. They're the things that make me feel better when a lot of other things don't. The orange of the flowers matches, nearly, the orange of the Ritz Crackers. A lot of people are talking about how they miss restaurants, but I don't really miss them. I miss food being free of stress. Our relationship to food is something that a still life can excavate. Earlier in the pandemic I did a series of photographs of the inside of my fridge and freezer and pantry. I'd organized everything. It feels a bit like something out of a post-apocalyptic novel. The beforehand of the scenes where the characters are rummaging in abandoned places for food. If we were to disappear today, later they'd find my cupboards well-filled, orderly. A lot of staples and canned goods. Sardines. Noodles and pasta. Tins of tomatoes, baked beans, soup. I want them to think well of me, these unknown future characters.

October 27, 2020

It is one week from the US election, and at the same time the politics in my home province, Alberta, are also terrible. The premier has taken notes on what has worked for Trump and is, in particular, ruining health and education. I don't want to say anything overtly about that, so I respond instead with a photograph of drying roses and a blue paper butterfly on a still life book titled, *Nature Morte*. I accompany my photographs with lines from Simone Weil and Olivia Laing.

Weil first: "Attention, taken to its highest degree, is the same thing as prayer. It presupposes faith and love. Absolutely unmixed attention is prayer. If we turn our mind toward the good, it is impossible that little by little the whole soul will not be attracted thereto in spite of itself." And I do think this is possible: to turn the soul to good little by little for those of us predisposed to attend to the world in this way. The more we go forward, the more I learn of the humans of this world, the less faith I have or the more jaded I am around this process. I suppose there was one point in my life when I thought that a lot more people would have this as a goal. I wasn't so naïve as to think that everyone had the improvement of the mind, soul, and the expansion of their heart along with the goal to become more compassionate and enlightened. No. But could it be so few? It feels that way some days.

I come across this in Olivia Laing's book *Funny Weather: Art in an Emergency*:

"Bothering to see beauty, making beauty freely available ... showing that beauty is unstable, coming and going, requiring effort. I mean political in the sense of how you choose to be in the world, what you are willing to look at, what keeps you alive."

October 28, 2020

Single dried flower hanging off the *Nature Morte* book on my stack of still life books.

"Learning
To believe you are magnificent. And gradually to discover that you are not magnificent. Enough labor for one human life."

— Czesław Miłosz

November 5, 2020

The results of the US election are still being tallied. Right before election day, November 3, I set up a still life on my stack of books with a cut cantaloupe, a halved orange, and a lemon with an unwinding peel. Rob had bought some pink-peach roses and two stems of snapdragons. I added paper butterflies, and I took two photos. In one I added the porcelain cat from Chloe's room, something she didn't take to college when she left home. In the other, I added the skull and taped two paper butterflies into the eye sockets. The cat is a symbol of trickiness in traditional still lifes. We might associate the cat's appearance in a still life as one of surprise.

The unexpected. The cat as opportunist or disruption of the current order of things. A reminder that a still life is not really so still. What is, can be changed. What seems set, might be unbalanced, changed, rearranged.

The cat seems to go nice with the butterfly, compositionally. If we think about how disruption also often occurs in tandem with a kind of rebirth, these things also make sense right now.

We certainly know that the skull is a motif from Vanitas—the futility of pleasure, the inevitability of death, the transience of life, the worthlessness of worldly goods—and of memento mori, "remember you must die." The butterfly in still life usually symbolizes the resurrection, but in our secular world, they are a symbol of rebirth, renewal, hope. New beginnings. Let's go with that, shall we?

I didn't set out to say anything about the political moment via still life, but it seems that one cannot help doing so. As people die in record numbers from COVID-19, and Trump refuses to concede, we hope for a new beginning, a disruption in this unholy state of the world.

November 13, 2020

The still life books themselves. A warm-up photo. It usually takes a photo or two to get the settings right. I've always been a bit of a trial-and-error photographer. I start by lining the books up just so, setting my black backdrop behind the coffee table which I've pushed to the wall having removed the chesterfield to the side. I'll snap a few shots to make sure it's even worth continuing with the setup. These books are on still life, in various configurations, but usually *Still Life: A History* is the anchoring object on the bottom of the pile. I don't know what I'm doing exactly, but I want to be taken seriously. I have the feeling that a lot of people think that I'm a lightweight. I sort of think that I'm a lightweight. Maybe I want to take myself seriously. At the same time, why take anything too seriously? We're all a bit ridiculous, aren't we?

Next, in comes the cake. Duncan Hines. Chloe and I made it last night. I wouldn't have made it if she weren't at home from college. It's a yellow cake with canned chocolate frosting. Chloe is an accomplished baker but I am not. I bought this cake mix at the beginning of the lockdown. We put cherry jam in the centre and then iced the cake with the frosting. We each had a piece of it, then put the rest in the fridge. When I took the first photograph, the cake had already been sliced into. After a couple of photos, I cut another slice. I took maybe ten photos in total, before sitting down to eat the slice that is in some of the photos. Then I put the empty plate with just the crumbs back on the books, and the fork, too. That's my favourite of the lot because it reminds me of a photo I took in the mode of Irving Penn of the empty plate with the white napkin. There's something about a plate with food remains on it that feels poignant to me. Definitely an indication of narrative. A more explicit human presence.

It's not really possible to think about a cake in still life without Wayne Thiebaud's painted cakes popping into my mind. I like what he says here: "If you stare at an object, as you do when you paint, there is no point at which you stop learning things from it." This is true for photography as well, and also for this entire project of mine. I learn something every time I set up a still life. There is no point at which I have stopped learning from it.

A cake is usually for a celebration or get together. One doesn't usually just make a cake for no real reason. Not a layer cake with frosting, anyway. There's too much of it, too much of a good thing. It feels a bit decadent, a bit indulgent. But right now, given the state of the world, maybe a cake also feels necessary. What are we here for if not to enjoy a slice of cake with creamy chocolate frosting?

November 16, 2020

The cat returns. I have taken a photo of a white pillar vase of a blue hydrangea, pink gerbera daisies, and yellow dahlias. A few faux butterflies are protruding from the flowers. But the flowers alone seem not enough, so I add a spiky shell and the nautilus shell. They are all crowded on my book plinth, so I end up taking the flowers away and shooting just the floral ceramic cat and shells horizontally rather than the vertical orientation that the tall vase requires.

Often when it feels as though one of my still lifes is missing something, the cat ornament, of which there are two in my daughter's room, is what I reach for. A real cat would be better, but we don't have one of those. Interestingly, in the last month or so a small grey cat has been visiting us, and we've been petting it on our back porch. It's obviously not a stray and is very affectionate. We've seen it walking around in the neighbourhood. One day we let it in and it seemed pretty happy. Sat in Rob's lap, and Chloe's for a while before we let it out again. While it was here though, it seemed perfectly at home. We still hope to travel at the end of this pandemic. We'd be in Rome right now if things were different. It seems like things will be like this until the spring at least, until there is a vaccine. I imagine it will take a long time for the world to right itself again. The symbolism of the cat seems pertinent, now more than ever. The disruption, the trickiness. Their intelligence and affection. Their otherworldliness, too. A certain unpredictability. If the table is a planet, as the comparison has been made, then a cat is a force from beyond. What will happen next? says the cat. Only the cat knows.

December 28, 2020

It's been over a month since I thought to jot something down here. I have taken some photos in this ongoing series. In mid-December I set up some fruit I bought at Safeway for that purpose—a dragon fruit, a persimmon, a lemon, and a passion fruit. The colours were very bright and uplifting and pleasing together. The different shapes and textures and the leaning all in a line really made me happy. There was the bouquet of rose and ranunculus that Rob brought home from our favourite florist too. I remember feeling as though I needed a therapy session with the flowers. It was a pretty deep need. I should consider myself lucky that this works for me, that our life makes the presence of flowers a necessity, at least at intervals.

Yesterday the cat came back, the neighbourhood cat. It meowed loudly and we let it in. We were having tea at the kitchen table, just the three of us. I had earlier in the day been thinking about whether I'd want to continue this project into 2021. Had I not already tried all the things? And there was the cat. The coffee table in our living room is kept ready with my usual stack of books. I got out my black backdrop, grabbed my bowl of seashells, an orange, a lemon, a dried flower in a vase and a tin of sardines from the cupboard. I set it up somewhat haphazardly, but also with practice and experience, as the grey cat did its usual walkabout. With no trouble I enticed the cat onto the table. One of the petals fell from the dried rose, and I crinkled it a bit, and tossed it on top of the book *Dutch Flower Painting*. The cat posed for a few seconds, then was done. I clicked the shutter perhaps six or seven times, and one of the shots seems quite good.

This is probably the least planned out of the series, to date. Hastily assembled, just grabbing what was available. I had no real hope of it actually working, no expectations, but the fun was in the attempt. Maybe there's a lesson here. It was either going to work or not but once the idea popped into my head to try, I brought what I could to the table.

January 15, 2021

I did a little riff on a painting by Floris Claesz van Dijck this afternoon. The painting has cheeses stacked up, as Dutch still life often does. Bread, a plate of olives, a small silver plate with an apple sliced in half, reflecting on it very sweetly. There is beer in a glass, some nuts, a plate of grapes, a bowl of apples, and a vessel for pouring with a long and narrow spout. I could improvise most of the items, but not grapes. The grapes at this time of year never seem to taste that good and I couldn't justify buying them at the grocery store just for a still life. I'd picked up some bread, cheese, nuts, apples. But those will all be consumed. Waste, right now, seems like a foolish thing.

I find it hard to believe a week has passed since the insurrection in the US. That the world has moved on so quickly is really unfathomable. I set this still life up as a sort of therapy. And it worked. Looking at it, you can't really tell that there is turmoil going on in the world, can you? Or can you? I don't know. I only know I feel shattered. My stomach hurts in the way that only worry makes your stomach hurt.

Along with the traditional still life items, I placed a box of Velveeta cheese under the wedges of gouda and edam. I want this still life to be about now so I place my usual Diet Coke can onto the table too. I know pop is bad for me but it's an indulgence. A splurge. It's a small, mostly harmless addiction. Floris did not, I don't think, drink Diet Coke. I can only imagine how repulsed he would have been by Velveeta.

A notable absence is my usual stack of still life books. Maybe that's symbolic. Personally so, if not in a larger sense.

January 21, 2021

This is where my still life project started, inspired this time by a seventeenth-century painting by Georg Flegel which is owned by the Metropolitan Museum of Art NYC. I had the desire to photograph a bird on some bread. You know, a perfectly normal impulse. So I dug out a bird ornament from our Christmas box (our tree theme is mainly birds) and I tore a loaf of bread in half. But that seemed too minimal, so I added what I had around the house.

There's whisky and chocolate in one of the setups, and a poured beer in another. The drink is definitely a reflection of this time. I don't think I've ever had such a need for alcohol. The contradictions that we dwell in as frontline customer service workers has quite honestly made me irate. One of the great silences of the pandemic. So many of us are beside ourselves with anger and have nowhere to put that anger.

But there is still still life. There is a good pour of whisky. Things to arrange and compose. So much of life is out of our control right now, and so this planet on the table, this world that I can amend, subtract and add to, compose with thought to symmetry, balance, colour, and with the occasional surprising element thrown in, is something to hold on to.

February 8, 2021

The composition started with the red carpet on our coffee table. Again, no books. The still life started with a cantaloupe and a small watermelon, the blue-and-white ginger jar, a remnant from one of Rob's old tabletop still lifes. I looked through images of seventeenth-century still life and added a beer, the unwinding lemon, the glass ball, the nautilus shell, some walnuts, an open seashell purse, a small silver plate, and a knife.

Afterwards, I was thinking about still life; the rearranging, composing, the precariousness, the adding and subtracting, the way it holds and falls apart, and all the small improvisations. It's not hard to compare the making of a still life to the way we are muddling through these pandemic days in our ordinary lives. Ordinary life has changed so much but also not as much as I thought it would have. That is to say, for me, it hasn't changed that much but I know for others it's changed a lot. Or it changed a lot and then stayed mostly the same. We're in a holding pattern of sorts and maybe that's if we're lucky. If you've lost someone then the world will feel as though nothing will ever be ordinary again. Still life has been referred to as a world on a table, a planet on a table, and that seems to help me sort out my thoughts. There's so much chaos in the world. At least on the table of things, order can be found or at least composed temporarily.

The first image I set up is usually not the best one. I add. I subtract. I rearrange. I cut into fruit; I slice. Sometimes things fall off the table. Others are propped up at a certain angle. I play. I hurry, I wait. The sun comes, the sun goes. I have the benefit of having watched my husband set up traditional still lifes for years for his paintings. He paints floral pieces mainly these days, but he spent years setting up tabletop stills. I was busy with a small child, busy getting an MA in English, writing books, working multiple jobs. I always envied him, but I was doing what I chose to be doing, at the same time. Him doing it really was enough for me. I got to live a bit vicariously. So, it's interesting that he's gone in a different direction now with his paintings, and I'm sort of coming up from behind, having a go with still life in photography.

In a still life, you move one object, and three more slide off the table. A glass gets broken occasionally, or the unwinding rind of the lemon becomes detached from the fruit and you stick it back on with a toothpick. Scotch tape is hauled out. A dish is propped up from behind by a couple of walnuts. Everything is too much. You start to subtract. You go minimalist, and that's fine for a bit too.

So yes, I keep thinking about how everything in our lives is getting arranged and rearranged on the regular. We get laid off from our jobs, we're called back, only to be laid off again. Or we're kept on, in my case, but the job is radically different. The COVID case numbers are high and we're told to stay home, then they drop and guidelines are relaxed, and it's all reversed. You had one plan, and now you have another. You looked forward to something, and now you tend to look forward to other smaller things, closer to home.

February 10, 2021

Vertical composition with blue-and-white ginger jar, cantaloupe, watermelon, lemons (cut and unwinding), and walnuts. Along with the glass photographer's orb, knife, silver plate.

"The spirit of the thing is the aura that surrounds the shapes of its body. It is a halo. It is a breath. It is a breathing. It is a manifestation. It is the freed movement of the thing."

"I make a great effort not to have the worst of feelings: that nothing is worthwhile. And even pleasure is unimportant. So I keep myself busy with things."
—Clarice Lispector

The interesting thing about being a writer or artist is that, as the poet Lorine Niedecker said, there is "no layoff / from this / condensery." Rob and I work pretty much seven days a week. Art often looks like play and yes, it is, but it's also work. He painted on Christmas Day this year. Today I'll be editing, photographing, writing, and probably grocery shopping. Half of my life is side hustle. Yesterday was the day job and tomorrow will be too. Our last holiday was Rome in November of 2019 and even that was a research trip. Like everyone else, I'm feeling the burnout.

February 20, 2021

Still life can be about so many things: surfaces, transience, consumption, class, desire, the ordinary, the ephemeral. A still life speaks to the overlooked details of ordinary life, to our wants and needs, to what we can have, and to what escapes us. When I asked Rob to go to our neighbourhood Sev and load up on sugary prepackaged sweets, the cashier said incredulously "This is all for you?" Just looking at this image I'm feeling the shame.

The first shots I took were on an old beach towel from Disneyland. The colours seemed to go with the sugar overload. I kept thinking about the fancy takeout everyone is posting to support local restaurants that isn't available to everyone. I think a still life like this says more than I can articulate with words but I'm hoping at first glance it seems pretty.

What is my 7-eleven still life about? Surfaces and empty calories, consumption, abundance. I wanted to make a still life that was pretty, but also a bit stomach-churning. I keep asking "what is ordinary life now?" in the pandemic and I guess partly this composition, this subject, is my answer at this precise moment in time.

February 26, 2021

I wanted to have another try at a fast-food still life. At the beginning of my still life project, I tried one with KFC and McDonald's. It was around the time Trump served the college football national champion Clemson Tigers a fast-food buffet at the White House and professors were likening the photo of him standing behind a smorg of Wendy's, McDonald's, and Burger King as a grotesque take on Da Vinci's "The Last Supper."

I don't always know why I'm compelled to shoot a particular thing, but I've had this on my list of things I wanted to revisit. One day when our groceries were getting a bit low, I decided to order both KFC and Burger King at about lunchtime. I ordered KFC on Skip the Dishes but my credit card was declined for the Burger King. I found out later the credit card company flagged my Instacart grocery purchase from a week previous as suspicious. It all seemed to be a sign of the times. Almost all our purchases of late are done online.

When many people are posting images of the fancy, high-end takeout they're getting to support local restaurants, a little bit of virtue signalling accompanies these posts, but that's fine. Who can deny anyone a bit of happiness right now? Even the rich people.

We live in the suburbs, far away from the indie restos, and our furnace just broke and needs to be replaced. It's cold, and we're just hoping the current one can hump through until next week when the replacement will be installed. It's funny how so much of life comes down to money. A not so hidden themes of still life: class, wealth, abundance, excess, broken furnaces, bills….

I wanted some of the traditional elements of a still life, so because we had lemons, I sliced into one and peeled it so that the rind would dangle over the edge of the table. I included my photographer's orb, and also a faux classical bust with a faux bashed in nose.

I didn't post it on social media for a week, because honestly, it was too much junk all at once and made me feel queasy to look at it. I spread onion rings and french fries around the table surface, cracked open a couple of Diet Coke cans, got the ketchup from the fridge. It's a bit surprising to me how much ketchup we go through these days, but I guess it's all the McCain fries we've been eating.

I tried to make the burger look "nice," like in an advert. But fast-food in real life doesn't look like the stuff in the advertisements. It's been squished into wrappers and placed into paper bags and, because it's travelled across town, lost its crispness or freshness. The person making it isn't thinking about the food being displayed or immortalized in a still life or photographed by some odd Instagrammer. There's just no way to make it pretty which is the point of this type of image. I wanted to give it a sort of monumental feeling all the same. Our exalted pile of greasy food.

The viewer looking at this set of photos might be thinking, ugh, yuck, but reader, we chowed down, and it was good. Weirdly satisfying.

March 8, 2021

Today's still life is about managing the fridge: image of groceries, fruit veggies, cup noodles, parmesan cheese, celery, tomato soup, bread.

Moyra Davey wrote about the fridge in her 2020 book, *Index Cards*. She wrote this pre-pandemic but it strikes a chord.

I had a houseguest once who told me that all of his cooking was about managing his fridge ... I think of a fridge as something that needs to be managed.

Once every ten days or so the fridge fills up with food and the Sisyphean cycle of ordering and chewing our way through it all begins anew.

Later in the same book Davey talks about how Sontag refers to photographs as memento mori and as an "inventory of mortality," which is something I thought about while taking the above photos. It was Sunday morning and I'd returned from taking some photos of downtown buildings. Our fridge was one big white and empty box. So in between editing photos, I ordered groceries online. I've been ordering online for the last month and having them delivered, which isn't something I would have imagined myself doing. But I'd needed to find strategies to remain calm and this was a decision I made when I hit the pandemic wall. It helps, is the thing. I go out to work three times a week and I can usually make that my only real contact with other humans.

Long story short. I order my groceries and they arrive on my front step only a couple of hours later. Is not that a small miracle? A privileged one, for sure, but what a lovely relief. I unpacked my vegetables and began "managing" them. What needs to be eaten first, what needs to go in the fridge, what needs to be chopped up. I have the whole week planned out with them. As one does. We are all in some ways, I imagine, captive to the contents of our fridge. The goal is to not waste anything, to time it so we don't have to shop for another ten days, to save a few good things for near the end so it feels like we're not eating strictly out of tins.

The still life this week feels very personal and of this time—despite solely being my groceries. The same revealing, naked feeling as when I posted a photograph of the inside of my fridge. I suppose I should have added the tins of chickpeas and boxes of pasta, the croissants I accidentally ordered too many of, the tube of tomato paste, the orange juice, and the eggs. I could have included the bag of spinach and the frozen corn and packet of bacon. You could have spent time wondering what recipes I had in mind.

Another interesting aspect of ordinary life in this time is the way we're managing it, the way we're chewing our way through it, over and again, sort of like background music we don't pay attention to. The shifting of this box in the pantry, and that one, and the way we make sure the new milk carton is behind the old one from last week. The new eggs below the older ones.

At the beginning of the pandemic, there was worry about surfaces, though now we know it's much less of a concern. We crave human touch, and yet, we've been conditioned to be wary of it. Even just the thought of someone touching our produce feels different these days.

The way we manage our fridge is the way we manage our lives during this pandemic, in some sense. We move, we shift, we hope for open space, we hope for replenishment, we slowly move through our abundance, we come to the end of the abundance, and if we're lucky it begins all over again. The fridge empties and fills, we make what we can of the ingredients, whatever it was that was available the day we went to the store. We stretch things out, we make them last, or we binge on ice cream, and eat all the chips in one sitting. We get creative. And sometimes it feels like a five-star restaurant, and sometimes it's hotdogs and french fries or a tin of beans on toast.

I hope that if we can dig our way out of our fridges, we can dig our way out of this pandemic. Spaces will open and become more defined. We will empty out, so that we can fill again in new and smarter and more creative ways.

April 5, 2021

Last week I was setting up one of my usual still lifes, that practice. And at the end, I thought, oh, I wonder what it would look like in my photographer's orb. I found the result to be delightful, and yes, wonderful. Seeing it upside down in the curve of the orb just made me go, huh! I guess I knew what I would probably see when I held up the orb, but still,

I was surprised. And it reminded me that this isn't such a bad lesson at all, a lesson in how we see things, how we understand them. I have so many questions, but rather than answers, this is a kind of response, isn't it?

April 15, 2021

Lemons in a ceramic bowl adorned with dragons, and wilted peonies leftover from Rob's shoot.

You are more than one thing. You live in multiple registers, now more than ever. And yet it's holding together, you are holding it together in a world tricky and challenging. You are here and you are wonderful and good.

July 17, 2021

This is not going to be over for a long time. The pandemic and all the other things happening in the world. I haven't taken still life photos for a while. Rob bought some pink-orange dahlias for me. He doesn't like them for his own still lifes, so these were strictly for mine. I had bought a can of Alphagetti a while back for the purpose of making a still photo, and it called to me. Dahlias and Alphagetti. Orange and pink were the combination I was craving, and really just an absurd juxtaposition. Dahlias are always Fantin-Latour for me. And Alphagetti is just a strange memory from childhood, which also speaks to class maybe, to everything we have and don't have or will never have. Intertwined with the 70s and the Rolling Stones and the way housewives would file their chocolate cakes. It was the time that Kraft Dinner maybe seemed like a miracle and cans of Beefaroni and Alphagetti were a big treat.

I read a letter from Henri Fantin-Latour to Whistler this morning that has nothing to do with Alphagetti but gets at how different we can feel from others: "My dear Whistler, It is very kind of you to write to me. I do not understand your silence you know all the same how interested I always am in what you are doing. You also know that there are not many of us who understand each other we have always got on well together. I have seen and I see every day how little people like us. Between ourselves there are things we cannot say to others …you cannot imagine how little I find myself in sympathy with other people."

Maybe I'm trying to say something about our time: the nervousness, the drag of it, the beauty and the yuck of it, the interest we have in each other combined with the distances… the inexplicable incongruities.

The practice of making a still life involves adding, subtracting, nudging, giving up, starting over again, trying one more thing, peeling lemons, adjusting things by one millimetre, then another, moving away, getting closer, waiting for the light. The world is on the table. Life, death, the unwinding, memento mori, the beauty, the sweetness, the sour, the mysteries. Being able to acknowledge all of it in this context has saved me, when in other contexts we have to be silent. We have to keep various contradictions to ourselves.

July 21, 2021

The game of still life. Trying to figure out the symbolism, the story that this scene might tell. Outside of narrative … but not really. Still life can make a little corner of order amid the chaos, even the still lifes that seem chaotic have been organized to be so. In paintings, the artist has deliberately composed the chaos or at least allowed it.

But you don't have to be an art historian to enjoy a still life or feel like you get it. It's open to interpretation. It can be several things at once, quite comfortably. You don't need to know the history of cards, for example, to enjoy cards in a still life.

Sometimes I think I'm choosing these elements randomly, or more for colour or composition, but playing cards, shells, cigarettes, ceramic birds, Rooster brand cup noodles, and the photographer's orb … maybe these are subliminal messages I'm sending myself. We've spent the last couple of weeks in first a heat wave and then under air quality warnings because of the fires in BC and Northern Saskatchewan.

September 19, 2021

Has it really been two months since I made a still life?

I went out into the yard and picked an armful of flowers and put them into a variety of vases, including the empty bottle of passata, and the Buddha Beer bottle. I also filled the flower orb with begonias, orange and yellow. The flowers are a bit of a motley crew so to speak. A bit weather-worn and an odd assortment of colours and stem length. This year the garden grew very well due to perhaps the heat wave? Who knows really? When we bought the plants in the spring, the variety wasn't the greatest.

All the various flowers went onto the table and that was one shot. After that the flowers were pared down and the skull needed to come in, and the nautilus shell. Every time I do this, I learn all over again: camera settings, light, composition. You would think that composition was something I would just "get," but no, I seem to need to relearn it every time by trial and error. So many errors! This is fine. There is time with a still life to blunder. Maybe this is why I enjoy the process so much—it has built in forgiveness.

I have been reading about still life as resistance in the book *Planets on Tables* by Bonnie Costello. She quotes John Berger: "We live in a world of suffering in which evil is rampant, a world whose events do not confirm our Being, a world that has to be resisted." And so, the still life can be a place to question the suffering, the aesthetic moment of a still life can be a place to situate hope. It offers order in the chaos and confusion, it reassembles from the disturbance of the world, a place of contemplation. Out of the brokenness and fragmented reality of the world, we can come back to a moment of goodness. The order, the concentration, the hopefulness evoked is a point of resistance.

Costello talks about the "immense pressure of public news" and how a personal engagement might aid in us not "collapsing from its force." What I'm wondering in all this is if we can see still life as an aesthetic moment, a disruption, a place of resistance with the objects as markers of the outside world and, if so, then what does that moment mean? That pause? Or is it enough that it is a pause? Is it enough that it stops the flow for a moment? Sure, it's going to come apart at the end, the composition will change, the flowers will fade. But once there is order, there will be again.

December 1, 2021

Cup noodles, spilling out of the container, a can of Spam, a Diet Coke, a tomato, a pear. The groceries aren't nearly as organized as they were at the beginning of the pandemic. I still try to go less often, or at least only once every week or two. Near the end of the week after a shopping trip, there are odds and ends. What could you possibly do with a tomato and a pear? Groceries are more expensive than they have been. I've really given up on cooking and I'm simply trying to keep the bills down. We like noodles, so it's not a big hardship. I'm not someone given to cooking fancy things anyway. Now I don't care about food or meals. I will cook but I try and make everything as easy as possible.

I want to let the still lifes speak for themselves, for the most part. I hope that they say something about this time. At one point I was quite preoccupied with what "pandemic life" revealed about class and social status and privilege. And maybe new layers in the social stratum have developed—the WFH (or work from home) class, for example. For the front facing social stratum (i.e., customer service), the information on aerosol transmission definitely gives you feelings. And those of us who regularly rely on side-gig income have seen that trickle away. How are we living differently? What are the things we've become used to? What have we given up and what have we gained? What things are we being quiet about now? How does exhaustion affect our analysis of all those things we're going through?

January 5, 2022

Still life of a skull smoking a cigarette, inspired by VVG, flipped on its side.

You can't really do a still life project without delving into the theme memento mori. The inspiration: Van Gogh's student work of the skeleton smoking a cigarette. The painting lives in the Van Gogh Museum in Amsterdam, which we visited when I was writing *Rumi and the Red Handbag* and researching handbags at the Museum of Handbags and Purses there. No one knows what joke VVG was making exactly but still life humour is like that sometimes.

I think right now, two years into the pandemic, we are sick to death of remembering death. It has been a low-grade fear, tamped down panic, and generalized trauma that I can't process any more. The whole point of memento mori is to prompt the viewer to remember how to live. How precious that is. Life! The importance of that is a constant. It's something I don't want to ever lose sight of.

Van Gogh was a big fan of smoking. For the record, me, not so much. I suffered a lot in making this art, since I can't even tolerate the secondhand smoke that well. I started a sub-project called "Pack of Cigarettes," but I still have more than half the pack left. I had intended to just incorporate a cigarette into a photo until the pack was gone but it's just too rough to smell the smoke.

January 10, 2022

Two stacks of books, one about photography, one about painting still life. I began by shooting an iPhone photo from above of the scene. Flowers in a metal urn: roses, ranunculus, and one bedraggled peony that the florist gave us for free. Pinks, yellows, peaches. My Pentax MX film camera on one of the stacks of books.

I think this photograph gets at how I'm in love with both still life and street photography. I love looking at images of all kinds: paintings, photographs, iPhone photos, film photos, digital. The books here aren't just for show; it's such a pleasure to sit and crack one open and just stare at one image for a while and think about it. The opposite of what we do on IG, which is where I imagine posting it as soon as I take it. I love IG, don't get me wrong. But it moves too fast.

There's that great line by Rumi (as translated by Coleman Barks):

I don't get tired of you. Don't grow weary
of being compassionate toward me!

For most of us, posting photos is not our job. Instagram does not employ us. I'm trying to remind myself to enjoy. Slow down and enjoy. Knowing that we're going to post the photo even before we take it is strange. But that's part of the process of making a photograph these days. What will it do for us? How will it change how others see us? What part of our story does the photo tell? What does it say that we don't even know it's saying? The way we post our photos is part of our story, whether we like that or not. We can't always know how we're perceived. There are a lot of bad photos that get a lot of attention. There are beautiful photos that should be blown up large on a screen. We should sit with them. But we don't. We can't. We have to get back to our day jobs.

I took this photo on the last day of my three-week holiday. It's not an elaborate setup. I did add a glass of carrot juice in a champagne flute for the colour and I peeled a lemon, let the rind unwind. I added a knife to reflect the lemon and angled it just so. I added the colourful bowl with the Chinese dragon that I had ordered from Amazon a year ago. I'm always trying to recreate the mood from a Willem Kalf painting without being overt about it. Why is that? What is it that I want from looking at an image, or making an image? The feeling I get when looking at the Kalf painting is one of awe at its beauty—the colours, the composition, the perfectly placed objects. These days, I think what makes me feel verklempt when I contemplate such a painting is that Kalf made this not knowing if it would last. Certainly not knowing that a couple of hundred years later someone would look at it and care about it and feel things before it. We can say all we want about a picture, but in the end, it would be honest to say that it makes us feel something.

January 19, 2022

Photograph of dried flowers in a Japanese bowl illuminated by the low January sun that only comes in that window thusly once a year.

Now, that is the magic of still life! Roses—orange, pink, magenta, yellow. Ranunculus in pink and yellow. Rob had taken photos of them when they were fresh. I also took a few. But time got away from me and I didn't get quite as many as I would have liked, and so they ended up in this bowl. Perfectly fitting to sit atop the book, *Nature Morte*. And that's memento mori! The colours have faded but when the light swung in and hit the table, I had the idea to get the bowl of flowers from where it was in the kitchen and to place it on the stack of books. Then it was a bit of waiting until the sun hit the flowers just so. Illuminating them so that they glowed, a colourful surprise! A shock of delight and beauty! Ta-da!

February 4, 2022

Still life with three fancy cocktails made over crushed ice. One made with Empress Gin (purple!) and Cinzano, layered. Another one that is pink made with Starlino Aperitivo. A third lemony yellow made with limoncello.

They are jewel-bright and saturated and juicy looking. They look delicious but afterwards needed a bit of doctoring. Bit of club soda, bit of simple syrup, that sort of thing. For the photo though, I wanted the souped-up colours. I had to work fairly quickly to photograph them because I didn't want the ice to melt too much. I tried them in a natural setting in our front room, with the glamorous paintings of Grace Kelly that Rob once did as a backdrop. I wheeled the bar cart into the frame as an element of interest and for colour. I shot them against the black background next with a cut glass bowl filled with colourful dried flowers that mirrored the colours of the cocktails. I photographed the three of them alone against the black and I also photographed them from above. All quite quickly and then, as it was 3:30 in the afternoon and bit early to be drinking alone, I popped them in the fridge where they sat until before dinnertime.

Which is to say, the photos I took were real, but they were also a setup. And I wonder if people are looking at such a photo know that? Do they care? Do they think about it? If they did think about it, I'm sure they'd know. I'm not concealing anything. My caption for the photo on Instagram was: "Photography: a magic or an art?" But what is my responsibility as a photographer in the age of digital photography? To try and make the viewer forget about the magic that goes on behind the scenes? To forget about everything going on in the world for a few seconds? And likely less, as the attention span of someone scrolling is infinitesimal. Is my role as the photographer to try and get them to pause? To forget, to feel delight? To care?

We know that social media is set up to both addict us and to make us feel like we're in some kind of competition. We talk about ways to disrupt this but then we're right back in the fray again. Posting a still life on Instagram versus a person commissioning a painting of tulips and a nautilus shell with a lemon in the seventeenth century to show off to the other businessmen who come to his house is interesting to think about.

Can I post a picture of three fancy cocktails and know that on Twitter it will be surrounded by news of illegal gatherings and convoys of foreign-funded truckers protesting vaccines, and be sanguine? I post the cocktails because I need to drink them. Not just because they're alcohol (though partly so) but because they're beautiful. Pretty colours, nice glass, crushed ice. They've been made with care. I want to think of them as potions. Perhaps I'll be transformed by drinking them. I drink them symbolically, beauty as an antidote to all the fuckery of the world. How did we even get here? Historians will be dissecting this time period forever. What happened to people? When did some of us stop caring about others?

If people can change, can they also change back? Is there a drink or a potion or a magic trick for that? Or is the real magic trick learning how to change going forward?

February 17, 2022

It's the middle of February and I have put together a still life of a bunch of spring flowers from Safeway (hyacinths and tulips), an orange plant (also from Safeway, an impulse buy), lemons and oranges, a blue hydrangea (leftover from Rob's recent photoshoot), a bird's nest, and two porcelain cats. Maybe it's just a bunch of objects thrown together or maybe it's a sign of hope mingled with the symbolism of the chaotic force of cats.

The blue hydrangea plant is in a Heinz Ketchup bottle that I saved from a while back, and the orange plant (the instructions on it were "decorative: do not eat") has been placed in a giant tin of San Marzano tomatoes.[23] I think I likely would have hung on to the ketchup bottle and the tin can at any time in my life, but it also seemed like a very pandemic thing to do. What's coming up in the future? What

---

23 My sister-in-law had ordered some tomatoes without looking at the size of the tin and it ended up being as big as one's head. She shared them out among family members, and we were lucky recipients.

things did we discard that we will wish we had kept? I believe this goes for physical as well as more abstract things. Hope, though, that's something that's hard to hold onto right now; it's hard to keep and keep still. The line by Octavia Butler that is the epigraph in the latest Rebecca Solnit book on Orwell, goes like this: "The very act of trying to look ahead to discern possibilities and offer warnings is in itself an act of hope." Is the very existence of a still life a measure of some hope? If you're looking at a still life you're already in its future. That's something.

If the cat typically symbolizes the force of chaos, here in the still life anyway, the chaos is stilled.

I think of the way we joked at the beginning of the pandemic about the line "I hope this email finds you well." And maybe every still life says this too, "I hope this still life finds you well." I hope it finds you hundreds of years in the future where things really are well. How's that for hope?

February 28, 2022

I post a photo of an arrangement we got from the florist. We don't normally buy arrangements because Rob isn't likely to paint them. But this one was like spring and we're still firmly in winter here. The news has been filled with the Russian invasion of Ukraine. We are witnessing from afar. It seems absurd to take photos of an exquisite arrangement of flowers while people are hiding, fighting, fleeing for their lives.

Historians will look at our time and wonder how when we knew Ukraine was being invaded, we arranged flowers and took still life photos. Maybe they will say of us, they were tired. They will say, for years they carried their worry on strings like dark clouds from a renaissance painting. In a relatively safe space, their moral goodness was eroded by the behaviour of some in the pandemic. What could the average person a world away do anyway? They did their laundry and watched hockey games and they waited for peace and quiet. They praised each other for resilience and preached their hearts out to the converted. They were accomplices of a sort but they said comforting things to each other. "It won't always be this way." "Most people are good." They weren't wrong to do any of this, historians will say. They weren't wrong to arrange flowers, find beauty, try to stay alive and cherish that they are still relatively carefree.

The future won't hold it against us, will they? Our ease at being in the world so far away from what we wish was unthinkable. It will depend on whether the future historians live in a place of peace or constant fear. It will depend on what traumas were passed down to our thoughtful historians. Are there still countries? Borders? Have the trees survived? The ozone? Are the historians beloved and able to love?

March 6, 2022

Taco Time still life. Did I think this still life series was going to bring me acclaim? That it would be recognized or loved by any but a very small audience? No, not really. Still, I'd be lying if I didn't often feel discouraged by the whole thing. But it continues to give me something, so I continue with it. Am I getting better or am I getting worse? Or does it even matter if no one is looking at it?

I have been wanting to take this still life of food from the Taco Time ever since a photo I took of the Taco Time sign had become popular on Twitter (over a thousand likes and 90 retweets). The CBC asked me to write an article about the suburbs, featuring this photograph.

Fast-food still lifes make me laugh but they also make me feel uneasy. I can never think of them any more without hearkening back to Trump's fast-food gala at the White House. He got McDonald's, Wendy's and Burger King. But no Taco Time.

Though COVID cases are still high, we are at that part of the pandemic where there is a move to be done with restrictions. Restaurants are fully open, for example. For two years, people have been relying on takeout, and for the poorer among us, fast-food has been a bit of a treat, a bit of a luxury. Using the Uber Eats or Skip the Dishes apps is now second nature. Before the pandemic I didn't have the apps on my phone. In the heyday of Dutch seventeenth century, still life exotic objects and fruits came via ship. But for this still life, the food came by way of a Skip the Dishes person driving a black Audi SUV on a Sunday afternoon. I try to fill in with my imagination the circumstances that would lead someone driving a vehicle worth that much to deliver fast-food, but the variables are far too many. And though I can google how much an Audi SUV costs and how much a Skip the Dishes driver makes and what the working conditions are like, the costs we have suffered for the last two years are incalculable.

We began the pandemic grabbing take-out because we weren't able to gather and restaurants were closed. Now they're open and it seems like the risk is even higher to dine out. A lot of people will do it anyway and you can't blame them. They're following the rules and guidelines given. In the seventeenth century, Rembrandt (a relatively well-off artist) lost three of his four children to plague. In an article from 2012 (before this current pandemic) in *The Guardian*, "Brush with the Black Death: how artists painted through the plague," Jonathan Jones notes after seeing a show of Van Dyck,

> It is a fascinating perspective, yet it is just the tip of an iceberg, for if you think about it, the entire story of the Renaissance and baroque periods in art is sealed inside the kingdom of the plague. Pestilence had all of Europe in its grip from 1347 to the late 17th century, with outbreaks in southern Europe recurring in the 1700s. This means the lives of all the "Old Masters" were experienced in its shadow: Michelangelo, Rembrandt and the rest all faced the danger that mortal contagion could at any moment seize their city.

It's not easy to depict those suffering from COVID-19. Much of the day-to-day suffering is internal for those living in fear of contracting COVID. We've lived with the fear for two years, but the myriad ways the illness seeped into our society is another thing altogether. And a still life of food from Taco Time doesn't say everything but it does say something about how we live right now. We all still like Mexi-Fries.

March 17, 2022

This is the two-year anniversary of being laid off from my job for the first few months of the pandemic. Though it had begun in other places before this, 17 March 2020 was the start of things for me.

I set up the toaster and fill it with chocolate and vanilla iced pop tarts, pour some chocolate and strawberry milk. I tie additional pop tarts to a string and have Rob hold them above, as the game or a piece of fruit would hang in a seventeenth-century traditional still life. The porcelain cat is perched atop my usual book stack.

This is the last still life for the purposes of this diary, though it's not likely my last still life. I thought I'd have a lot to say about this image. It's a bit of a still life joke, echoing the themes from the past with modern junk food. The suspended sugary overprocessed pastry filled with preservatives dangling over an already full toaster—does that speak to our time of denial, disinformation, bad choices, full hospitals? I don't know. I made it to be frank, because it was fun to make. Times are grim. There is a war in Ukraine. Soon the cat will knock everything off the table, bob for the pop tarts as though they were balls of yarn. No one will feel healthy after eating all those pop tarts. The table will be cleared. The still life will begin again.

April 1, 2022

No, wait, this is the last one.

I was at the Safeway and saw a pre-packaged macaroni and cheese loaf sliced meat. As a kid, this was actually a specialty thing, even though now it's probably going to have a gross-out factor for a lot of folks. I had Rob hold the packaged meat from a string. Below I had arranged a tin of sardines, KD, baked beans, sardines, Ichiban noodles, cup noodles, and a bowl of the new Miss Vickie's spicy ketchup chips, all on my usual stack of still life books.

I wanted it to say something about our time and about how weird groceries have been for the last two years. Because even though some people want to call this the end of the pandemic, it's not. Food prices have gone up. We stock our cupboards, still, with food for the apocalypse. With cheap food, affordable stuff. Not necessarily nutritious stuff. There is a nostalgia going on in this image, too. The foods from my childhood to some extent. We were poor then, without really knowing it. The world was ending then, but not the way it's ending now.

April 25, 2022

No, this is definitely the last one. Two photos.

Photo one. Vase of flowers on the stack of still life books. Just the beauty of the flowers. We deserve that, too.

Rob and I both tested positive for COVID-19 this past week after two years of doing everything possible to not get the virus. So, we sent ourselves flowers to commemorate getting COVID. Or we ordered them to console ourselves, as a way to be creative even while isolating. We feel like rubbish but we're fine. At about this time, two years ago, Rob ordered some flowers for my birthday from our go-to florist, and he ended up painting them. He'd been painting flowers before but he'd also been working on a series of stills from movies at the time. When the pandemic hit, he went deeper into his study of flowers, and it turned out, people really wanted beauty, and they loved his flower paintings. And isn't it lovely when what you want to give is what people want to receive?

Photo two. Stack of books, roses and ranunculus in pinks, corals, yellow, cream, bowl of seashells, nautilus shells, playing cards, pack of smokes, bird's nest, and skull wearing a crown. Siri Hustvedt: "...the canvases are drenched with meaning, but they cannot be reduced to 'messages.' The great allegorical paintings of the Dutch are not one-liners." The works "draw from and play with a known pictorial vocabulary through which they produce complex meanings."

At the beginning of the pandemic, I would often leave the skull out of my still lifes. A traditional reminder of memento mori, I thought it would be too visceral and unsettling, given the number of COVID deaths. I found it unsettling. These days many don't even blink an eye at the number of COVID deaths. For me, the cigarettes remind me of how at the beginning of the pandemic someone said to think of the aerosol of COVID as the smoke from a cigarette, the way it lingers even after the smoker has left the room. But that message wasn't as widely disseminated as it could have been. And the playing card is about the luck of things. The luck of what class you happen to belong to, which race. Rich, white people aren't immune but fared better, which has always unfairly been the case. The deck is stacked, you could say. The empty nest is a symbol of all those homes missing a human now, and the shells, too, empty of whatever creature once lived in them. The flowers are always beauty, the persistence of beauty, but a reminder that our vows to beauty have to be constantly renewed, constantly grown and cultivated.

The Practice of Still Life

The subject of a still life is never the subject. The subject is light, or time. The subject is our mortality. The subject is mystery. The subject is inexhaustibility. The subject is incorruptibility. The subject of still life is dream and reverie.

The practice of composing still lifes can be grounding. The practice can be what Audrey Flack says of the act of painting, that it is a "spiritual covenant." The act of composing a still life is what matters. The process and the practice. The hand reaching out, adjusting, arraying, caressing, holding, hefting, setting things out.

The subject of a still life is hunger. The subject is how things are just out of our grasp. The subject of a still life is you can almost touch the apple, almost taste it. You can almost smell the flowers. The subject of a still life is almost.

The practice of still life is keeping things company. Things persist, things remain, things abide. The practice of still life is staying with. The practice of still life is seeing flowers through to the end. The practice of still life is waiting, silently, patiently. The practice of still life is petal by petal.

The subject of a still life is the immutable. The bowl is a shape that has been in existence for thousands of years. A rose is delicate and will fade, but roses were found in ancient Egyptian tombs. The subject of a still life is the mutable. A young person leans into the frame and blows a large bubble near the fresh caught fish on a platter, the lemons and oranges, the ripe cheese. The subject of a still life is precariousness. The plate of sweets is balanced perilously on a stack of leather-bound books.

The practice of still life is steadiness but also innovation and problem solving and a working knowledge of the TV show MacGyver. Strawberries are pyramided on a silver platter one at a time, balanced each to each, affixed with toothpicks. A plum is secured to the edge of the table with poster putty. A pink carnation is held in place with Scotch tape.

The subject of a still life is hanging on by a thread. The subject of a still life is how hanging on, even so, we can be shattered. Our innocence taken. The subject of a still life is a shattered roemer with all the shards placed inside the salvaged remains of the vessel, overlapping, hurting, cupped.

The practice of a still life is deleting digital images. The practice of still life is taking more photographs than are necessary. The practice of still life is arranging things little by little, adding, subtracting, nudging, tweaking, inching this forward and that backward.

The subject of a still life is what Rilke called the inexhaustibility of objects. The subject of a still life is that it is never done, always unfolding. The subject of a still life is the overlooked, the ordinary, the quotidian, the everyday, the way things repeat and repeat. The subject of a still life is attending, appreciating, paying attention, deep meditation, prayer. The subject of a still life is a blessing. The subject of a still life is a lesson in seeing with magic eyes. The subject of a still life is seeing ordinary things with ordinary eyes and then seeing things as magical. The subject of a still life is an approaching. The subject of a still life is experiencing fragrance through your eyes.

The practice of still lifes is walking in and out of rooms noticing the light. The practice of still life is monitoring decay, drooping, levels of water. The practice of still life is custodial. The practice of still life is pinching deadheads, bending stems slowly, plucking leaves that obscure the flower or other objects. The practice of still life is contriving shadows to fall in patterns.

The subject of a still life is sensuality. Sexuality. The subject of a still life is a flower opening, stamens, petals, pollen pollen pollen pollen.

The practice of still life is gesture. The practice of still life is letting remain a trace of the felt gesture or movement of the hand that placed the object on the table. The practice of still life is in telegraphing gestures of objects, swaying stems of flowers, petal kisses, the undulating and riffling pages of books, the delectable unravelling of a lemon, the sighs of a peeled orange. The practice of still life is rarely still.

The subject of a still life is memento mori. Everything dies, darling, just ask Bruce.

The practice of still life is learning f-stops. Focal distance. Lightroom. Editing. Contrast. Desaturation. Clarity. Exposure.

The subject of a still life is beauty, unapologetically. The subject of a still life is astonishing Paris with an apple. The subject of a still life is living. We are alive!

The practice of still life is unpredictability. In flies a butterfly or a housefly. The housecat leaps up and bats at the sweet peas and poppies, bats at the lemon, and ogles the fish. The practice of still life is intrusion. Yapping dog, a parrot, a small child.

The subject of a still life is loss. Loneliness. Being alone. The subject of a still life is breathing in and breathing out. The subject of a still life is so quiet you can scarcely hear it when you lean in.

The practice of still life is knowing the poetry of emptiness and loneliness and howl. The practice of still life is reciting Wallace Stevens's "Anecdote of the Jar" or sitting in the backyard reading Charles Wright deliberate on the vessels of Giorgio Morandi.

The subject of a still life is the threads of connection that run everywhere and in and out of the maze, which is to say the world. The whole world. The subject of a still life is the chaos and the order of the universe back and forth ad infinitum.

The practice of still life is remembering that bowl you got as a wedding present thirty years ago and bringing it up from the basement storage and into the light and putting three plums, a lemon, and a lime in it.

The subject of a still life is the wilderness of the mind. The subject of a still life is that it is untameable, unfinishable, always resurrecting. The subject of a still life is the endless permutations.

The practice of still life is feeling things through things.

The subject of a still life is the frequency and vibrations of the universe. It is about realms. The subject of a still life is the vibrations between things and juxtapositions. The subject of a still life is the spirit and aura. The subject of a still life is the way things appear in your dreams and also the way things dream your presence into existence.

The practice of a still life is watering flowers, arranging and rearranging them, ordering seeds from the seed catalogue in the middle of winter. The practice of a still life is dropping a penny into the vase.

The subject of a still life is the thingness of things. The simple description. The magic of things. A deepening. A mercy. A grace. Mystery. The subject of a still life is intimately learning what these are experientially, by sitting, opening, not thinking.

The practice of still life is visiting museums and homing in on the small paintings of flowers and fruit or homing in on the details of larger paintings that contain still lifes. A vase of lilies by the virgin Mary, a pink carnation, an orange and a pomegranate, a loaf of bread, a book.

The subject of still life is poverty and luxury. The subject of a still life is extravagance except when it is about austerity. A still life swings back and forth between being the subject for a monk's meditation and contemplation, and the humble-brag of a noble person. When the subject of a still life is profound and sparse, it still speaks about abundance and over-the-top lavishness and luxury.

The practice of still life is about your own absent body at the same time as it is about being present. The practice of still life is sinking down into yourself so that the viewer will be able to do same.

The subject of a still life is that we have all lived one or two flowers, as Hélène Cixous said. We have all lived through one or two still lifes. The subject of a still life is that it is, as Anthony Gormley said about art, "useless but vital." The subject of still life is the acknowledgement that we live, we are yet alive.

The practice of still life is standing on a chair to get the flat lay view. It's crouching down and sitting with your back up against a wall. It's squinting with one eye; it's looking at everything with an eye toward still life. The practice of still life is stopping everything to take a photo. The practice of still life is your dinner going cold. The practice of still life is being late for the coffee date because the light raking across the table will not last and nor will it ever be quite like that again. The practice of still life is when your friends bring over their things for you to borrow for your potential still life and when they also always bring flowers or an apple with an odd stem.

The subject of a still life is that beauty is relative, that things are relative to things. That my idea of composition and notions of symmetry and balance regarding colour and shape may not be your jam or cup of tea. The subject of a still life is if you don't like the way things are arranged you can change them. The subject of a still life is that some things are drab until the light reaches low and wedge-like onto the table in mid-winter. The subject of a still life is that we knew not what would haunt us, make us shiver, silence our inward turmoil, delight us, or what we would find beautiful in this astonishing and ravaged world.

Why Still Life Might Speak to You Now

Still life is my jam. I'm married to an artist who has spent most of 30 years painting still life in one form or another. There are a lot of themes and subsets to still life—always more going on than meets the eye. Still lifes are in many ways about the extraordinary nature of ordinary life, everyday existence. And these days when we are steeped in the ordinary life, I think it makes sense to look at the genre of still life and the stills in our everyday life. Odds are you have been doing this, whether you've noticed or not. But my guess is that you are noticing. You are baking bread and cinnamon buns and loaves. You are setting up your cocktails and ingredients into pleasing arrays. You are stacking your books and instagramming your lipsticks. You are setting your wine beside the bread and grapes and wedge of cheese. You are filling bowls with lemons and cutting up your cantaloupes and maybe you are arranging flowers, tulips, roses, hyacinths. Your children are bored, perhaps, and reminding you a thousand times a day of the passage of time, of transience. Maybe you are frothing your beautiful coffees and admiring them. Still lifes, all.

The beauty of a still life is that while it may more overtly say "memento mori" (in the case of my skull photographs), many traditional still life objects, especially flowers, remind us that tempus fugit. We have the beauty of the blooms in floral still lifes, which will not last, often in combination with perishable food and fruit. Often precarious items are placed and because life is precarious, full of unknown interruptions, disruptions, and loud noises, so is the unexpected.

Still lifes remind us that everything is always happening at once. There are terrible sad things right beside sensual and lovely things. We are learning every day that the so-called ordinary life is in the details, it's in the numbers.

It seems absurd that you can scroll through social media and see death tolls, stories of the effects of this terrible illness, and reports of the most horrific mass murder in Canada and interspersed with that are photos of bread and baked goods and flowers and the new leaves and blossoms in some parts of the world.

It's a lot to process but we can hold it. We can, we do. Still lifes have always held all these difficult and brutal and beautiful things in the palm of their hand. The French call it Nature Morte, but even so, still life is on the side of the living. It's on the side of poetry and prayer, on the side of contemplation and patience and the long-settled gaze. Still life is on the side of love, transforming all of the truths about death and the precariousness and preciousness of our existence into love, and into beauty. Still lifes are full of imperfections and limited by the parameters of the genre. A still life may include objects, a table, various degrees of light and shadow. But it is also the magic show that can turn our everyday life, complete with fear, frustration, spills, awkwardness and failures, into something that takes your breath away. Something you can sit with for a long spell and see your way into and back out of.

A still life has the potential to hold, if not everything, a lot of we're experiencing right now. I have a strong belief in the power of words, but when words are difficult, we can find a lot of expression in things. A still life can be a place to express and experience hard to say and even unsayable words in a difficult time. And perhaps later, through them, we can come back and formulate more thoughts. We will remember the sorrows and those we lost, but we will also remember the original joys, our faithfulness to the details of small things.

ART(IST) LIFE

Artist Studio

Let's begin with Alberto Giacometti's studio. Address: 46 Rue Hippolyte-Maindron in Montparnasse. Giacometti was in this studio since 1926. In a photo essay by Ernst Scheidegger, the studio is described thus: "With an area of twenty-three square metres and a high ceiling, the Parisian studio was extremely simple and bare. There was no running water until the late 1950s and the lighting was dim. The floor was made of cement and the roof leaked. Even later, when his more comfortable economic circumstances allowed it, Giacometti never thought of transforming or leaving this studio which was 'the prettiest and humblest of all'." And then Giacometti is quoted as saying, "It's funny, when I took this studio … I thought it was tiny … But the longer I stayed, the bigger it became. I could fit anything I wanted into it." Looking at the black-and-white photos, the place is covered in plaster and plaster dust. The writer Jean Genet remarked on how precarious the studio felt. The grey powder everywhere, the way it could float in the air or, with the water from the leaky roof, be turned into porridge. Genet said, "And yet it all appears to be captured in an absolute reality. When I leave the studio, when I am outside on the street, then nothing that surrounds me is true." Of Giacometti's studio, the art historian Michael Peppiatt says,

"… And then suddenly, improbably, towards the end of the sculptor's career, a small but sturdy tree erupted, unbidden but unopposed, through the studio wall, stretching its luscious green leaves in the grey plaster-filled air."

Hélène Cixous writes of the artist in the studio in her book *Stigmata*. She loves the process, whether of writing or art-making. She says, "I want the forest before the book…" and "I love the creation as much as the created, no, more." She says, "I want the tornados in the atelier." She finds ecstasy in the technique, and is drawn to art being born, arriving. I can't help thinking about the forest, or at least the tree, that erupted into Giacometti's studio, here.

Often, in photographs of artists' studios, the studio has been sanitized, tidied. A non-messy studio seems unworthy of recording, I suppose. "Do artists imprint themselves on remains left behind after they have gone? Or do we project our own version of their presence into those empty rooms?" asks Simon Schama in the introduction to the book of photos Sally Mann has taken of her friend and neighbor Cy Twombly's studio. Schama notes that she captures the "explosion of fecund mess," though there are "a few documents of improbable discipline: tubes of paint laid out in rows; cleaned brushes reporting for duty in their pots." Sally Mann says, "…the hope is that it holds a greater sense of manifold truths about a life, through both the evidence and inspiration."

Maybe the most famous artist studio is Francis Bacon's. He's quoted as saying he'd return to Dublin only "once I am dead." And so, his 7 Reece Mews studio in London moved posthumously to Dublin seems to fulfill that (even if Bacon is rolling his eyes in the afterlife). Catalogued, mapped, documented to the nth degree, the staggering assemblage even includes the original dust from the notoriously chaotic studio. Visitors can now view the mess through windowpanes, but there's nothing like walking through an artist's studio not knowing what substance will affix itself to you. You'll leave with paint on your sleeve or hand, dust on your pant legs, some kind of oil or grime on your shoes. I don't imagine too many folks left Bacon's original studio without a trace of where they'd been.

Joel Meyerowitz photographed Cezanne's studio in Provence, which Cezanne had only moved to in the last five years of his life. Maybe the most striking feature of that studio is the tall and narrow opening in the wall through which he could pass a large canvas out into the garden. Meyerowitz photographs the painter's smock and hat on hooks, skulls, a cane. He captures wide views of the studio as a whole but mainly the book is settled on a series of objects in the studio, taken in the same spot against the grey-green wall. The photos are beautiful and seem to speak through the long corridor of time. They're so removed from the chaos of studio that they seem almost unbearably honest. There is no pretense that we can experience the objects in the same way Cezanne did.

Lovers of art make pilgrimages to artist studios: Frida Kahlo shared a studio with Diego Rivera in Mexico City (two studios connected by a bridge), and she also had a blue studio in Coyoacán named "Casa Azul." Georgia O'Keeffe's studios in New Mexico are a tourist destination. I can see why people would want to look at the studio of a favourite artist. It's safe to say that I myself wouldn't make a special trip to see one.

I've looked at a lot of photographs of studios, but the one in my basement is the one I'm most familiar with. I love the line by Cezanne, "the sugar bowl changes every day," and you can also say that the studio changes every day. I enjoy seeing the haphazard and inadvertent still lifes in an artist's studio, but I also know that the next day there will be another arrangement. The tubes of pigment and brushes will have been used and moved around. Paint cloths will adorn the floor, dropped in the heat of painting. A new photo or colour swatch will be tacked to the wall for inspiration. Who knows what storms will have moved through the artist's belongings, or what desire for order?

Between each painting, Rob does a bit of a cleanup. The colourful bits of paper towel he wipes his paintbrushes on are tossed out. The garbage is emptied, the floor swept. The glass palette he uses is scraped off with a razor blade. He removes the photograph from which he works from its cardboard backing. I've taken photos of his palette and easel and him painting often enough, but maybe I'm too close to the subject. I tend to want to edit out the debris and the cardboard boxes that are often stacked up in his space.

The studio space holds also the less romantic business part of art-making. Down there he boxes his paintings, he varnishes them, he might stretch a canvas or construct a stretcher. There are hammers and wrenches and plyers, the wire he affixes to the back of the painting when it's complete, and there are waybills and invoices and notebooks and calendars and planners. He has an old drawing table as a desk, and there are sticky notes reminding him of what he needs to send to which gallery and various requests and dates that must be remembered—ship this by this date. There are bills to pay stacked up neatly, and invoices. It's not at all a glamorous space. The walls are mainly drywall and in places not even that; you can see the yellow insulation covered with plastic. The ceilings are similarly unfinished, so you can see the pipes running through. It's definitely humble. Couple that with the fact that we live pretty far outside the accepted art centres of the world, and it's even more uninteresting.

I've always wished Rob had a nicer, more well-lit space in which to paint; there was a point when I might have imagined him in something magazine-worthy. But he never complains. Maybe the magic of it is that he creates such beautiful pieces in such a grungy, subterranean, utilitarian space. And that's the magic of all art studios. That you can make something so layered and rich and colourful, something so beautiful, in what would otherwise be an ordinary space.

Luck, Still Life, Looking at Art

We happened to be in Rome, luckily, at the same time as a still life exhibition at the Corsini Gallery in 2019. And maybe a lot of still life, like a lot of life, is reliant upon the lucky moment. In street photography, there is the idea of the decisive moment, a concept associated with Henri Bresson, in which a gesture is caught in a split second, before or after which it is gone, that encapsulates so completely what the photograph is saying. In still life, because the setup is under fewer time constraints and is more methodical and contrived, it seems as though luck would play less of a factor. The gestures are made by the artist, setting up the composition, hoping it all coheres, that nothing tips over, that the cat doesn't come into the frame and create chaos.

Artists talk about happy accidents, and these are really a result of showing up, doing the work, taking risks, being in a state for learning, a state conducive and receptive to creative sparks. The trick is to know what to do with those happy accidents, to make use of them. Luck in art has to do with being in a place and making the effort to be there waiting.

It's overwhelming to think of all the luck it takes to get to both a physical place and the mental place required to make art of any sort. In constructing a still life, there are the artistic circumstances: which fruit is in season or not, which flower is blooming, what objects are at hand. And then, there is the light, that magic, that luck.

It's two plus years into the pandemic as I write this. And it's a little more than that since we were in Rome and saw the art exhibition titled "Timeless Nature" at the Corsini Gallery. I took a lot of photographs of the still life paintings, some iPhone videos, and we visited the exhibition at the beginning of our trip and then three weeks later, at the end of the trip. Of course, we had no idea then that the pandemic would hit in the spring of 2020, and that we'd see no paintings outside of the stuff being made in our home by my artist husband for a couple of years. At the time, I might have had a vague idea that I could write an essay about this show. I have loved essays written about art in the era of the blockbuster show. What intrigued me about this show, though, was that it was the opposite of a blockbuster art exhibit. No "star" artist, no well-known works. The only painting that I'd heard of before attending was a still life in the adjacent room by Christian Berentz from the Corsini's permanent collection, known as *La Mosca* or "The Fly." Beyond this, though, there were still lifes of lemons, pomegranates, a plate of peaches, vases of abundant flowers, game, plums, often brightly lit against a dark background.

As much as I loved the show, I knew I wouldn't find a place for such an essay in a magazine. I'm not an art historian, or a famous enough writer, or any kind of influencer. I haven't any kind of cachet that would give weight to my hot-take on a show of mostly unattributed still lifes that would be over by the time I'd get anything written down. Sometimes it's enough to just see something because you want to see it, and to absorb it, and let it live in you. Not everything has to be dissected or shared. Some things you can see and just keep for yourself. Regardless, I couldn't coordinate the timelessness of the subject matter with an article requiring timelines.

Had there been no pandemic, no two years without much travel, I perhaps wouldn't now be thinking about this still life exhibition. It meant a lot to me at the time but it has come to mean more. The images from that trip scroll on my screensaver including, of course, the photos from the still life show. I work a bit on my computer in the mornings, then move to the chair in the corner of my study to read a bit or write things in my journal or on a steno pad. Eventually the screensaver kicks in and usually one or two of the images I took at the Corsini still life exhibition fade in and out.

The exhibition was the collection of one person, Geo Poletti. He collected still lifes (among other works) from the seventeenth and nineteenth century. The forces that brought the work together initially, and then into this room in the Corsini, must have been operated on by so many various pieces of luck that one can hardly fathom. But isn't luck composed, in part, of deliberation, sometimes obsession, an interest, a curiosity pursued?

Many of the pieces in the show were anonymous works by "Caravaggesque Painter" or "Painter Working in Rome" or "Tuscan Painter" or "Emilian Painter." The style was typical of the Baroque with chiaroscuro and/or tenebrism for which the period is known. By the time we made it to the still life exhibit in Rome, Rob had been painting his flowers on a black background back in Edmonton for about a year, though the subject matter and process felt very new for him. We were both registering the way the backgrounds worked in the still lifes we were seeing and were certainly struck that many of these breathtaking and beautifully executed works were by unknown artists. Both humbling and funny, the two of us unknowns wandering and sitting, looking long and hard at these unattributed still lifes.

Would we have looked at the exhibition differently had we known about our upcoming isolation? More thoroughly? Through a different lens? Maybe. But we did know that the exhibit wasn't permanent. We knew it would be the last time we'd see it. And so, in a way, we did have that feeling of "never again" built into our viewing. I remember looking at the bright lemons so carefully in one of the paintings at the Corsini, and afterwards sitting across the street with a view of a lemon tree full of the fruit. At home, we'd heard it was snowing and, while it was about plus 20 in Rome, it was well below zero in Edmonton. In the winter, we have lemons in the grocery store and they seem like such a miracle. But in other parts of the world, they're just part of ordinary existence. I've probably only seen maybe three lemon trees in my entire life.

We didn't go to Rome just to see this still life show. We went to see the art of Rome, because Rome called to us, both of us, and we answered the call. When we were there, we would wake up each morning and decide where to go and what art we wanted to see. We had been to Rome the year before and this time we wanted to look at the art slowly. We didn't have to rush to see anything. Seeing something for the second or third time is such a different experience. So many people asked us if we were going to take day trips, but we just felt the pull to sink further into the offerings of the Eternal City.

You could say that we followed the pollen path. Even in a museum, we would meander from one work of art to another. What experience were we hoping for? An eloquent expression of who we are together? A witnessing of the beauty of the world as it exists in this one time and place and reverberating back in time and into our futures? We wanted to spend enough time so that we might feel the vibrations of a room, a corridor lined with paintings. To feel the echoes and resonances between pieces. To get at the energies of the place.

After thirtyish years of looking at art together, Rob and I have rhythms, we know how long we each want to look at this or that. Sometimes I will go ahead, and Rob will lag looking at one piece for a greater span of time. It's a bit of a dance. I take photos of rooms, paintings, furniture, arrangements, and he will be looking carefully at brushstrokes. I stop and ask him for some bit of art historical information, which he invariably knows, and he listens to my feelings about a piece, my thoughts on the poetic realm as it pertains to what I'm seeing.

In between our two viewings of the still life show, we spent our days looking at the art of Rome. Every day we'd pick one or two museums or churches, and head there. One of the threads of the trip was looking at Caravaggio paintings. In Rome, there are twenty-three of the sixty paintings attributed to Caravaggio and we've seen all of them except the ceiling painting at Casino Ludovisi. On each of our three trips to Rome, we'd seek out the Caravaggios. My favourites are the one with the dirty feet (*Madonna of Loreto* in the Chiesa di Sant'Agostino), the one with the horse's posterior (*The Conversion of Saint Paul* in Santa Maria del Popolo) and the one with the angel covered in drapery (*Saint Matthew and the Angel* in The Contarelli Chapel of San Luigi dei Francesi). But Rob loves them all and has studied the work of Caravaggio all of his life as an artist and read every book he could get his hands on about him. Besides Vermeer, Caravaggio is the artist most mentioned in conversation in our household.

In an article by Tara Lloyd on Caravaggio and chiaroscuro, she writes that

"Not much is known about Caravaggio's early life. He was born Michelangelo Merisi, on September 29, 1571, in Milan, Italy. When he was five years old, his family moved to the Caravaggio countryside to escape an outbreak of the bubonic plague, though by 1577 Caravaggio lost his father, younger brother, paternal grandparents, and uncle to the disease. His mother died in 1584, just after Caravaggio began an apprenticeship with painter Simone Peterzano."

Caravaggio wouldn't even be called Caravaggio if the plague hadn't prompted his family to move there.

What portion of life is luck that has some people surviving a plague and some not? For whom does the fly alight?

Which paintings are kept and collected, and which lost to history? Which artists are remembered and why?

While Caravaggio didn't invent the techniques of tenebrism and chiaroscuro, he was influential in popularizing the technique in the baroque. His biography is one of drama—murder, brawling, various high-profile quarrels, fleeing from one place after another, until his death at 39 years of age. The events of his life are always connected in any work about him to his affinity for dramatic lighting.

Rob and I have been to Rome three times together, and each time we sought out the Caravaggios in churches and museums. Back home, Rob continues his study of the work and life of Caravaggio. I've happily gone along, though my interest isn't as keen. What I do find interesting is when someone is deeply pulled toward a subject and goes toward it, following it ever deeper. We've seen Caravaggios in other places, too. London, Paris, New York.

Caravaggio painted two versions of *The Fortune Teller* and one is in Paris at The Louvre and the other earlier version is in Rome. The Louvre version has more dramatic lighting and was painted a year later, highlighting the emotions and the deception more immediately for the viewer. The storytelling is what we think of these days as cinematic—she strokes his hand to tell his fortune… as she removes his ring. *The Fortune Teller* illustrates a whole story, but a poet contemporary to Caravaggio compared the tale of the charming woman's deceit to that of Caravaggio's own illusionism, the way he tricks the viewer into believing the scene is real. The story in the painting is one of bad luck; read another way, the painter has tricked his patrons out of their valuables too with his skill and cleverness. The poem by Gaspare Murtola goes, "I don't know who is the greater sorcerer / The woman you portray / Or you who paint her. Through sweetest incantation."

Here is the way I'm writing this essay: I sit and remember what it felt like to be in the rooms with all the still lifes. I jot a thing or two down in a notebook and usually cross them out. How did I feel looking at the still life? There was this deep feeling of being in conversation with not just an unnamed artist but a place in history. Wandering around Rome, looking at art, we certainly didn't know then that the plague was coming in our time. If you'd told me then, I'm sure I wouldn't have believed it.

I began writing this book before the pandemic started in 2020. We knew it was coming, though many of us were in denial when we saw the videos of people in Italy in lockdown, singing from their balconies. It was beautiful, the way they came together, and also surreal. I didn't believe it would happen here, even though our friends in Europe were warning us. Starting in March of 2020, we too were isolating at home for three months, after which I returned to work, though most people continued to either work from home or be laid off. All this time, Rob continued to paint his flowers, and I attempted to photograph a still life most weeks.

After we got vaccinated, things felt a bit more normal for a while, and then new variants of COVID-19 arrived. We are all living differently, we have been changed, and by now we know that nothing will really ever be the same. As with the Spanish flu, COVID isn't happening exclusively—the news delivers something staggering to us every day, some previously unthinkable thing. To list a few in the USA: an insurrection, the overturning of Roe v. Wade, the continuing climate crisis. Here in Canada: protests by COVID-deniers, anti-vaxxers, and spreaders of disinformation. The disinformation crisis is one that hits home for me in particular given my part-time work in a library. How will the future sift through all this information and facts interspersed with falsehoods? How we knew things and didn't know things? Will they be able to chart the waves of knowing and not knowing, the darkness, the light?

When both Rob and I caught COVID, luckily, we were protected by the vaccine to a goodly extent, but it still wasn't wonderful to have. Months later I'm still feeling the effects of it. Fatigue, difficulty in concentrating. And an ongoing low-grade depression from having to be in the midst of an-ti-vaxxers in our daily lives. Every day we're navigating the varying levels of comfort in coping with the pandemic, the varying levels of belief in how the pandemic—a moving tar-get—should have been handled.

Rob has spent the morning painting, as he always does, and I spent the morning writing, or more accurately, trying to write. I'm distracted these days. It's hard to settle in. Post-COVID, brain fog. Hard to see where one subject connects to another. Gut instincts tell me they do, thanks to years of practicing. I try to trust in that. We sit for twenty minutes as I pepper Rob with questions about Caravaggio. He's into it, telling me all about the latest used book he's found online about the Baroque artist. These kinds of conversations seem so dear right now. We're not having them very often with anyone else as we're not socializing as we once did. As artists we've always been fairly isolated, but these days it's more so. We're out of practice, we're brittle, we're fine but we're stranger than usual. We have things to offer, and no one to offer them to.

A few days later I'm looking at the photos I have of the still life show in Rome in a folder on my desktop. I call him up from his studio and ask him what he'd call the colours of the walls, the permanent ones in that room of the Corsini. Terra-cotta? We look at the blue installation walls of the ex-hibit, placed in front of the terra-cotta ones. We spend time looking at blue paint colours to try and match it. Phthalo, Antwerp blue. None are quite right, or maybe some versions are—there are so many versions online of the same colour name. This sort of ends up being besides the point. The talk about the colour is the thing. That enjoyment.

Do artists look at art differently? I've usually viewed art with an artist or someone who would become an artist, Rob and our daughter, Chloe. Audrey Flack, a realist still life painter, wrote about a Cezanne opening at MOMA, a preview for artists only, saying, "Artists look at paintings dif-ferently." She goes on:

"They discuss the quality of light and the handling of space and color:

"Did he use vermillion or cadmium orange?"

"Look at those brushstrokes."

"See how he had the guts to leave the area seemingly unfinished."

She talks about how in a room full of artists, a lot of them would want to get up close to the paintings. And how, in a rather animated space, there is respect for anyone who wants to just be alone with a painting for a bit. And this all tracks for me, and my experience of looking at art with Rob.

Siri Hustvedt, in her book *Mysteries of the Rectangle* quotes David Freedberg, "I was concerned, above all, by the failure of art history to deal with the extraordinarily abundant evidence for the ways in which people of all classes and cultures have responded to images." I think this is such an overlooked aspect of what images mean, how we interact with art, and how and why we are drawn to art as just regular average human beings. We need art, but a lot of people think you have to have an art history degree to look at it or you'll make an ass of yourself. But you won't. All you need is to be open to what you see and start there. Or maybe, just look at art the way you imagine an artist would.

At the beginning of the pandemic, immediately there was no theatre, no live performances. Movies were being filmed but in closed lots, their own worlds. There was testing, masks, tracing, isolation. Our first awareness of it in Canada were those video clips of people in Italy singing to each other. There was a lot of love shown to healthcare workers and support even for grocery store workers. That seems so quaint compared to what happened later: the protests by supposed "freedom" lovers, the spread of disinformation, the general disrespect for those who had before garnered praise. Our lives seemed less like live drama or movies, and more like a series of stills. Our everyday narrative had stopped, and everyone became obsessed with hoarding food items, toilet paper, hand sanitizer. People posted photographs on social media of their groceries, their cocktail mixing stations, their takeout dinners.

At the start of the pandemic we wondered and worried, would people even still want art? Our own yearning for art told us that they probably would, but there was a lot of uncertainty. The world was shutting down, and we had no idea how the economy would be affected.

An artist needs to look at the art of others to be inspired. Like all the chefs who weren't able to be in their kitchens or musicians who didn't get to play or hear others play, artists were deprived of art. Luckily, those working in mediums that required solitariness fared well enough, as Rob did.

I have a photograph of Rob in the threshold to the room with the still lifes in 2019. He's standing in the doorway to a small adjacent room looking back at where I'm taking photos. I wanted to record the light coming in through a recessed floor-to-ceiling window, the light blue velvet chairs for docents or visitors. The details of the door, the fire hydrant, the patterns on the floor, the deep orange and blue colours of the wall, the ornamental painted designs on a closet, and of course, the installation of the exhibit, and details of the paintings. Part of me must have known I'd want to remember this time in some depth.

When I took the picture, I had no way of knowing how often I would refer to it in the following years. I return to it for several reasons, I suppose. To remember what the room was like, to remember how lovely it felt, looking at art with Rob. To remember that looking at art is more than just the art but also how it is presented, the textures and colours and ambiance of the room. That each painting will make you feel differently about the following one. The order you view them in, who else was in the room, the time of day, and maybe even if you're hungry or thirsty, will also be part of the art viewing experience.

In the photo, at first you might not even see Rob, recessed as he is in the doorway, his face, left leg, hand, emerging into the light of the larger room. He was coming into the light. But my eye goes first to the greater light coming through the window, to the blue chair, to a painting to the left of the window almost entirely in shadow, before swinging back to the right of the frame, to the figure in the doorway. And then, once you see the figure, it holds the gaze, or at least mine. It's a quiet photo and really, it's just a family photo, a personal one, that's all. A vacation photo. One for the memory books, for us. It's the kind of photo you take because you know you're not going to remember some of those very small and quiet moments. I don't think I would have without this image.

Still life draws attention to the overlooked. Still life is the minor genre. But for me, still life is aligned with the way things are now. It tells us how our small acts matter. My favourite still lifes are small holy moments. My other favourite still lifes quietly say openly secret things about the time in which they are made. Siri Hustvedt has said: "Still life is the art of the small thing, an art of holding on to the bits and pieces of our lives." And isn't that the truth? Our lives, slowed down as they have been in so many ways, are carried a bit differently now, with more awareness, maybe of how small they are, how easily shattered.

Making a still life, we adjust one thing, then another. We add an orange and take a rose from the vase and set it on a book. To make a still life is to compose and recompose. Small gestures, small adjustments are made. We figure things out one way, and then we figure them out in another way. Assembling objects reminds us of the myriad of possibilities in a single framing. Each still life could very well have been a different still life even though once the painting is made or the shutter is clicked, there is also the sense of inevitability or fated-ness.

Whenever I make a still life, I remember how many small acts led to the final picture. I nudge a shell closer to the edge of the table, I turn the glass just so. Had I not, it would have been a different image. I'm reminded of how in Hitchcock movies, for example, he had the knack of dwelling on a phone, a scarf, a doorknob, or a matchbook, something still, which would convey so much about the action at hand. But movie watchers might only think about these meanings after the movie is over, while strolling down the street with the remnants of a bag of popcorn. It's interesting to remember that before we had the movies, we had paintings. Paintings have been used to holding a lot for the viewer. They know how to do that work.

I believe that whatever it is we're making in this time is connected to the time we live in. This is always true, though, isn't it?

George Oppen wrote of poetry:

"Poetry is related to
music and cadence and therefore to the force of events."

Those things that we are making may seem small, but at some point, they may seem much larger, saying things that we don't even know they're saying, connected as all art is, to the force of events. I often think of the lines by Rumi:

"Look at your eyes. They are small, but they see enormous things."

Rob's first exhibition of his flowers on a dark background took place in May 2021 and he called it, "Flowers Help." I think his work spoke to people because it portrayed the beauty and poetry of flowers but without denying the darkness of our time. We were trying to see what was happening, to understand. We were walking in the darkness of the present, squinting into the future at all we didn't know. There was goodness, too, people trying to see by the light of flowers.

This time has changed us, yet I'm not trying to change back so much as change forward. Our memories of looking at the show in Rome feel almost cinematic from our current vantage point. Will we look back at the pandemic ten years from now, or twenty, and will it seem like a movie or a series of still photos, still lifes? What will we remember?

I do know that things we experience act upon our memory and affect us and impact our art-making sometimes years later, playing out slowly, subconsciously, and almost inevitably. It feels mysterious right now, this making of still lifes, flowers emerging into light from a place of darkness, but later, perhaps it will feel like an obvious reaction to our time.

When we first viewed the still life show in Rome, there was the delight of knowing that we had three more weeks ahead of us in the city and that we'd be back. We were free from that low-key urgency that this would be the only time we'd see something. And the experience of viewing the paintings was so different from what we'd experienced in all our years of looking at paintings.

I remember being in Paris in 1996 and being almost bowled over by people, often in pairs, bolting past us, running to go see the "hits" of The Louvre. *The Mona Lisa.* The same occurred years later, in New York City, at The Met, looking at Vermeers, being hovered over by docents. In Rome, we were left to our own devices, or at least it felt that way. There were blue velvet seats in the one room. And a blue chair in the other. But there were no docents, no anxious tour groups, or people storming around, ticking paintings off a to-do list.

I wonder what the attention span for looking at art will be in the future? There are already correlations being made between COVID and our experience of trauma in the pandemic, on our ability to concentrate. Brain fog is something many of us have had to contend with. Perhaps it will affect our future abilities to focus, and maybe it will affect how we remember things that are happening to us. I keep wanting to still things, to take photos, so that I might remember a specific moment in time and to attach my feelings to that pictured moment. I don't want to forget all those things that this time has made me feel: ethical concern, anger and, at times, despair. I want to remember how at first, I found the theme of memento mori unsettling, but later embraced it because it reminded me to not just walk through this time in a stupor but to live it as well as I could.

My memories for these past two years will be forever entwined with my memory of looking at the still life exhibition in Rome those two times, bookending our trip. Two years of having it in the back of my mind, seeing the photos on my screensaver. The details and threads of my particular experience of the pandemic is forever entwined with remembering the Caravaggesque still life paintings at the Galleria Corsini. Everything we make from here on in will be influenced by the pandemic, whether we want it to or not. This time will always be looked at through that lens of what was going on in the larger world.

Pandemicists and historians note that there is relatively little art or writing about the Spanish flu, as if people didn't want to think about it. If you got through, you got through, and at a certain point people just pretended it was over. Maybe the Spanish flu wasn't written about that much because it's not a narrative like, say, a war is a narrative. In an article titled, "The 1918 Flu Pandemic Changed Literature More Than You Think, It was just hidden," Molly Schwartz notes:

> One of the things that Virginia Woolf says in that essay is that illness doesn't have a plot. It can be, as you say, the same thing day after day. I think it's why we like stories that have miracle cures or some sort of resiliency. There's a lot of literature by survivors who say, Could we stop with the health journey motif? It's not like that, and it puts too much pressure on people. Most of it is this mundane trying to get by.

In another article that mentions Woolf, by Jeremy Eichler, titled, "How did artists respond to the Spanish flu? Searching for traces of a forgotten catastrophe" he writes: "On top of all this, Woolf says, consider the curious impoverishment of our language itself when it comes to describing the inner experience of pain. 'English,' she famously writes, 'which can express the thoughts of Hamlet and the tragedy of Lear, has no words for the shiver and the headache.'"

What would the language of COVID-19 even look like? It's hard to write about brain fog while in it, yet afterwards, in a clearer frame of mind, it doesn't seem quite real either.

It's odd to make beautiful things and talk about beauty, and making, and looking at art, when all around you people are dying of COVID-19. Regardless, we will leave behind a record of our small gestures, small observances with our small eyes that see enormous vistas. A lot of it will have been luck. That we were here on earth at all, looking, squinting our eyes at what is partially obscured, coming out of darkness. We will have left our mundane gestures in art, in the art of the everyday, in the art of our still lifes. So much of what we've experienced is mundane; we've simply been trying to get by, and to move forward into an unknown light.

We don't typically think of Caravaggio's paintings as coming out of the bubonic plague, reacting to the suffering and illness, nor do we think of the still lifes of the Italian baroque as a kind of response either. I know that my attraction to making my still life photos is in how the process acknowledges the darkness. It acknowledges the luck and chance of how we can make things happen. A still life is an instant, things coming together by force of imagination and sometimes out of a dream-like foggy tired state, things cohering momentarily. A still life comes into being one gesture at a time, out of a chaos that feels like an emergency, and into another ordered place, somewhere neither here nor there, into a frame or window of possibility. In the moment the objects are perishable and subject to a light source to make them visible to one degree or another. But in the art of the still life, the moment holds.

A good artist will leave openings in the work for it to speak its own mind, to be of its own time. The bonsai masters speak of leaving a space for the birds to fly through in their work, and it's like this with art, too.

How will the future receive one's art? What will last? Who will be remembered? We don't know. But maybe what is left will mean something. Maybe our art holds meaning we can't yet see or understand. Yes, the future art historian will say, these paintings were made when there was a plague, a pandemic, and 6.4 plus million people died worldwide. See how they hold grief and the worry of the unknown near future.

During the last couple of years, a piece I wrote titled "In Lieu of Flowers" became reasonably popular on the internet. It has been shared countless times, read at countless memorials. I very often receive emails or messages asking me if the poem might be read at a funeral, or thanking me for it, or sharing a story. The poem is about: instead of sending flowers on the occasion of someone's death, that we mark it with a simple ritual that would have appealed to the person no longer with us. It asks the readers or listeners to contemplate a flower for themselves. I think part of the appeal of Rob's flower paintings is that they fulfill a similar purpose. They mark this time as a remembrance for people and are perhaps part of a new ritual of contemplation in a home.

All this time, were we coming into the darkness or going out of the darkness? What were the bewilderments, as Plato called them, of our eyes? I'm always thinking about the bewilderments of our eyes from *The Parable of the Cave, Plato's Republic Book VII*:

> "Any one who has common sense will remember that the bewilderments of the eyes are of two kinds, and arise from two causes, either from coming out of the light or from going into the light, which is true of the mind's eye, quite as much as of the bodily eye; and he who remembers this when he sees any one whose vision is perplexed and weak, will not be too ready

to laugh; he will first ask whether that soul of man has come out of the brighter life, and is unable to see because unaccustomed to the dark, or having turned from darkness to the day is dazzled by excess of light. And he will count the one happy in his condition and state of being, and he will pity the other; or, if he has a mind to laugh at the soul which comes from below into the light, there will be more reason in this than in the laugh which greets him who returns from above out of the light into the den."

I think these pandemic days, the bewilderments of our eyes are what we're navigating at a dizzying degree. We are going into and out of the light at breakneck speeds. It's difficult to focus or remember if we ourselves are squinting because of the excessive light or the excessive darkness. And those we encounter! How much darkness have they been dwelling in? For how long? Or are they in the light? How many times back and forth? And what does that passage do to their souls?

For me, it reminds me of what we can know, what is hidden and what is visible. It reminds me that there will always be some darkness, there will always be light. It reminds me to be a bit curious and a bit more caring, a bit more open. It also reminds me that there is beauty that may come out of the darkness, quite unexpectedly. And maybe that's really what we need right now, the kind of beauty that jumpstarts my heart, which is honestly a little worn and tattered.

I like what John Berger has said about photography and time: "What makes photography a strange invention—with unforeseeable consequences—is that its primary raw materials are light and time."

I think a lot about the settings on my camera, how much light to let in, in relation to how much light is available. The time that the shutter operates determines what the image will mean, how it will seem. But paintings are also interesting to think about as objects in relation to time. I always find it somewhat curious when someone asks Rob how long it takes to paint one of his works. Do they want an answer like, "112 hours," or do they want to think about the number of times the brush has touched the canvas, the hand of the artist moving over that space, the number of years the artist spent before even arriving before the painting? Often people will ask one question, when they mean to ask another, or they veil the question they really want to ask, because they think it will make them appear a certain way. Maybe what they want to know is, what did you go through to get to those two weeks of laying paint onto a canvas? I always wondered how long it takes to look at a painting and merge into the mystery of it. How long will a painting stand up to scrutiny and affection and a dreaming soul looking?

I'm writing this as a record for myself because I know that my memories are already fading. I'm writing this because I want to convey the way that a still life composed of mundane and ordinary objects holds all sorts of secrets—plagues, darkness, light. Sometimes a still life will say all that we're too tired to utter. It was difficult living through this time, they'll say, but there was joy and light, too. The energies from a room full of paintings resonated and fed my soul for a couple of years after seeing them. Their vibrations move through them and through me and into the work both Rob and I have produced since seeing them. My feelings collected around the experience of seeing that still-life exhibition in Rome and I can't seem to let them go.

Still life is persistent in that it sends its messages again and again, even when no one is looking. A still life is patient, it will wait for its viewers. For me, the messages of still life I held dear to me are that it's difficult to tell if the objects are coming out of the dark or receding into it, that life is fleeting, and time is embedded into all the art we make. One day we will be forgotten, and the drama of the world will hold most of the attention of historians. But there will be little pockets and unnoticed corners, tabletops, and niches, and there we might contemplate persistent, eternal themes: time, the brightness of being alive, memento mori. The small gestures we make in a life do matter, and still life is here, quietly telling us so.

When setting up a still life I continue to think about possibilities. I'm hoping to be lucky in spite of whatever odds. I keep trying, anyway. What if this is the order of things that speaks of beauty with the most clarity? What if this composition is the one that creates a necessary feeling of calm in the viewer? What if this is the one you love? What if by arranging this here and that there, a particular layer of the universe rhymes and resonates? If I can get this arrangement to spark a few shocks of beauty, what else can we see by its light?

Poetry and Still Life

In the place where poetry and still life meet there is a radiance. Poetry resides in many places but I have loved spending most of my life being astonished by this confluence whenever it occurs. The everyday, the ordinary in poetry, meets the everyday and ordinary in still life.

If you're a poet, you've likely taken a run at saying what poetry is. (I did myself in my book, *Asking*). W. H. Auden wrote: "Poetry is the clear expression of mixed feelings." When I'm in the presence of poetry, and this isn't always through a proper poem per se, I feel as Rumi did:

"This is how it always is
when I finish a poem.

A great silence overcomes me,
and I wonder why I ever thought
to use language."

Hélène Cixous, one of the major influences of my creative life, said, "I call 'poet' any writer, philosopher, author of plays, dreamer, producer of dreams, who uses life as a time of 'approaching.'" Cixous says that "the soul is the magic of attention" and "attention is magical matter." Poets are attentive, they are attuned, they put unlike things together and a magic happens. It's a way of thinking: a human with poetic intelligence is a kind of magic in a room that is almost always invisible, though. This is fine. We can pick each other out across a space, across time.

I have trouble explaining to people why it's important to have poetry in their everyday lives. But in fact, I think that it's probably (after the basics) the most important element. When I talk about poetry, I'm not necessarily thinking about it in some tangible form. There's a passage by Teju Cole in his book, *Blind Spot*, where he talks about the filmmaker Tarkovsky, who says that poetry is "the link that allows different kinds of excellence to understand one another." If you're interested in a thing, anything, it's probably the poetic essence in that thing or activity to which you are drawn. Cole says, that "if everything else succeeds but the poetry fails, then everything has failed." He talks about mystical relationships and the "inarticulable realms." And honestly, we need more of that kind of language and not less. We need more quiet meetings in the inarticulable realms. And really, isn't it a kind of mind-blowing thought: that poetry is how and where we can meet—one type of excellence meeting in the poetry of another.

There is a shocking and beautiful clarity in excellent poetic language. A complex idea mixed with feelings and nuance in such a way that just goes straight to your heart—pow! The language might appear simple, it might be elegant, or complex, or ornate. There is not one single path to what Joseph Campbell called aesthetic arrest. But for the artist or poet it arrives after one has plumbed those proverbial depths. The simplest line of poetry will undoubtedly have a decade of learning and feeling behind it so that it looks easy.

As someone who is interested in both poetry and still life, I'm always excited by poetry that gets still life, gets art. When it misses the mark, granted this is heartbreaking for me, but done well, what a thrill! And Charles Wright is one of those poets who gets it. From Appalachia, his poem "Basic Dialogue" begins:

"The transformation of objects in space,
                              or objects in time,
To objects outside either, but tactile, still precise …
It's always the same problem –
Nothing's more abstract, more unreal,
                              than what we actually see.
The job is to make it otherwise."

And this is in part a nod to Giorgio Morandi (who Wright often writes about) who said, "there is nothing more abstract than reality."

There is poetry (potentially) in a still life. The magical matter, the ineffable, inarticulable life-juice of stuff, isn't a given. Anne Bogart talks about making art, any art, as well as making a life in art, in terms of still life: "We are debris arrangers. Equipped with what we have inherited, we try to make a life, make a living and make art. We are assemblers. We forge received parts into meaningful compositions." She quotes Jasper Johns, and this is pretty much the through-line of my existence: "Take something. Change it. Change it again."

The question that I am obsessed with these days is by adrienne maree brown from her book *Emergent Strategy*: "What is the next most elegant step?" And this is the way one composes a still life. You put something on a surface, you move it, you add things. You take away. You compose. You arrange the debris, the rubble. What is the next most elegant step? What is the step that taps into the magical matter? If you've composed a lot of still lifes, you know when you strike upon that magical combination. At least usually you do—sometimes it's revealed to you later. With photography, I usually know when I've caught some primo light. I know when the sparks are flying. But it's later when I upload the photo to my computer that I know for sure. And that's a fun and exhilarating moment. You hope! But you don't know for sure. And then funnily, you think you've got some magic down and no one responds to it at all when you post it. Maybe it's not magic to anyone else. That's fine. It was magic to you.

Brown says the elegant next step "acknowledges what is known and what is not known." This is also very like the still life process: you compose into the unknown. And what you get, the aesthetic rapture, that moment of sudden clarity, it turns immediately to ash. You must begin again.

Not all poetry is about the everyday, the quotidian, but very often the everyday in a poem speaks to the everyday in still life. Both art forms try to distill or convert the seemingly insignificant into a higher substance. It's that golden transformation, when the sap of existence is turned into Cohen's ashes.

Robert Creeley wrote a perfect short poem that goes:

One day after another –
Perfect.
They all fit.

We arrange our chocolate pots and dog-eared books and beer-filled roemers and ripe cheeses and cascading flowers and brief butterflies and dead game until something clicks. A moment of poetry has happened, escaped into the world. An aesthetic arrest, a moment of radiance, rapture. The arrangement falls into place. It fits. Later it is disassembled, refrigerated, consumed, distributed. But something remains. We have the ash, we have the spark, the shock, the beauty. The poetry remains. O thank you poetry! for staying.

Still Life vs. Real Life

There are the still lifes that are set up deliberately and meditatively and contemplatively and precisely and then there are the still lifes that appear; they happen, they emerge, they erupt out of our daily lives. Sometimes those real-life still lifes are captured in a photograph or in paint but they might just move in and out of our peripheral vision. We might not think about the shelf in our bathroom with soap and razors and a knock-off Chanel No. 5 bottle as a still life. Every morning at breakfast there is a still life: coffee cup and sugar bowl, spoon, croissant, box of cornflakes, milk, phone, a book, the newspaper, a crossword puzzle and pencil. And when we go to bed on the table beside: a book, eyeglasses, water glass.

Looking for or recognizing a still life takes practice—picking it out of the debris and chaos of our everyday lives is an artform. Looking at a still life also takes practice. Traditionally, art students learning to paint will begin with a still life, composing it with dust-covered vessels and discarded maquettes from the sculpture students, and perhaps a plant or vase of flowers. This is a way to practice the techniques of oil paint, and also train the eye and hand to form shapes, how to create shadow and light, with the substance artist Chuck Close called coloured dirt.

Student still lifes are places of trial and error, trying things out, learning. There is something clunky and off-kilter in these practice pieces, which have a charm of their own. Such earnestness, such dedication and desire. Occasionally the student will go on to find success as a painter but not always. We are interested in the student works of artists who went on to be great because we want to see the beginnings of their seeing. How did they start off looking at a thing? How did looking at a group of things and arranging them transfer to the work that came later? What sensibilities were already there, and which came later?

A still life that occurs naturally in our homes is a step back from the inadvertent composition. What did Chardin's room look like if you took several steps back from the basket of strawberries? In real life you'd have a larger context, other small arrangements, messes, maybe even a bit of chaos.

I'll go out and buy flowers. I'll think for a few days about a theme. Is there a visual pun to be made? What allusions to the history of still life? What should I riff on? What do I want to say about my small part of the world? What does a tin of sardines say? What about a Big Mac? A bowl of Kraft Dinner? What about the fruit imported from Chile or Florida? A deliberately created still life might feel completely removed from those that occur in our ordinary lives, but the objects will yet hold traces of their usual resting places.

Anyone who spends a decent amount of time looking at still lifes will simultaneously train themselves to look at the world more attentively. If we can draw out the meaning in the details and nuances and threads of a still life, maybe we can also see things with a certain clarity in real life. The details here in this still life of seashells, fruit, books, and wine glass, allow us to see the details out there, in the larger world. Wallace Stevens wrote a poem titled, "Planets on a Table." The still life has been noted to be a place of resistance, a reordering of the chaotic world. Bonnie Costello, in a book named after the poem by Stevens, says that "the planet on the table serves to evoke, not to cover up, a broken, beautiful, unmasterable, heterogeneous reality."

I look at still life as a way of knowing myself. I arrange formal still lifes because I want to say something about the world, but I want to do it with the objects I have at hand. In doing so, I say something about myself. I exist. I'm here, too. This is how I'm getting through. If we can be attuned to the way a still life can say more than one thing at once, maybe we can also be attuned to the contradictions of the world. Or maybe when it's difficult to speak about certain things, we can put them into a still life as covert messages. Still life is about time but maybe it's also a form of time travel, a way of sending messages into a more receptive future.

Do we find the arranged beauty of a still life to be more compelling than what appears to be a found still life? Is one more honest or true than the other?

In our household these two kinds of still lifes speak to each other. Reconciling the ordered, framed moment, with the life that goes on outside the frame or behind the scenes. They're of course deeply connected, one feeding the other. We need both. There's always a lot going on that we can't know about in someone's life. If we have made something approaching art, though, perhaps the behind the scenes is felt in the more formal presentation.

I've been making still lifes through our twenty-first century pandemic as a way of telling myself that everything will be fine, it won't always be like this. But it's always been like this. Things have always been this way. We look at things and then we look away. We read about genocides and holocausts and mass graves and look at photographs of them. We read about the death tolls of plagues and pandemics. We look at these things and then feel hungry. We cut up an apple. We sit by the window looking out at the birds at the birdbath and eat our apple.

John Berger says that the "aesthetic moment offers hope." Can we also find hope in these haphazard still lifes that we come upon in our daily lives? The fresh laundry on the bed, the spoon on the edge of the pasta sauce pot, the band of light that the cat nestles into on the corner of the couch.

We see things in one way and then we see them in another. I think about that expression, "o see in a new light," and comparing the real-life objects to the objects in a more formal still life. Where is there overlap? What are the things being left out? What are the things added?

Real life: I bought the plums with a specific recipe in mind, setting them in a bowl on the cupboard for when I had time. The light arrives, unexpectedly. I run for the camera.

Still life: I flip through a book on seventeenth-century still life and remember that I have a similar glass. What kind of juice is in the glass? How could I get that colour?

Real life: Light falls on an open book I'd been reading with my breakfast. I left the plate from my toast and the light does nice things to the toast crumbs, too.

Still life: I buy pop tarts and strawberry milk for an idea I have. I dislike strawberry milk. And pop tarts are just so much sugar. I'm too old and sedentary to burn off the calories of pop tarts.

Real life: Stepping back from composing a still life on the table, I notice the other still lifes: camera, upended bowl of fruit, the pineapple on the floor propped up against the coffee table, the flower that broke off sitting in a bit of spilled water.

Still life: Still life holds the secret little joys, and sorrows, and funny and sometimes rubbish plot lines of our lives with a quiet mystery.

Real life: The plot lines of our lives erupt into still lifes: heaps of clothes from the laundry, the spaghetti pot in stove light, wine glass in the sink from the night before, the plate filled with cookie crumbs we forgot on the coffee table, the dregs of the popcorn bowl on the couch where we watched the movie last night.

Still life: Constructing a still life is a way of working things through.

Real life: We can find ourselves here in the haphazard leavings and tracings of the life we live, in those little shocks and delights of beauty that appear.

The Most Lost Vessel

I'm going to reveal one of the secret tricks that I've used these many years of my writing life. It is the secret of the most lost vessel. It is the secret I use to dispel doubt, banish fear, and calm my despair.

I learned this trick from Hélène Cixous. And I think it works well for writers but it's one of those things that transfers to anything that we love making but we put off due to doubt or that feeling of futility. There was a moment in my life when I had four unpublished manuscripts stacked up and sitting on my desk. I even took a photo of them at some point that has been lost. Four manuscripts are a lot of paper! They were on my desk, then I moved them crosswise on my bookshelf; they reclined there as one might at a first appointment on the chaise longue of a psychiatrist. But that first appointment lasted a shockingly long time. I was ready to throw in the towel. Long story short, three of those four manuscripts did eventually get published, though not in the order they were written.

What got me through that period of extreme despair (and I do not use the word *extreme* lightly) was this line by Cixous:

> "It is really the fantasy of the poet who confides his written heart to a vessel but the most lost vessel in the world, to the smallest chance."

I made a drawing of a vessel, a scribble really, and Rob framed it for me. I keep it in our bedroom on a small storage chest. And though we have moved our art countless times in the years since I drew that desperate little vessel, it has never left its perch. It's not art, that scrap of paper torn from an old notebook, but a reminder of what Cixous calls "an act of faith and self-assurance." The messages we send out into the sea in our bottles, to "a distant eternity," she says, are "a form of incredible courage."

Ever since that time I have always addressed my work to the most lost vessel in the world, to the smallest chance. And maybe that is where my courage to continue comes from. It arrives and is sent out in that vessel and goes out with the tides and miraculously returns, sometimes, on the waves. I say all this as a person completely unfamiliar with the sea, as a woman raised on the land-locked prairie.

I have been thinking of my camera as some kind of vessel. One that fills up with images and then empties out. Writing is like that, too. We pour the words out of ourselves and hope upon hope that after we rest and read some more, we will have more words to once again pour.

Giorgio Morandi is known for his still lifes of bottles and jugs and various other vessels. His still lifes were almost architectural, certainly mysterious, pared down to the point of becoming mystical. They remind us that we don't need a lot of stuff to make art but that we can just keep rearranging and reordering and going deeper into what we do have.

I was sitting on the couch before writing this, reading a beautiful book I have of photographs by Joel Meyerwitz of Cezanne's studio. The photographs are of the vessels Cezanne painted and which were in his last studio. The photographs are simple, profound: a single object against a grey-green wall. They elicit a kind of reverence. The simplicity of the depiction allows for a lovely contemplation of each object. While the photographer likely held and placed them very carefully, you can imagine the artist not thinking twice about propping them in precarious positions. What were the chances that these vessels painted by Cezanne remained?

I appreciate the everyday vessels in my home. On one table in our living room is an assortment of such containers. None of them are worth anything, per se. They're just knick-knacks picked up from Winner's, mainly. But I enjoy noticing the shadows they cast, the sort of cityscape they form at a certain time of the day, the architecture of them. I rearrange them and enjoy the play of shapes as they overlap, rhyming with each other. Sometimes I remove one from the array and just look at it alone on my stack of books on the coffee table. It's quieter, then. The silence of these vessels, the way they hold, even when empty, reassures.

I invite you to draw a vessel and whilst doing so, imagine what message you are sending out into a distant future. Remind yourself how courageous you are to be creating anything at all! The image of the message in the bottle reminds me that I only really need one future person to receive what I'm casting out there to make it worthwhile doing. Perhaps it will have other resonances for you. Whenever I look at a still life with a pitcher or vase or glass, I remember that all art is that: messages in bottles, containers of hope, gifts into the future unknown. Everything we make is addressed to the smallest chance, but it is a chance.

Acknowledgements

This book is as much about living a life as a reader as it is about living a life with art and still life. I've been in conversation these past many years with so many amazing minds through their writings. Some of these are quoted from and engaged with in my text more extensively, others were good companions as I wrote and thought and pushed objects around on a table, but they're all pretty deeply embedded in my subconscious. I'm grateful to the following books and authors:

Ordinary Affects by Kathleen Stewart
A Chorus of Stones by Susan Griffin
The Eros of Everyday by Susan Griffin
Shooting the Works by W.S. Di Piero
Born to Run by or Bruce Springsteen
A Defense of Ardor by Adam Zagajewski
The Mysteries of the Rectangle by Siri Hustvedt
Stigmata by Hélène Cixous
A Breath of Life by Clarice Lispector
Art and Soul: Notes on Creating by Audrey Flack
What's the Story by Anne Bogart
Let's See by Peter Schjeldahl
Attention Equals Life by Andrew Epstein

Index Cards by Moyra Davey
Planets on Tables by Bonnie Costello
Still Life with Oysters and Lemon by Mark Doty

I gratefully acknowledge the support of the Alberta Foundation for the Arts during the writing of this book. "By the Still Life Painter's Wife" was published on *LitHub* as "The Painter's Wife vs. The Poet's Husband: Portrait of a Marriage." "The Practice of Still Life" was published in *The Antigonish Review*.

Thank you to Aimée Parent Dunn and Palimpsest Press for their stellar work. Thank you to Ellie Hastings for the cover design. Thanks to Sohini Ghose for the copyedits. Books are shaped by many people and I'm grateful to you all.

Thanks to literary and library friendships: Kimmy Beach, Lisa Martin, Angie Roos and to friends in art, Jennifer Annesley and Neil Zinger.

This book is dedicated with love to the beauties of my life, Rob Lemay and Chloe Lemay.

Works Consulted

Ordinary Affects by Kathleen Stewart. Duke UP, 2007, p. 19, 127, 36.

A Chorus of Stones by Susan Griffin. Doubleday, 1992, p. 151.

The Eros of Everyday by Susan Griffin. Doubleday, 1995, p. 192, 194.

Shooting the Works: On Poetry and Pictures by W.S. Di Piero. TriQuarterly, 1996.

Born to Run by Bruce Springsteen. Simon & Schuster, 2016, p. 391.

A Defense of Ardor by Adam Zagajewski. Farrar, Straus and Giroux, 2005, p. 10.

The Mysteries of the Rectangle by Siri Hustvedt. Princeton Architectural Press, 2007, p. xx, 29, 36, 58.

Stigmata by Hélène Cixous. Routledge, 1998, p. 20.

Coming to Writing by Hélène Cixous. Harvard UP, 1991, p. 73, 114.

Rootprints by Hélène Cixous. Taylor and Francis,2012, p. 102.

A Breath of Life by Clarice Lispector, translator Johnny Lorenz. New Directions 2012, p. 70.

Hour of the Star by Clarice Lispector, translator Giovanni Pontiero, New Directions, 1986. P. 26, 62

Art and Soul: Notes on Creating by Audrey Flack. Penguin, 1991, p. 48.

What's the Story by Anne Bogart. Routledge, 2014, p. 6, 21, 31, 141.

Let's See by Peter Schjeldahl. Thames and Hudson, 2008, p. 65.

Hot, Cold, Heavy, Light by Peter Schjeldahl, Abrams, 2019.

Attention Equals Life by Andrew Epstein. Oxford UP, 2018.

Index Cards by Moyra Davey. New Directions, 2020, p. 1.

Planets on Tables by Bonnie Costello. Cornell UP, 2008, p. 107.

Still Life with Oysters and Lemon by Mark Doty. Beacon, 2001.

Ten Windows: How Great Poems Transform the World by Jane Hirshfield. Knopf, 2015, p. 151.

Letters on Life by Rainer Maria Rilke. Modern Library, 2006, p. 23, 36.

The Woman Who Fell From the Sky by Joy Harjo. Norton, 1994.

Look at Me by Anita Brookner. Penguin, 1983, p. 19.

Bruce Springsteen: The Stories Behind the Songs by Brian Hiatt. Abrams, 2019.

The Waves by Virginia Woolf. Penguin Books, 1992, p. 227.

An Origin Like Water: Collected Poems by Eavan Boland. Norton, 1997.

Still Life and Trade by Julie Berger Hochstrasser. Yale UP, 2007, p. xiv.

The Assumption of the Rogues and Rascals by Elizabeth Smart. Harpercollins, 1995, p. 57.

The Butterfly's Burden by Mahmoud Darwish. Copper Canyon Press, 2007, p. 133.

Funny Weather: Art in an Emergency by Olivia Laing. Norton, 2021.

Appalachia by Charles Wright. Farrar, Straus and Giroux, 1999, p. 5.

Emergent Strategy by adrienne maree brown. AK Press, 2017, p. 220.

The Wife by Meg Wolitzer. Scribner, 2003, p. 184

"By the Still Life Painter's Wife" from *All the God-Sized Fruit*, 1999 by Shawna Lemay quoted with permission from McGill-Queen's University Press

Articles

"Why are men still in charge in book titles?" by Judith Evans. *The Guardian*, Wednesday, 21 November, 2007.

"Why the Art World Ignores Wives" by Jessica Dawson. *Daily Beast*, March 17, 2014.

"Where are all the women artists?" by Erin Spencer Sairam. *Forbes*, March 1, 2019.

"'Sponsored' by my husband: Why it's a problem that writers never talk about where their money comes from" by Ann Bauer. *Salon*, January 25, 2015.

"The Instagram-Husband Revolution" by Taylor Lorenz. *The Atlantic*, January 11, 2019.

"Annie Leibovitz, in Camera" by Russel Smith. *The Globe and Mail*, November 10, 2017.

"Bruce Springsteen's Memoir Beautifully Dissects His Own Masculinity" by Rebecca Traister, *Vulture*, September 28, 2016.

"Stars, they're just like us" by Kate Lee, February 27, 2013.

"Flowers or Vaginas: Georgia O'Keeffe Tate show to challenge sexual cliches" by Hanna Ellis-Petersen, 1 March 2016.

"From Black Death to fatal flu, past pandemics show why people on the margins suffer most" by Lizzie Wade. *Science*, 14 May 2020.

"In Dutch Still Lifes, Dark Secrets Hide behind Exotic Delicacies" by Julia Fiore. *Artsy*, 4 September, 2018.

"Brush with the Black Death: how artists painted through the plague" by Jonathan Jones. *The Guardian*, 15 February 2012

"The Chaotic life of Caravaggio, chiaroscuro, and the card-sharps" by Tara Lloyd. Singulart Magazine, November 2019.

"The 1918 Flu Pandemic Changed Literature More Than You Think, It was just hidden" by Molly Schwartz. *Mother Jones*, May 2020.

"How did artists respond to the Spanish flu? Searching for traces of a forgotten catastrophe" by Jeremy Eichler, May 6, 2020.

"Inside Giacometti's Studio, The Tate. Photos" by Ernst Scheidegger, text by Cecilia Braschi, Michael Peppiatt, 2017.

Shawna Lemay is the author of *The Flower Can Always Be Changing* (shortlisted for the 2019 Wilfred Eggleston Award for Non-Fiction) and the novels, *Rumi and the Red Handbag*, which made Harper's Bazaar's #THELIST, and *Everything Affects Everyone*. She has also written multiple books of poetry, a book of essays, and the experimental novel *Hive*. *All the God-Sized Fruit*, her first book, won the Stephan G. Stephansson Award and the Gerald Lampert Memorial Award. *Calm Things: Essays* was shortlisted for the Wilfred Eggleston Award for Non-Fiction.